Convergence Issues in the European Union

This book is dedicated to the memory of

Ellen Van Hauwermeiren,

University of Antwerp student of the
2000-2001 class of the
MA Economics of International Trade
and European Integration

Convergence Issues in the European Union

Edited by

Wim Meeusen
Professor of Economics, Universiteit Antwerpen, Belgium

José Villaverde
Professor of Economics, Universidad de Cantabria Spain

Edward Elgar

Cheltenham, UK · Northampton, MA, USA

Published by
Edward Elgar Publishing Limited
Glensanda House
Montpellier Parade
Cheltenham
Glos GL50 1UA
UK

Edward Elgar Publishing, Inc.
136 West Street
Suite 202
Northampton
Massachusetts 01060
USA

A catalogue record for this book
is available from the British Library

Library of Congress Cataloguing in Publication Data
Convergence issues in the European Union / edited by Wim Meeusen, José Villaverde.
    p. cm.
    Includes bibliographical references and index.
    1. Convergence (Economics)—European Union countries. 2. European Union countries—Economic integration. 3. European Union countries—Economic conditions—Regional disparities. 4. Finance—European Union countries. 5. Labor market—European Union countries—Regional disparities. 6. European Union countries—Economic policy. 7. European Union countries—Social policy. I. Meeusen, Wim, 1945– II. Villaverde, José, 1950–

    HC240 .C61814 2002
    337.1'42—dc21   2002021387

ISBN 1 84064 666 7

Printed and bound in Great Britain by Biddles Ltd *www.biddles.co.uk*

Contents

List of Figures

List of Tables

List of Contributors

Filip Abraham
Centre for Economic Studies
Katholieke Universiteit Leuven
Belgium

Nick Adnett
Economics Division
Staffordshire University Business
School
UK

John Ashworth
Department of Economics
University of Durham
UK

Manuel Balmaseda
Research Department
Banco Bilbao Vizcaya Argentaria
(BBVA)
Spain

Frank Barry
Department of Economics
University College Dublin
Ireland

Alain Borghijs
Department of Economics
Universiteit Antwerpen
Belgium

Philippe De Lombaerde
Department of Economic Theory and
Policy
Universidad Nacional de Colombia
Colombia

José García Solanes
Department of Economics
Universidad de Murcia
Spain

Aoife Hannan
European University Institute
Firenze
Italy

Bruno Heyndels
Faculty of Economic, Social and
Political Sciences
Vrije Universiteit Brussel
Belgium

Ramón María-Dolores
Department of Economics
Universidad de Murcia
Spain

Wim Meeusen
Department of Economics
Universiteit Antwerpen
Belgium

Eric J. Pentecost
Department of Economics
Loughborough University
UK

Glenn Rayp
Department of Economics
Universiteit Gent
Belgium

Blanca Sánchez-Robles
Department of Economics
Universidad de Cantabria
Spain

David Taguas
Research Department
Banco Bilbao Vizcaya Argentaria
(BBVA)
Spain

André Van Poeck
Department of Economics
Universiteit Antwerpen
Belgium

José Villaverde
Department of Economics
Universidad de Cantabria
Spain

1. Introduction and Outline

Wim Meeusen and José Villaverde

Economic convergence is a hot topic for at least three clearly distinct reasons. The first is that it has become obvious, now also to the lowest form of political intelligence, that on the planetary level the gap between the rich and the poor is not getting smaller, and that this not only is an insult to the human race but, after the events of 11 September 2001, is also a threat to world peace.

On a smaller and less dramatic scale, convergence – secondly – is a big issue within that part of the rich world that is the European Union. It is at the same time a necessity for the Union to survive and grow, but also – in the eyes of a majority of commentators, economists and politicians – an expected outcome of the creation of the internal market and its ultimate expression, monetary union. If convergence does not come about and a two- or multi-speed Europe unfolds, then the most ambitious political project in Europe since the French Revolution will have failed.

Thirdly, on a still more modest scale, the convergence issue is at the centre of the discussion between the supporters of the traditional neo-classical growth theory based on the Solow-Swan model and the advocates of the theory of endogenous growth. Although Kaldor had already mentioned the divergent growth rates of output per capita across countries as one of his 'stylised facts' (Kaldor, 1961), most economists, including growth theorists, using the traditional growth model, seemed largely to have taken economic convergence for granted as a natural consequence of this model. The underlying, usually silent, assumption was that knowledge and therefore technology have the characteristics of public goods that are freely available to all countries. The mechanisms that, at least in the long-run, are responsible for this are so-called knowledge spillovers. Unless these are sufficiently important, models of the Solow-Swan type, as is now well understood, only predict 'condi-

tional' convergence. That is, the lower the actual level of income per efficiency unit of labour, *relative to the particular steady-state value of the
economy*, the faster the economy will be moving towards this position. Conditional convergence therefore only means convergence in the formal, not the
actual, sense of the word. Since the equilibrium value of per capita income
(expressed in efficiency units) depends on the savings rate, the growth rate of
the population and the form of the production function (the technology), rich
and poor countries converge to different steady states. If, on top of this, the
rates of Harrod-neutral technological progress are not equal in the different
countries or regions of the world, the equilibrium positions themselves may
diverge. Obviously, what the world and for that matter the EU need is 'absolute', not 'conditional', convergence.

The contributions in this book address the second of the three convergence
issues that we mentioned, also touching on the third. What is the convergence
record in the EU so far? Is there a sign of Baumol and Quah's 'convergence
clubs' and 'Twin Peaks' (Baumol, 1986; Quah, 1997)? Have the 'Structural
Funds' of the European Commission made any difference? These are the
topics dealt with in Part I. Part II discusses fiscal and monetary aspects. Can
we expect the monetary policy of the ECB to have similar effects in the EMU
member states, or is it in itself a source of asymmetric shocks? Has EU
membership made any difference with respect to the initial differences in tax
revenue structures? Part III focuses on social and labour market issues. Is
global economic convergence compatible with sustainable differences in national social protection levels? Does European globalisation force labour
markets to 'de-institutionalise'?

In the first chapter of Part I *Filip Abraham* reviews the theoretical and
empirical literature on national and regional convergence at the macro-level.
He concludes that, so far, there is no reason to believe that Krugman's theoretical economies-of-scale argument on the possibility of divergence has ma-
terialised (Krugman, 1991). The growth record in both the EU at large and in
the subset of countries forming the EMU is such that relocation of industries
in the proximity of large and rich regions, as a result of which a destabilising
positive feedback process might lead to increasing income inequality between
the rich and the poor regions, could not have taken place on a large scale.
Abraham concludes that, on the whole, the 40 years of post-war European
integration have brought high and low income regions closer together, albeit
slowly and discontinuously.

On the same broad question of actual real GDP and growth rate convergence *Eric Pentecost* has brought to bear the power of the Kalman filter approach to a convergence equation with time-varying coefficients. Following
Haldane and Hall (1991) and Hall *et al.* (1992), but also continuing his own
work on the subject (Button and Pentecost, 1993; 1995), the author, on the

other hand, finds some evidence of divergence within the group of countries participating in the monetary union, the reason, in his view, possibly being the stringent economic policies that were applied in a number of candidate countries in order to meet the Maastricht criteria. Pentecost warns, however, that real convergence may take a long time, and that it is too soon to draw firm conclusions.

José Villaverde and *Blanca Sánchez-Robles* in their chapter continue on the same theme, but specialise in the regional convergence issue within the borders of Spain. They apply Quah's Markov chain methodology, sharing his interest in the possible existence of 'convergence clubs'. Although no lasting 'Twin Peaks' are discernible, there seems to be a tendency whereby the richest provinces – as a result of a Krugman geographical externality effect? – tend progressively to concentrate in the North-east of the country. There appears otherwise to be a large degree of persistence through time in the relative positions of the Spanish provinces.

In the light of the foregoing, *José García Solanes* and *Ramón María-Dolores* in the next chapter address an obvious question: did the Structural Funds of the European Commission make any difference? The answer according to them is 'yes'. β-tests of (conditional) convergence reveal an important and statistically significant positive effect on the speed of convergence. The biggest impact, in terms of the category of funds, corresponds to funds assigned by the European Regional Development Fund (ERDF) and the European Agricultural Guidance and Guarantee Fund (EAGGF).

In the last chapter of Part I *Philippe De Lombaerde* re-examines the theory on optimum currency areas in the light of recent experience, concentrating on dynamic aspects and on the question of time-consistency. With respect to the latter aspect, his most striking conclusion is that in a process of monetary integration that is gradual in terms of membership, the theory of optimum currency areas does not yield time-consistent recommendations.

Part II deals with monetary and fiscal issues. *John Ashworth* and *Bruno Heyndels* examine the impact of EU membership on tax revenue structures. They found that the effects are ambiguous: while membership itself lowers tax 'turbulence' (measured as the degree of tax structure change within a given country), the member countries are less able to react to external shocks and so turbulence is increased. They also found some evidence of the fact that the tax structures of the newer member countries are moving towards those of the founders.

The propagation of monetary policy is the subject of the chapter authored by *Manuel Balmaseda* and *David Taguas*. They use a VAR framework to estimate the dynamic effect on domestic interest rates of a change in the monetary policy of the German Bundesbank under pre-EMU conditions, and also of innovations in domestic monetary policy in different EU member states on domestic real GDP, the inflation rate and the interest level. Their main tentative conclusion is that, on the basis of simulations with their model, key variables in each EMU member country respond differently to monetary innovations. This result might be bad news for the EMU, but may however, according to them, be partly attributable to the observation period used, through necessity including the late 1970s and early 1980s during which time structural changes taking place in the countries considered may have distorted the evidence.

Part III of the book focuses on social and labour market problems. *Wim Meeusen* and *Glenn Rayp* use a two-country Grossman-Helpman type of model of monopolistic competition with product innovation (Grossman and Helpman, 1991), in which the equation expressing equilibrium on the labour market has been replaced by an equation imposing equilibrium on the social security budget. Their aim is to examine the long-run sustainability of different levels of social protection. The closed-form solution for the common long-run rate of innovation in a monetary union that is obtained by the authors suggests that the levelling of social protection is not a necessary outcome in a situation where, among other things, R&D productivity between countries differs.

Alain Borghijs and *André Van Poeck* approach the 'social convergence' issue from a different – but immediately policy-relevant – angle, more directly focusing on labour market characteristics. They examine the case for more nominal wage flexibility and the ensuing necessity of labour market reform, starting from the reality of continuing differences in the unemployment rate among EU members. They also try to answer the question on the significance of the creation of the monetary union in this respect.

Frank Barry and *Aoife Hannan*'s interest is again more theoretical. They try to verify whether the new industrial specialisations of the so-called 'peripheral' EU economies (Greece, Ireland, Portugal and Spain), following their entry into the EU, are in line with traditional Heckscher-Ohlin-Samuelson theory. They make use of the European Commission's revealed comparative advantage method, and find that, although Greece and Portugal seem to conform, Ireland and Spain do not, appearing – counter-intuitively – to move towards more capital-intensive sectors. They point out, however, that this is still consistent with HOS-theory once the model is amended to allow for labour market distortions.

The final chapter is by *Nick Adnett* who discusses the economic rationale behind the so-called 'Third Way' model of the labour market (in the broad sense). He argues that since policy changes in a democratic society, including those relating to the labour market, are by definition gradual, reforms have to recognise the constraints imposed by existing institutions. In other words, enforced policy convergence would be costly in both economic and social terms. The political 'Third Way' model seems to have some popular support at the EU level, but its union-wide application should take national specificities into full account.

REFERENCES

Baumol, W.J. (1986), 'Productivity Growth, Convergence and Welfare: what the long run data show', *American Economic Review*, **76**, 1072-1085.

Button, K.J. and E.J. Pentecost (1993), 'Regional Service Sector Convergence', *Regional Studies*, **27**, 623-636.

Button, K.J. and E.J. Pentecost (1995), 'Testing for Convergence of the EU Regional Economies', *Economic Inquiry*, **33**, 664-671.

Grossman, G. and E. Helpman (1991), *Innovation and Growth in the Global Economy*, Cambridge, Mass.: MIT Press.

Haldane, A. and S.G. Hall (1991), 'Sterling's Relationship with the Dollar and the Deutschmark', *Economic Journal*, **101**, 436-443.

Hall, S.G., D. Robertson and M. Wickens (1992), 'Measuring Convergence of the EC Economies', *Manchester School,* **60**(Supplement), 99-111.

Kaldor, N. (1961), 'Capital Accumulation and Economic Growth', in F.A. Lutz and D.C. Hague (eds), *The Theory of Capital*, New York: St. Martin's Press, pp. 177-222.

Krugman, P. (1991), 'Increasing Returns and Economic Geography', *Journal of Political Economy*, **99**, 483-499.

Quah, D. (1997), 'Empirics for Growth and Distribution: stratification, polarization and convergence clubs', *Journal of Economic Growth*, **2**, 27-59.

PART I

Convergence between Nations and Regions
in the EU: General Issues

2. Regional Adjustment and Convergence in Euro-land

Filip Abraham[1]

1. INTRODUCTION

The member countries of the euro-zone are getting used to living with a single currency. The euro was successfully launched in 1999 and has taken its place as a world currency whose relationship to the US dollar is followed closely on international financial markets. The European Central Bank (ECB) is at the centre of the new macroeconomic framework, conducting a monetary policy that is targeted at internal price stability in the euro-zone.

With EMU safely on track, the attention is gradually shifting from shorter-term operational problems to a fundamental reflection on the longer-term costs and benefits of the newly established system. One important issue was frequently voiced in the run-up to the introduction of the single currency. In the post-Maastricht, pre-EMU period, several leading critics of EMU argued that monetary union could widen the gap between countries and regions with strong and weak economic growth (see, for example, Feldstein, 1997). This pessimistic scenario was motivated by research showing that Euro-land did not constitute an optimum currency area and that – in a macroeconomic setting without national sovereignty in exchange rate and monetary policy – rigid labour markets in Europe would fail to achieve a smooth adjustment to asymmetric shocks.[2]

It is clear that a euro landscape with widening growth disparities would undermine the long-run prospects of EMU. We see two problems which we want to discuss in more detail in this chapter. First there is the issue of *macro-economic adjustment*. The ECB's task is to conduct an effective monetary policy for the whole euro-zone. This policy cannot be targeted at the specific needs of individual member countries. In the event of diverging national growth patterns, it is unlikely that the ECB policies will be appropriate for the economic conditions of individual countries. Hence countries and regions must look for other adjustment mechanisms to deal with aggregate shocks at the national and regional level.

The second problem involves *cohesion* within the EU. Political support for European integration would seriously decline if EMU were to systematically raise the growth rates of leading regions while lowering growth rates in lagging regions. The latter would blame the integration process for their problems while the former would object to the rising costs of interregional redistribution.

How realistic is the prospect of diverging economic performance in the euro-zone? Evidently, it is too early to tell. At the time of writing, detailed information on the convergence process in the EU after the introduction of the single currency is not yet available. And with the prevailing robust growth in Euro-land, policy-makers did not yet face the acid test of coping with a recession. On the other hand, the experience of the first two years of EMU is instructive. Moreover, recent research yields new insights that advance the academic debate well beyond the ideas found in the literature of the pre-EMU era. In this chapter we bring together research and recent experience. Section 2 focuses on macro-adjustment in monetary union. Section 3 deals with regional cohesion. In Section 4 we briefly assess the policy options available to address undesirable growth differentials between countries and regions. The chapter ends with some concluding comments.

2. MACROECONOMIC ADJUSTMENT IN EMU

Monetary union is a new macroeconomic regime with a substantial growth potential. A credible commitment of the ECB to price stability eliminates the risks of high, volatile and uncertain inflation throughout Euro-land. This stable, low-inflationary macroeconomic environment facilitates rational economic decisions by households, businesses and government. In addition, the introduction of the single currency banishes nominal exchange rate variation among member countries. It is safe to say that exchange rate fluctuations do not always reflect economic fundamentals and that persistent exchange rate misalignments cannot be ruled out. If so, the adoption of one currency may contribute to a sound macroeconomic framework conducive to economic growth.

What does this imply for growth *differentials* across countries? The benefits of exchange rate and price stability depend on the characteristics of each individual country. The growth response to EMU will therefore vary across countries. This should not worry us for two reasons. Variation in growth rates is the natural outcome of the interaction between countries and regions. For instance, cross-country differences in the share of non-traded and traded goods are one cause for diverging growth paths according to the well-known Balassa (1964) effect. Moreover, divergence in growth rates is perceived as less of a policy problem when most countries and regions experience solid economic growth. To the extent that monetary union achieves a widespread improvement in growth prospects, tensions between countries and regions are likely to abate.

Monetary union becomes more of a problem when the growth potential fails to be realised or is achieved in some countries and not in others. Such an unfavourable scenario is emphasised in the literature on optimum currency areas (see Obstfeld and Peri, 1998 for an overview). Trading partners may face asymmetric shocks which need to be translated in adjustments of the real exchange rate. A sustainable macroeconomic set-up should not impede such real exchange rate changes. Critics of EMU argue that the monetary union will do just this. With imperfectly functioning labour markets, European countries need the monetary and exchange rate instrument to cope with country-specific shocks.

The combination of an asymmetric growth performance in Euro-land and the inability of member countries to deal effectively with their domestic economic problems cannot be solved easily by monetary policies of the ECB. Countries with a booming economy will pressurise the ECB to raise interest rates in order to keep inflation under control and slow down the economy. Member states with sluggish growth prefer a cut in interest rates to revive the economy. Given its mandate to set interest rates for the whole euro-zone, the ECB is most likely to opt for an intermediate position between the preferences of economies with strong and weak growth patterns.[3] This policy choice strengthens the expansion in the booming economies and thus enhances the probability of a real exchange adjustment with a 'hard landing'. In the slowly growing countries, this intermediate solution hampers the 'take-off' of the economy. Taking for granted that wages and prices in many European labour markets respond slowly and partially to adverse economic conditions, unemployment may have to go up a lot before the required adjustment in the real exchange rate takes place.

An extensive body of empirical research assesses the importance of asymmetric shocks in European countries (see De Grauwe, 2000 for a discussion). The bad news for proponents of EMU is that the 11 euro countries did not constitute an optimum currency area in the 1980s and early 1990s. In many studies a clear distinction is established between the 'core' countries of the EU and the 'periphery' (Southern Europe, Ireland, the UK and – to a lesser extent – Scandinavia). The periphery faces asymmetric shocks with respect to the core. The good news is that the core is gradually expanding to include more EU member countries and that the contrast between core and periphery has been diminishing in recent years. Other good news is that aggregate country-specific shocks may not be as important as optimum currency area theory would want us to believe. Sector-specific shocks appear to matter much more than developments at the national level. Marimon and Zilibotti (1998) establish for a sample of ten European countries that almost 80 percent of the long-run employment growth differentials across countries and industries are accounted for by sectoral effects and only 20 percent by country effects. Abraham and Van Rompuy (1999) find that sector-specific shocks in the Belgian economy dominate national and regional developments.

Table 2.1.   *Real growth rates in the euro-zone (in %), 1991-2001*

	1991-95	1998	1999	2000 (forecast)	2001 (forecast)
Belgium	1.5	2.7	2.3	3.5	3.3
Germany	2.0	2.2	1.5	2.9	2.9
Spain	1.3	4.0	3.7	3.8	3.4
France	1.1	3.2	2.8	3.7	3.2
Ireland	4.6	8.9	8.3	7.5	6.2
Italy	1.3	1.5	1.4	2.7	2.7
Luxembourg	5.4	5.0	5.0	5.6	5.7
Netherlands	2.1	3.7	3.5	4.1	3.7
Austria	1.9	2.9	2.3	3.2	3.0
Portugal	1.8	3.5	2.9	3.6	3.5
Finland	-0.7	5.0	3.5	4.9	4.2
Euro-zone	1.5	2.7	2.3	3.4	3.1

Source: European Commission, 2000.

It is worthwhile to take a look at actual growth rates in the Euro-11 countries (see Table 2.1). It is clear from this table that there are indeed pronounced growth differences in the EU. Ireland, Finland, Sweden, the Netherlands, Luxembourg and Spain are growing at a robust pace. By contrast the German and Italian economies are experiencing sluggish growth. Of course, the existence of a heterogeneous growth pattern in the EU is nothing new: growth rates varied considerably before the euro was introduced. Moreover, there are signs that growth rates of euro members are coming closer together at least if the forecasts of future growth rates in Table 2.1 turn out to be correct. Most importantly, the move towards monetary union coincided with a return to solid growth. This fact does not prove that EMU *causes* long-term growth. But it undoubtedly facilitates macro-management at the ECB and at the national level.

So what should one conclude? In our view, the EMU macroeconomic framework is solid and can contribute to sustained long-run economic growth. This does not mean, however, that the challenge of diverging growth rates should be cast aside lightly. Instead, policy-makers should look for adjustment mechanisms that allow countries and regions to deal effectively with economic shocks. This point is taken up again in Section 4 of this chapter.

3. INTEGRATION, COMPETITION AND CONVERGENCE

Monetary union is not only a macroeconomic event but also a leap towards the full integration of EU markets. EMU extends the Single Market Project and promotes competition by taking away foreign exchange transactions and by enhancing the transparency and comparability of prices. In turn, this may stimulate growth by a better allocation of production factors, the exploitation of economies of scale and perhaps even more innovation and diffusion of improved technologies and methods.

3.1. Convergence or divergence: some theoretical considerations

Do market integration and stronger competition also reduce the divergence in national growth performances? The international trade literature links market integration to cohesion, that is, to the difference in real income *levels* across countries and regions. One distinguishes between the proponents of the convergence and the divergence school who come to diametrically opposed conclusions.[4]

The convergence school predicts that real income levels in an integrated economic area will come closer together. The theoretical background for this strong result is the Heckscher-Ohlin-Samuelson (HOS) model and its extensions. The driving force of this convergence result depends on the type of model considered. If factors of production are mobile across countries and regions, factor mobility guarantees convergence. In the European context of limited labour mobility, one usually thinks about capital mobility when companies decide to invest outside their home market (Braunerhjelm *et al.*, 2000). Such foreign direct investment contributes to the transfer of knowledge and new technologies from the more advanced to the lagging regions.

If factors of production do not move across countries (regions), convergence obtains as a result of international (interregional) trade. Countries or regions specialise in products that use intensively the factors of production that are abundant and cheap in that country or region. As a consequence of those trade relations, the theory predicts that abundant production factors in each country will become more expensive, that countries will adopt the same technology and that income levels will fully converge.

A very different picture of regional adjustment is offered by theories of regional agglomeration. Taking up an old tradition in regional economics, Krugman (1991) elegantly formalises some key driving forces of regional agglomeration. His work has been the starting point of a renewed interest in the forces that drive regional agglomeration and clustering (an overview of the current state of the art is found in Fujita *et al.*, 1999).

In Krugman's initial model, equilibria with regional convergence and regional divergence are both possible. Regional wage differentials foster regional convergence of income levels. Lower wages offer an incentive for companies in high wage regions to relocate. In this way, the regional wage gap is gradually closed. This convergence process is, however, counteracted by mechanisms that lead to regional divergence in income levels. This possibility of regional divergence has received considerable attention in academic and policy circles.

In the simple Krugman set-up, proximity to a large market with high-income levels attracts companies to locate in richer regions. In those markets, firms are close to their customers and are able to exploit economies of scale, which lower their average costs and strengthen their competitive position. In addition, firms in those locations benefit from the presence of a skilled workforce and from the contacts with other firms in the region. Therefore firms tend to flock together, which may trigger a self-enforcing process of regional clustering. This agglomeration process is more likely in an integrated economic area because firms can more easily exploit economies of scale and because workers, capital and firms face fewer restrictions on mobility.

The stylised Krugman model has been extended in later work to incorporate intermediate inputs and innovation. Regional expansion leads to increased demand for intermediate inputs and attracts companies supplying those intermediate goods. The regional clustering of firms stimulates innovation, which reinforces the competitive advantage of the expanding region even more. A self-reinforcing process of rising regional income levels, innovation and clustering of companies and their suppliers takes place. The prospering region leaps ahead of the other regions. While this process cannot go on forever, it can continue for a long time.

The consequences for cohesion are not so positive. It is straightforward to come up with a scenario with divergent growth rates between regions that benefit from agglomeration and those that do not. The implications for macroeconomic policy-making are equally problematic. Regional clustering leads to asymmetric shocks. Particularly worrisome from both cohesion and macroeconomic management point of view, would be a situation where the single currency deepens the existing core-periphery pattern in the EU.

3.2. Empirical evidence on convergence and divergence

By now a large amount of empirical work is available that focuses on the convergence-divergence debate. It is clear from this research that reality is more complicated than the strong convergence result would lead us to believe. Strict empirical tests of the HOS theory are no great success. Trefler (1995) considers a wide sample of 33 countries and 9 production factors using the American input-output technology for every country. He finds that the theory does not perform much better than the toss of a coin. The main culprit for this disappointing result is the assumption that countries use the same technologies. If technological and demand differences are taken into account, the theory does much better. This indicates that inter-sectorial specialisation and convergence factors may interact with technology to determine the world-wide distribution of income levels.

A paper by Davis *et al.* (1997) compares the performance of the HOS theory for a sample of countries and a sample of Japanese regions. They find stronger convergence in income and technology between Japanese regions than between countries. This should not be too surprising because Japanese regions are geographically closer and belong to one country without barriers to trade and factor mobility.

Translating this to the European case, one would expect that convergence is far more likely between regions that have been integrating for a longer period of time. There is indeed evidence that points in this direction. Several studies trace the evolution of regional income differences during the 40 years following the signing of the Rome Treaty (see Abraham and Van Rompuy, 1995; Neven and Gouyette, 1995). The global picture is one of slow convergence between higher and lower income countries and regions. This result is confirmed by Barro-type regressions that put the conditional convergence rate in the EU at 1 percent to a maximum of 2 percent a year, below the speed of regional convergence in the USA (Vanhoudt *et al.*, 2000 and Sala-i-Martin, 1996). According to Fatas (1997) shocks that are affecting EU regions are becoming more similar over time.

Nevertheless, convergence in Europe has not been a smooth process over time. Years of divergence alternated with periods of regions growing closer together. Moreover, the broad convergence trend does not mean that each and every lagging region was able to catch up. According to Quah (1996) proximity matters in the convergence process. The author emphasises the importance of regional spillovers between neighbouring EU regions, which are more important than macroeconomic factors at the national level. He also shows that convergence in per capita income between neighbouring regions occurs at a faster pace than the average convergence process for all EU regions.

Recent empirical research takes a closer look at clustering and agglomeration effects that are the key phenomena of the divergence school. Amiti (1999) finds an increase in geographical concentration in 30 of the 65 manufacturing industries of her sample between 1976 and 1989. Only 12 industries recorded a fall in geographical concentration. Factors contributing to geographic concentration of industries are economies of scale and strong intermediate linkages with other industries. Turning to the specialisation of countries instead of individual industries, the industrial structure of Belgium, France, Germany, Italy and the UK have become more similar between 1968 and 1990 although the opposite evolution occurred between 1980 and 1990.

Hallett (2000) analyses trends for EU regions in the period 1980-95. Measures of regional specialisation, concentration and clustering are highly stable over time and, if anything, show a slight downward tendency. The degree of clustering and concentration varies across sectors with stronger concentration and clustering in traded goods, credit and insurance services, and other market services. A clear core-periphery pattern emerges with the wealthier central regions specialising in banking, insurance and high value-added manufacturing while the more traditional labour-intensive sectors tend to be located in peripheral regions with lower income levels.

Deriving the main message out of this empirical evidence ultimately boils down to beliefs about whether the glass is half empty or half full. In our opinion, the burden of proof is still on those who argue that monetary integration will lead to a pronounced widening of the gap between higher- and lower-income regions and countries. Admittedly, this scenario cannot be ruled out a priori in the future. Nor do we deny that individual regions and perhaps countries might be confronted with structural adjustment problems. But the history of European integration does not support the hypothesis of broad-based divergence so far.

4. ECONOMIC POLICY AND REGIONAL ADJUSTMENT

Suppose our cautious optimism happens to be misguided, and that Euro-land is confronted with divergent growth patterns that complicate macroeconomic management and threaten cohesion. Or assume, more positively, that policy-makers want to avoid a disruptive divergence scenario. What is to be done?

A first important caveat is that we should not expect the ECB's policies to cope with growth differentials between countries. The objective of the ECB's monetary and exchange rate policy is to guarantee low and stable inflation for the whole euro-zone. The ECB will therefore not resolve country-specific problems nor address asymmetric shocks in euro-zone countries. It is not the task of the central bank to achieve cohesion by actively trying to close the gap between prospering and lagging regions or countries. The ECB's best contribution to managing growth differentials is to create a stable and transparent macroeconomic framework that is conducive to economic growth.

A second essential point is that we should not overestimate the role of regional transfers to achieve convergence. Admittedly, transfers may help to close part of the gap in purchasing power between leading and lagging regions. While this takes away some of the political pressure that rising regional income equality generates, regional policy only offers a structural solution in the long run if it is accompanied by other policy measures. The recent success of Ireland, for example, may have been facilitated by EU subsidies but would not have been achieved if Ireland 'did not get its act together'. And it seems that for every success story in regional policy one can point to a failure like the Italian Mezzogiorno. This is also the conclusion of the academic research on the effectiveness of regional policies. If the recent evaluation of Vanhoudt *et al.* (2000) is to be believed, regional redistribution that takes the form of public capital investments actually reduces economic growth in the EU. While all observers do not share such gloom and doom, excessive optimism is equally misplaced. This is surely the case in the light of the ongoing reform of EU regional policy where, in an effort to extend the EU towards Central and Eastern Europe, regional funds are more thinly spread over the current recipients of EU structural aid.

The previous arguments lead to the inevitable conclusion that, to a large extent, countries and regions should address their own problems. There is no alternative for sound policies at the national and the regional level. When countries face asymmetric shocks they have to adjust. If regions lag behind, they should do something about it.

We pointed out in Section 2 that the macroeconomic toolkit of EMU member countries contains fewer instruments due to the loss of monetary and exchange rate policy. Countries and regions will have to rely on other policies to address asymmetric shocks and to promote convergence. Labour market and wage adjustments immediately spring to mind. Recent work by Wyplosz (2000), Daveri and Tabellini (2000), Blanchard and Wolfers (1999), Abraham (1999) and Nickell (1997) identify the rigidities that labour markets of several European countries still have to overcome. Those rigidities include generous unemployment benefits that are allowed to run on indefinitely, combined with little or no pressure on the unemployed to obtain work, and low levels of active intervention to increase the ability and willingness of the unemployed to work. Rigidities are furthermore generated by sectoral wage bargaining when unions do not take into account the consequences of their wage decisions for the rest of the economy. Likewise, high labour taxes pro-duce unemployment.

Research on European wage flexibility shows that wages and labour costs did not react sufficiently to adverse economic conditions in order to prevent unemployment from going up. A small wage response to changes in unem-ployment is a well-known result in the literature on European wage flexibil-ity. While unemployment elasticities of wages vary from country to country and from study to study, macroeconomic wage adjustments to unemployment do not usually exert a *strong* moderating impact on wage outcomes (see for instance Layard *et al.*, 1993; Eichengreen, 1993). At the regional level, Blan-chard and Katz (1992) for the USA and Abraham (1996) for the EU find that there is only a very small role for regional wage adjustment to unemploy-ment. In many European countries regional wage setting is strongly influ-enced by bargaining at the industry or national level and therefore does not sufficiently respond to region-specific developments.

As far as we can judge, membership of EMU brings about a greater awareness in euro-land that the evolution of national labour costs is a key determinant of unemployment and international competitiveness. Unfortu-nately, few signs are pointing to a similar switch in mindset at the regional level. In short, there is still some way to go before the functioning of national and regional labour markets will be fully adjusted to the reality of Euro-land.

5. SOME CONCLUDING COMMENTS

This chapter casts an old European debate on regional adjustment and con-vergence in the new setting of Euro-land. In doing so, we concentrate on the impact of EMU on macroeconomic adjustment and regional cohesion.

The existing theoretical literature sharply identifies the challenges for a balanced regional development in the years to come. Countries and regions must learn how to handle macroeconomic shocks and different growth per-formances in a setting without national exchange and monetary sovereignty. They must realise that a single currency pushes forward market integration and that this integration process unleashes forces that may lead to either more convergence or increasing divergence.

This is as far as theory can go. The empirical facts inspire some cautious optimism. The experience of the first two years of EMU does not point to a widening divergence in growth rates among euro-zone countries although economic growth obviously varies from country to country. On the whole, 40 years of post-war European integration brought high and low income regions closer together. But this convergence process was slow, discontinuous in time and did not benefit all lagging regions.

What will the future bring? Economic theories of regional adjustment and convergence are an uncertain guide because they are consistent with a wide range of optimistic and pessimistic scenarios. And the time elapsed since the introduction of the euro is too short to tell. There is no doubt though that flexible regional adjustment and a strengthening of regional cohesion will depend on the quality of the policy choices that will be made in the years to come. EMU is a new landscape that policy-makers are gradually discovering. Succeeding in Euro-land requires a careful guiding hand and skilful crafts-manship in Brussels, in Frankfurt, in the capitals of the participating member states and at the regional level. To achieve regional convergence and to prevent unsustainable growth differentials from undermining EMU, there is no substitute for competent policy-making.

NOTES

1. Katholieke Universiteit Leuven. This text is based on my presentation at the conference organised by the National Bank of Belgium on 'How to Promote Economic Growth in the Euro Area' and on my lecture on 'Regional Competition in the European Union' at the eleventh European Advanced Studies Institute in Regional Science in Munich.
2. Pessimism about EMU went quite far sometimes, in particular at the other side of the Atlantic. Feldstein (1997) raises the prospect of a European central bank unresponsive to local unemployment and the emergence of a political union that removes competitive pressures within Europe for structural reform. All of this would prompt protectionism and conflict with the United States. According to the author, war is also a distinct possibility.
3. Depending on the economic weight of the different countries and overall inflationary expectations.
4. This discussion is based on Abraham (2000).

REFERENCES

Abraham, F. (1996), 'Regional Adjustment and Wage Flexibility in the European Union', *Regional Science and Urban Economics*, **26**, 51-75.
Abraham, F. (1999), 'A Policy Perspective on European Unemployment', *Scottish Journal of Political Economy*, **46**, 350-366.
Abraham, F. (2000), 'Regional Competition in the European Union', in P.W.J. Batey and P. Friedrich (eds), *Regional Competition: Advances in Spatial Science*, Berlin: Springer, pp. 247-259.
Abraham, F. and J. Van Rompuy (1999), 'Is Belgium ready for EMU? A Look at National, Sectoral and Regional Developments', *De Economist*, **147**, 337-352.

Abraham, F. and P. Van Rompuy (1995), 'Regional Convergence in the European Monetary Union', *Papers in Regional Science*, **74**, 125-142.

Amiti, M. (1999), 'Specialisation Patterns in Europe', *Weltwirtschaftliches Archiv*, **135**, 573-593.

Balassa, B. (1964), 'The Purchasing Power Doctrine: a reappraisal', *Journal of Political Economy*, **72**, 584-596.

Blanchard, O. and L.F. Katz (1992), 'Regional Evolutions', *Brooking Papers on Economic Activity*, **1992**(1), 1-61.

Blanchard, O. and J. Wolfers (1999), 'The Role of Shocks and Institutions in the Rise of European Unemployment: the aggregate evidence', *NBER Working Paper* no. 7282.

Braunerhjelm, P., R. Faini, V. Norman, F. Ruane and P. Seabright (2000), 'Integration and the Regions of Europe: how the right policies can prevent polarisation?' *Monitoring European Integration*, **10**, London: CEPR.

Daveri, F. and G. Tabellini (2000), 'Unemployment and Taxes. Do Taxes Affect the Rate of Unemployment?', *Economic Policy*, **30**, 47-104.

Davis, D.R., D.E. Weinstein, S.C. Bradford and K. Shimpo (1997), 'Using International and Japanese Data to Determine When the Factor Abundance Theory of Trade Works', *American Economic Review*, **87**, 421-446.

De Grauwe, P. (2000), *Economics of Monetary Union*, Fourth edition, Oxford: Oxford University Press.

Eichengreen, B. (1993), 'Labour Markets and European Monetary Unification', in P. Masson and M. Taylor (eds), *Policy Issues in the Operation of Currency Unions*, Cambridge: Cambridge University Press, pp. 130-162.

Fatas, A. (1997), 'EMU: Countries or Regions? Lessons from the EMS Experience', *European Economic Review*, **41**, 743-752.

Feldstein, M. (1997), 'EMU and International Conflict', *Foreign Affairs*, November/December 1997, pp. 60-73.

Fujita, M., P. Krugman and A.J. Venables (1999), *The Spatial Economy: Cities, Regions and International Trade*, Cambridge: The MIT Press.

Hallett, M. (2000), 'Regional Specialisation and Concentration in the EU', *Economic Papers of the European Commission*, No. 141.

Krugman, P. (1991), 'Increasing Returns and Economic Geography', *Journal of Political Economy*, **99**, 483-499.

Layard, R., S. Nickell and R. Jackman (1993), *Unemployment: Macro-economic Performance and the Labour Market*, Oxford: Oxford University Press.

Marimon, R. and F. Zilibotti (1998), 'Actual versus Virtual Employment in Europe: is Spain different?', *European Economic Review*, **42**, 123-154.

Neven, D. and C. Gouyette (1995), 'Regional Convergence in the European Community', *Journal of Common Market Studies*, **33**, 47-65.

Nickell, S. (1997), 'Unemployment and Labour Market Rigidities: Europe versus North America', *Journal of Economic Perspectives*, **11**, 55-74.

Obstfeld, M. and G. Peri (1998), 'Regional Non-adjustment and Fiscal Policy: lessons for EMU', *NBER Working Paper*, No. 6431.

Quah, D. (1996), 'Regional Development Clusters Across Europe', *European Economic Review*, **40**, 951-958.

Sala-i-Martin, X. (1996), 'Regional Cohesion: evidence and theories of regional growth and convergence', *European Economic Review*, **40**, 1325-1352.

Trefler, D. (1995), 'The Case of the Missing Trade and Other Mysteries', *American Economic Review*, **85**, 1029-1046.

Vanhoudt, P., T. Mathä and B. Smid (2000), 'How Productive are Capital Investments in Europe?', *European Investment Bank paper*, **5**, 81-106.

Wyplosz, C. (2000), 'The Role of the Labour Market', Working Paper no. 8, Brussel: Nationale Bank van België.

3. A Quarter of a Century of Real GDP and Growth Rate Convergence and Divergence in the EU

Eric J. Pentecost[1]

1. INTRODUCTION

The European monetary union (EMU) has given rise to a common monetary policy for the 11 economies that are members of the euro area. This common policy is set to address the needs of the euro area as a whole and not of the specific countries within it. For this policy – defined as delivering low levels and dispersion of inflation and unemployment rates, and high levels and growth of output per capita across member states and regions – to be successful, it is important that the economies of the euro area converge. Without economic convergence the costs for some regions or countries of remaining within the euro-zone could become sufficiently high – in terms of high unemployment rates and falling per capita GDP – for an individual state to contemplate leaving the euro area (see, for example, Buiter, 1999). While a 'voluntary quit' is the worse case scenario, the convergence issue is important for the success and sustainability of the euro area.

Economic convergence has two distinct facets: nominal convergence and real convergence. The Maastricht Treaty (1992) and the joining conditions for membership of the euro area were essentially about the former type of convergence. Hence the Treaty explicitly set targets for inflation, nominal interest rates and exchange rates (see for example De Grauwe, 1997; Pentecost, 2001). Now that the single currency has been adopted and a common monetary policy is operational, it is very important that the real economies of the member states converge. Real convergence has, on the one hand, been fostered by the Single Market, but is, on the other hand, potentially handicapped by the single currency, since lagging regions or countries are no longer able to engage in demand-side stimulation. Without specific national economic management, remembering that fiscal policy is also severely constrained by the somewhat misnamed Stability and Growth Pact (SGP), short- or even medium-term divergences in national economic performance may be the initial consequence of EMU. This scenario gains credence particularly from the fact that there is still little evidence of labour market integration between the member states of the euro area. This lack of labour market integration could harbour productivity differences and even lead to longer-run real economic divergence and ultimately to a disaster for the EMU project.

This chapter is therefore concerned with the convergence and divergence of the real side of the economies in the European Union (EU). During the 1990s a large empirical literature has emerged on convergence, stemming from the tension between the traditional neo-classical model of economic growth that suggests long-run convergence of the real economies and the new endogenous growth models that suggest sustained divergence between economies (see Hermes, 1994). The seminal empirical work is that of Barro (1991) and Barro and Sala-i-Martin (1991), which examined the convergence hypothesis for regions within the EU by a time-series of cross-section data on output per head. The conclusion that convergence occurred at the rate of about 2 percent per annum has been challenged on both measurement and methodological grounds.

In terms of measurement, Barro and Sala-i-Martin compared regional GDP per capita with national GDP per capita, rather than with EU or world output per head. Thus the convergence they refer to is really national, rather than continental or global convergence. Button and Pentecost (1995) re-examine this model using EU-wide data and find that unconditional convergence is much faster – about 3 percent per annum within the EU between 1975 and 1988, although this finding is highly dependent on both the sample period chosen and the structure of the regional economies. Convergence is also shown to be much weaker during the 1980s than during the 1970s, perhaps partly due to the expansion of the EU to include Greece, Spain and Portugal.

The Barro and Sala-i-Martin methodology has also been much criticised in the literature since it assumes a common aggregate production function across economies (Islam, 1995; Lee *et al.*, 1997). Lee *et al.*, for example, show that steady-state growth rates differ across countries. Once this heterogeneity is allowed for, the estimates of beta – the convergence parameter – turn out to be substantially higher than those of Barro and Sala-i-Martin, although one should add that they are imprecisely estimated and difficult to interpret. Using a panel data framework, Bjorksten (2000) also examines real convergence in the EU over the period 1977 to 1997 and finds evidence of conditional convergence, but to different steady states. This in turn is shown to be consistent with the existence of three 'convergence clubs' (see Quah, 1993) in the EU. Canova and Marcet (1995) use a Bayesian approach to estimate convergence rates and the steady states of the European member countries of the OECD and European regions. They find that the average estimates of the rate of convergence are much higher than those of Barro *et al.*, at about 11 percent for countries and 23 percent for regions. Moreover, countries and regions have different steady states and, most importantly, the initial conditions are the most important determinant of the cross-section dispersion of steady states. That is, poor regions stay poor and rich regions remain rich over time, with the differences reduced by only a small amount.

In contrast to these cross-section and panel data studies this chapter concentrates on aggregate time-series data. Recent work by Mills and Holmes (1999) distinguishes between short-run and long-run convergence and finds that output levels diverge, but that there is convergence of EU growth rates of industrial production. The use of industrial production as a measure of output enables a monthly data set to be used, but since industrial production includes only about a third of all economic activity, this may be a misleading indicator for the economies as a whole. Moreover, given the global structure of industrial activity, the industrial production series may exaggerate the degree of national interdependence and hence convergence. Given this dependence of the EU economies on the service sector and the geographical dispersion of industries between economies, it is much more important that GDP per capita shows convergence than industrial production. The problem with the former series is that it is only available at an annual frequency, which greatly reduces the scope for dynamic analysis. To help overcome this problem a time-varying parameter framework is used, following Hall *et al.* (1992), to estimate the convergence and divergence between real GDP per capita in the 15 member states of the EU over the last quarter of a century.

The structure of this chapter is set out as follows. Section 2 reviews the theoretical mechanisms by which real economic convergence and divergence can occur. Section 3 then reviews the methodology used to measure economic convergence. Section 4 describes the data set and Section 5 presents the empirical results from the econometric analysis.

2. THE THEORETICAL BASIS FOR REAL CONVERGENCE

There are two principal mechanisms for real economic convergence: the Heckscher-Ohlin-Samuelson (HOS) model of international trade and the neo-classical growth model. Both of these approaches assume that all markets, including factor markets, are perfectly competitive.

The HOS model of trade assumes that in addition to competitive factor markets the economies have similar relative factor endowments and that countries engage in free trade. International trade between the economies will then result in goods price and factor price equalisation, due to arbitrage, without necessitating any movement of capital or labour across national boundaries. Allowing for international factor mobility speeds up productivity and wage and price convergence in an absolute sense. Thus the effect of closer economic integration should lead eventually to price and wage convergence. With increased trade, however, economic growth would be enhanced through greater specialisation according to the principle of comparative advantage, which may lead in turn to more divergent industrial structures (see for example Baldwin, 1989 and Krugman and Venables, 1990), thus working against economic convergence.

The second mechanism for real economic convergence across countries (or regions) stems from the traditional neo-classical growth model of Solow (1956) and Swan (1956). The neo-classical model assumes perfectly competitive factor markets, but in addition perfectly malleable capital and a freely accessible, common technology. Because capital is assumed to exhibit diminishing marginal returns the model predicts that, although growth in per capita terms cannot be sustained permanently, convergence in relative GDP per capita will occur. The mechanism for convergence is through decreasing returns that imply that the marginal product of capital will fall, reducing both the incentive to save and the contribution of output growth for a given volume of investment. As a result growth will gradually slow down. Because poorer countries are 'capital scarce', they will have a relatively higher marginal product of capital than the rich countries and hence have a greater incentive to save. With higher savings being translated into higher investment, they will enjoy a temporary higher rate of growth and gradually reduce the gap between themselves and the rich countries.

The introduction of exogenous technical progress allows for sustained growth in the basic neo-classical growth model, but does not affect the convergence result, providing the technology is common to all countries. In this context a possible important factor in the convergence process is technological catch-up (Abramovitz, 1979; 1986). According to this hypothesis the possibility of imitating at low cost, technologies developed elsewhere should allow poor countries to grow faster than rich ones, other things being equal.

The new growth theory due to Romer (1986) is, however, less optimistic about economic convergence. With increasing returns to reproducible factors, such as human capital, the return on investment is an increasing function of the accumulated stock of capital. As a result the growth rate will increase with time and the level of income. Romer (1990) shows that positive growth rates may be sustained indefinitely in models in which the rate of technical progress is endogenously determined by decisions by private agents to invest in human capital, providing such activities are not subject to diminishing returns. This leads to the rich becoming richer and the poor remaining poor.

The differences between the neo-classical and new growth theories are, however, not as large as may first appear. In particular the neo-classical model assumptions are very restrictive. In Solow (1956), for example, long-run income levels are functions of investment rates and the rate of growth of the population and, of course, these can differ across countries. Similarly Abramovitz emphasises that the catch-up process is far from automatic. The degree to which catch-up takes place in a given country depends upon on its 'social capability' to absorb foreign technologies (effectively schooling and education) and to adapt them to its own needs and to a conducive political and macroeconomic environment. Thus the convergence that emerges from the neo-classical model is only conditional convergence: that is, there is convergence in the sense that relative income levels are eventually stabilised.

There are also demand-side factors that may assist the catch-up of backward regions. Until 1991 member states of the EU were in control of their own monetary and fiscal policies, which could be used to stimulate regional or national economies as necessary. After the Maastricht Treaty, the monetary and fiscal policies of the candidate countries to the EMU were constrained by the need to meet the nominal convergence criteria set out in the Treaty, and so monetary and fiscal policy became the slaves of convergence rather than the tools of demand management (Button and Pentecost, 1999a and 1999b). Furthermore, since 1999 and the adoption of the euro by 11 of the 15 member states,[2] there is no scope for independent national monetary policies. Fiscal policy is also constrained by a balanced budget rule, set out in the SGP. Thus neither monetary nor fiscal policy is able to respond to regional imbalances without compromising the primary objective of price stability, which in the opinion of the European Commission is out of the question. The only adjustment mechanism that remains, whereby regional or even national imbalances are resolved, is through real sector adjustments in labour and product markets, which is believed to be a very slow process. Indeed one of the greatest concerns of economists has been that the generally poor functioning of European labour markets will cause most economies (and especially the peripheral ones) considerable suffering at one time or another under a common monetary policy. Despite a number of suggestions as to how to improve the functioning of EU labour markets (see for example Coe and Snower, 1997) progress has been slow and is expected to remain slower than is desirable.[3]

3. MEASURING CONVERGENCE

Convergence between two variables occurs when one variable gradually ap-
proximates to the other. More formally, convergence occurs when the difference between two or more time-series becomes arbitrarily small (or conver-
ges on some constant α) as time elapses, such that $\lim_{t \to \infty}(X - Y) = \alpha$. This
definition gives rise to a non-stochastic measure of convergence, known as
σ-convergence. In this context σ-convergence exists if there is a fall in the
dispersion of real GDP per capita over time. It is measured by the coefficient
of variation in GDP per capita across countries or regions at various points in
time, and is given as:

$$\sigma_t = \left(\frac{1}{n} \sum_{i=1}^{n} (X_{it} - \overline{X}_t)^2 \right)^{1/2} / \overline{X}_t \ , \tag{3.1}$$

where $\overline{X}$ is the mean of the series X and n is the number of countries.

For random series the concept of convergence can be extended to the notion of stochastic convergence, whereby the probability of the two series to
differ by a specified amount is required to become arbitrarily small, that
is $E\{\lim_{t \to \infty}(X - Y)\} = \alpha$ (Hall *et al.*, 1992). Moreover, this definition of
convergence can be extended to systems or to subsystems. For example, the
authorities may achieve inflation convergence, but only at the cost of higher
unemployment. This is not economic convergence in any meaningful sense.
Thus there is said to be *strong* system convergence where every pair of variables in a system or subsystem have converged, and *weak* convergence where
some variable pairs have converged without the others showing any change
in behaviour. Thus consider a vector of variables X, defined for countries i
and j. Then when

$$E\{\lim_{t \to \infty}(X_i - X_j)\} = \alpha_X \tag{3.2}$$

holds for all X, there is strong system convergence. Similarly, when (3.2)
holds for only some X there is weak system convergence if the time-series
relationship between the remaining variables does not change.

Following Haldane and Hall (1991) and Hall *et al.* (1992), this definition
of economic convergence can be made operational in this context by considering the differences between real GDP (per capita) of any two countries and
the difference between one of the countries and a third country with the help
of a regression model with time-varying parameters. The convergence of a

series Y, say, representing the log of real per capita GDP, can therefore be assessed by estimating the equation:

$$[Y_i - Y_j](t) = a(t) + b(t)[Y_i - Y_k](t) + e(t) \quad .$$ (3.3)

$a(t)$ and $b(t)$ are the time-varying parameters. If Y_i refers to a specific economy, Y_j to the EU average GDP per capita and Y_k to real GDP per capita in the USA, then convergence between UK and EU real GDP per head can be examined.

Table 3.1.   *Convergence rules*

Coefficients	$a \& b \to 0$	$\begin{array}{c} a \to c \ \& \\ b \to 0 \end{array}$	$\begin{array}{c} a \to 0 \ \& \\ b \to 1 \end{array}$	$\begin{array}{c} a \to c \ \& \\ b \to 1 \end{array}$
Type of convergence	$Y_i \to Y_j$	$(Y_i - Y_j) \to c$	$Y_j \to Y_k$	$(Y_j - Y_k) \to c$

Table 3.1 shows that there is a dual requirement for convergence. First, a necessary condition is that $a(t)$ tends to a constant c, which may be zero if per capita GDPs are identical. Second, $b(t)$ must also tend to zero. If $b(t)$ tends to unity then the GDP per head of the EU has converged to that in the USA. Because both $a \to c$ and $b \to 0$ are required for convergence, the validity of the alternative hypothesis for $b(t)$ is not important, since if $b(t)$ converges neither to zero nor unity, then $a(t)$ is unlikely to be a constant, or a stationary process. It is important to emphasise that $a \to c$ is a necessary, but not a sufficient condition for convergence (see Hall *et al.* (1992) for a more detailed discussion of the different possibilities).

Equation (3.3) refers to the level of real GDP per head, but the same analysis can be applied to growth rates in GDP per head. This is important because if economies are initially far apart in terms of GDP per capita then they may still be a long way away from converging on GDP per capita by the end of the sample period, although there may have been some convergence in growth rates. If it is indeed the case that poorer economies grow faster than rich economies in a context of conditional convergence, then it should be the case that a and $b \to 0$, denoting that economy i initially grows faster than j. In this case a will be declining over time as the national economy catches up with the EU average.

4. THE DATA SET

The data set is taken from the OECD Historical Statistics and is annual, real GDP per capita is measured in US dollars and runs from 1960 to 1999 for most countries. The data set is collected for all 15 EU member states and the United States (US), which is used as the relevant country for the alternative hypothesis in (3.2). As an average measure of real EU GDP per head the weighted average of the 11 euro-zone member states (EU-11) was computed using the official weights, which are noted in Table 3.2.

This series for weighted EU-11 real GDP per head from 1960 to 1999 is shown in Figure 3.1. The series shows steady growth from 1960 to 1979, after which it falls steadily until 1986. From 1986 until 1999 there is an up-ward trend punctuated by three short-term reversals in 1989, 1993 and 1997. These reversals correspond to the reunification of Germany and the collapse of the planned economies in Eastern Europe in 1989, the ERM crises in September 1993 and the quest by the EU-11 to meet the criteria for euro-zone membership in 1997. Real GDP per capita peaked in 1996 and although it has risen since, the 1999 level is still below that of the 1996 peak for the EU-11.

Figure 3.1.   Average real GDP per capita in EU-11, 1960-99

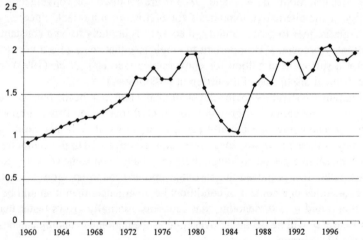

Table 3.2.   Weights used to compute average EU GDP per head (EU-11)

Austria	0.029	Italy	0.188
Belgium	0.040	Luxembourg	0.002
Finland	0.015	the Netherlands	0.051
France	0.211	Portugal	0.018
Germany	0.345	Spain	0.091
Ireland	0.010		

5. EMPIRICAL RESULTS

The results are presented in two parts. The first section refers to the measures of σ-convergence and the second section to the convergence of the time-varying b's to zero and the a's to constants.

5.1. σ-convergence

The results for σ-convergence are shown in Figure 3.2. These three measures of convergence based on the EU-6, EU-11 and EU-15 all show a similar pattern: increasing convergence through the 1970s as the coefficient of variation declines, a period of stability in the 1980s and then increasing divergence in the 1990s. The range in the coefficient of variation is smallest for the EU-15 and largest for the EU-6, but the dispersion of real GDP per capita is smallest for the EU-6 after 1974. This is consistent with the fact that new members have raised the standard deviation of the level of real income. The period of the EMS prior to 1989 and the idea of a common currency, is the decade of greatest real economic convergence between the member states.

Even on the most favourable measure of income dispersion, based on the EU-6, there are however sharp increases in per capita GDP dispersion in 1994 and 1998. Thus on the EU-6 measure, σ-divergence increases from about 16 percent of average real GDP per capita in 1991 to 44 percent in 1999. This suggests that the moves towards greater nominal convergence in the EU as set out in the Maastricht Treaty (1991), leading to EMU in 1999, have been associated with increasing real economic divergence. The fact that there has been a decade of real economic divergence suggests that this is more than a short-run cyclical phenomenon. Indeed the trade theory model set out in Section 2 suggests that this is what should be expected with increased economic integration. With comparative advantage, the production patterns of countries will become more specialised leading to greater economic diversity, in the absence of extensive labour migration or an active regional policy.

*Figure 3.2.   σ-convergence in the EU with respect to real GDP per capita,
1960-99*

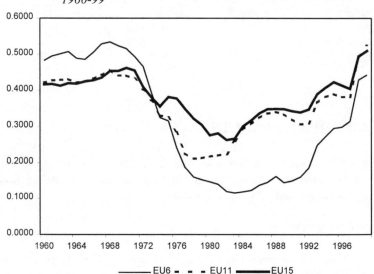

5.2. $a(t)$- and $b(t)$-convergence

The time-series convergence results are obtained by estimating equation (3.3) by using the Kalman filter, to obtain time-varying coefficients for $a(t)$ and $b(t)$ defined above.[4] The results are largely given in the various figures that follow. The model set up in Section 3, however, assuming that $b \rightarrow 0$, shows convergence towards EU average GDP per capita, providing also that $a \rightarrow c$, where c is a constant, or at least, a variable stationary in the mean. Thus the first test is to consider the stationarity of the time series $a_i(t)$ for each country i, using the augmented Dickey-Fuller (ADF) statistic.

The results are shown in Table 3.3. The unit root hypothesis is not rejected for all countries, and so these economies may be regarded as strictly non-convergent, even if $b \rightarrow 0$ over the sample.

The economies that are not converging on the EU-11 average level of real GDP per capita are: Finland, France, Greece, Ireland, Luxembourg, the Netherlands, Portugal, Spain and Sweden – over half of the sample. This includes all of the more recent members, except Austria, but the presence of France, Luxembourg and the Netherlands in this group is perhaps surprising.[5] To confirm these results, given the small sample problems of the ADF statistics, the $a(t)$'s were plotted against time. The $a(t)$'s for France, Luxembourg and the Netherlands showed a pronounced upward trend over the sample period and those for Ireland a downward trend – indicative of non-stationarity. The fact that the newer members do not show convergence may partly be a reflection of the short time period that they have been in the EU and partly a reflection of the different economic structure of the largely 'Mediterranean' character of these economies.

Table 3.3.   *Unit root stationarity tests on the* $a_i(t)$ *'s*

$a_i(t)$	ADF	$a_i(t)$	ADF
Austria	-4.049**	Ireland	-0.976
Belgium	-4.946**	Italy[#]	-2.900*
Denmark	-2.803*	Luxembourg	-1.668
Finland	-2.283	the Netherlands	-2.071
France	-1.632	Portugal	-1.253
Germany	-5.379**	Spain	-2.099
Greece	-0.539	Sweden	-0.662
		UK	-3.385**

Notes: Critical values for the ADF statistics are -2.945 (5%) and -2.611 (10%);
         # Sample period for Italy is 1974-99.
         '*' denotes statistical significance at the 95% level, '**' at the 99% level.

Therefore our investigation of what we shall call '*b*-convergence' (as different, but clearly related to the usual β-convergence) must begin with the remaining six economies. Figure 3.3 shows that for these economies there is evidence of $b \to 0$. The overall pattern is similar to that of the coefficient of variation, with the b's – fairly diverse in the 1960s and 1970s – becoming more closely aligned around zero in the mid-1980s, but with divergence increasing again in the 1990s. Figure 3.3 shows that as of 1999 Germany and Austria are fully converged, probably reflecting to some extent the high weight of German GDP in the computation of the EU average. Italy and Denmark are also converging to the EU-11 average, albeit still with some way to go. The $b(t)$'s for UK and Belgium seem to be diverging in opposite directions away from $b \to 0$ in 1999. This suggests that UK growth has been higher than the EU average, but not as high as in the USA. Thus as of the end of the twentieth century, and the adoption of the common currency notwithstanding, it is only Germany, Italy, Austria and, to a lesser extent, Denmark that show real convergence to the mean EU-11 levels of GDP per capita. It is interesting to note that neither Denmark nor the UK are members of the euro-zone.

Figures 3.4a-d show both the time varying a's and b's for the new members of the EU, defined as those joining in the 1980s and 1990s. The first two figures refer to the level of real GDP per capita and the last two to the growth rates of GDP per capita. Since the newer members are likely to be poorer in terms of levels of GDP per head, in this context it is likely that there will be less convergence both in income levels and in growth rates.

Figure 3.3.   b-*convergence for Austria, Belgium, Denmark, Germany, the UK and Italy, 1962-99*

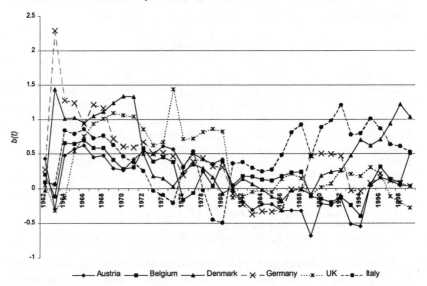

Figure 3.4a.   a(t) *for the new EU-members (GDP per capita), 1972-99*

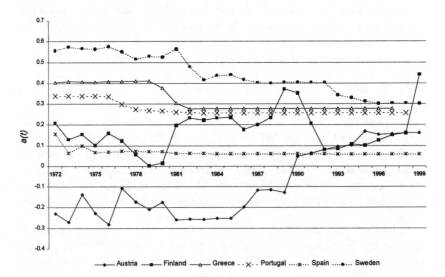

Figure 3.4b. b(t) *for the new EU-members (GDP per capita), 1972-99*

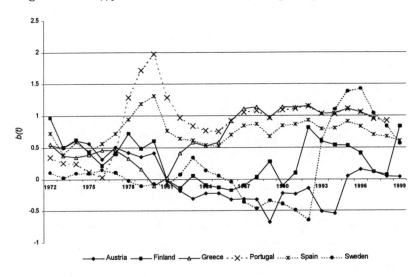

Figure 3.4c. a(t) *for the new EU-members (growth rate of GDP per capita),*
1972-99

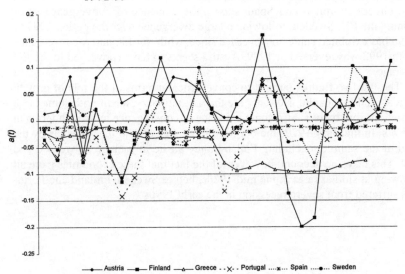

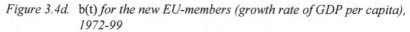

Figure 3.4d. b(t) *for the new EU-members (growth rate of GDP per capita), 1972-99*

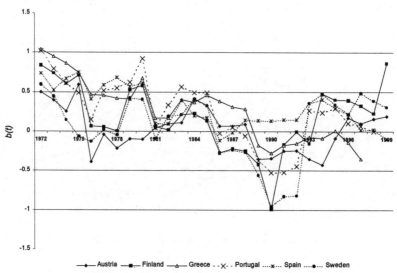

In terms of the levels of real GDP per head the *a*'s, with the exception of Portugal and Spain, are non-constant, showing divergence. In terms of the *b*'s, Greece, Portugal and Spain show little evidence of convergence since joining the EU. Sweden, following a large divergence over the period 1993 to 1996 has exhibited some convergence since, while for Finland *b*-convergence from 1992 was reversed in 1999. Austria seems to have converged to the EU average.

The last two figures purport to convergence in terms of the rate of growth of real GDP per capita. Not only are the *a*'s stationary, albeit with some large variations, but there is also some evidence of convergence in growth terms in the *b*'s. In the early 1970s the *b*'s were in a range of 1 to 0.5, whereas by the end of the sample, excluding Finland, they all lie in a range between 0 and 0.4. This takes no account, however, of the fact that these economies were all growing at similar rates in the mid-1980s, before Sweden, Finland and Portugal suffered from severe recession in the early 1990s.

6. CONCLUSIONS

This chapter has used time-series techniques in an attempt to make some judgements about the convergence or divergence of the EU economies over the past 25 years with respect to GDP per capita. According to the coefficient of variation there has been a divergence of GDP per capita during the 1990s between the EU-15. This descriptive measure is, however, not really appropriate for stochastic economic data. Therefore the approach pioneered by Hall *et al.* was used to try to uncover evidence for convergence or divergence in GDP per capita. The findings from this analysis show that there is more evidence of divergence than convergence in EU national GDP per capita. Indeed, only six economies seem to be convergent in the sense that $a \rightarrow c$, of which only Austria, Germany, Denmark and Italy show true convergence of per capita GDP, with $b(t)$ also tending to zero.

Combining the results from the σ-convergence and b-convergence suggests that one potential cause of the divergences could be the decision in the early 1990s to establish a common currency in the EU, which necessitated a stringent economic policy in many countries, in order for them to meet the entry criteria. That is, the quest for nominal convergence has contributed to greater real divergence. This result must, however, be regarded as provisional on at least two accounts: first, real economic convergence may take a very long time and can not be judged on the basis of only 25 years of data. Second, the process of real convergence is not necessarily monotonic and thus there will be periods when the real economies are temporarily diverging, although over a longer period of time their paths for real GDP per capita may turn out to be convergent.

NOTES

1. The author is at the Department of Economics of Loughborough University. His e-mail address is e.j.pentecost@lboro.ac.uk. Funding from the Wincott Foundation and research assistance from Kate Morrison are both gratefully acknowledged.
2. Twelve members from 2001 onwards, when Greece eventually joined the euro-zone, having initially failed to satisfy the criteria in 1998.
3. See for example IMF(1999), European Commission (1999).
4. See Haldane and Hall (1991) and Cuthbertson (1988) for a discussion of this methodology, which is also summarised in Button and Pentecost (1993).
5. This may be due to the experimental macroeconomic policy in France in the early 1990s (see Morin and Thibault, 1998). The Netherlands, on the other hand, is a country that has undertaken fundamental structural reforms and Luxembourg has an exceptional economy, both in terms of its size and its unique position within the EU.

REFERENCES

Abramovitz, M. (1979), 'Rapid Growth Potential and its Realisation', reprinted in M. Abramovitz, *Thinking About Growth and Other Essays on Economic Growth and Welfare*, Cambridge: Cambridge University Press, 1989, pp. 187-219.

Abramovitz, M. (1986), 'Catching Up, Forging Ahead and Falling Behind', reprinted in M. Abramovitz, *Thinking About Growth and Other Essays on Economic Growth and Welfare*, Cambridge: Cambridge University Press, 1989, pp. 220-244.

Baldwin, R. (1989), 'The Growth Effect of 1992', *Economic Policy*, **9**, 247-283.

Barro, R.J. (1991), 'Economic Growth in a Cross-section of Countries', *Quarterly Journal of Economics*, **106**, 407-443.

Barro, R.J. and X. Sala-i-Martin (1991), 'Convergence across States and Regions', *Brookings Papers on Economic Activity*, **1991**(1), 107-182.

Bjorksten, N. (2000), 'Real Convergence in the Enlarged Euro Area: a coming challenge for monetary policy', Bank of Finland, Economics Department Working Paper No. 1/2000.

Buiter, W.H. (1999), 'Alice in Euroland', *Journal of Common Market Studies*, **37**, 181-209.

Button, K.J. and E.J. Pentecost (1993), 'Regional Service Sector Convergence', *Regional Studies*, **27**, 623-636.

Button, K.J. and E.J. Pentecost (1995), 'Testing for Convergence of the EU Regional Economies', *Economic Inquiry*, **33**, 664-671.

Button, K.J. and E.J. Pentecost (1999a), *Regional Economic Performance within the European Union*, Cheltenham, UK and Northampton MA, USA: Edward Elgar.

Button, K.J. and E.J. Pentecost (1999b), 'Fiscal Policy and Regional Policy: complements or substitutes?' Paper presented at the European Regional Science Association Conference, Dublin, July 1999.

Canova, F. and A. Marcet (1995), 'The Poor Stay Poor: non-convergence across countries and regions', CEPR Discussion Paper nr. 1265.

Coe, D.T. and D.J. Snower (1997), 'Policy Complementarities: the case for fundamental labour market reform', *IMF Staff Papers*, **44**, 1-35.

Commission of the European Communities (1999), *Employment in Europe in 1998*, Luxembourg: European Commission.

Cuthbertson, K. (1988), 'Expectations, Learning and the Kalman Filter', *Manchester School*, **56**, 223-246.

De Grauwe, P. (1997), *The Economics of Monetary Integration*, 3rd edition, Oxford: Oxford University Press.

Haldane, A. and S.G. Hall (1991), 'Sterling's Relationship with the Dollar and the Deutschmark', *Economic Journal*, **101**, 436-443.

Hall, S.G., D. Robertson and M. Wickens (1992), 'Measuring Convergence of the EC Economies', *Manchester School*, **60**, Supplement, 99-111.

Hermes, N. (1994), 'Financial Development and Economic Growth: a survey of the literature', *International Journal of Development Banking*, **12**, 3-22.

International Monetary Fund (1999), *World Economic Outlook*, Washington DC: IMF.

Islam, N. (1995), 'Growth Empirics: a panel data approach', *Quarterly Journal of Economics*, **110**, 1127-1170.

Krugman, P. and A. Venables (1990), 'Integration and the Competitiveness of Peripheral Industry,' in J. Braga de Macedo and C. Bliss (eds), *Unity with Diversity, within the European Economy: The Community's Southern Frontier*, Cambridge: Cambridge University Press.

Lee, K., M.H. Pesaran and R. Smith (1997), 'Growth and Convergence in a Multi-country Empirical Stochastic Solow Model', *Journal of Applied Econometrics*, **12**, 357-392.

Mills, T.C. and M.J. Holmes (1999), 'Common Trends and Cycles in European Industrial Production: exchange rate regimes and economic convergence', *The Manchester School*, **67**, 557-587.

Morin, P. and F. Thibault (1998), 'French Macroeconomic Performance and Policy Mix: some questions on the years 1990-95', *Revue d'Economie Financière*, **45**, 63-95.

Pentecost, E.J. (2001), 'The Political Economy of the Transition to Monetary Union in Western Europe', in E.J. Pentecost and A. Van Poeck (eds), *European Monetary Integration: Past, Present and Future*, Cheltenham, UK and Northampton MA, USA: Edward Elgar.

Quah, D. (1993), 'Empirical Cross-section Dynamics in Economic Growth,' *European Economic Review*, **37**, 426-434.

Romer, P.M. (1986), 'Increasing Returns and Long Run Growth', *Journal of Political Economy*, **94**, 1002-37.

Romer, P.M. (1990), 'Endogenous Technical Change', *Journal of Political Economy*, **98**, S71-S102.

Solow, R.M. (1956), 'A Contribution to the Theory of Economic Growth', *Quarterly Journal of Economics*, **70**, 65-94.

Swan, T.W. (1956), 'Economic Growth and Capital Accumulation', *Economic Record*, **32**, 334-361.

4. Convergence or 'Twin Peaks'? The Spanish Case

José Villaverde and Blanca Sánchez-Robles[1]

1. INTRODUCTION

The issue of convergence among countries and regions has been at the fore-front of the economic debate in the last two decades, both among researchers and policy-makers. From the point of view of the former, the existence or absence of convergence is an important test for the validity of neoclassical models when confronted with endogenous models of the AK type. Policy-makers, in turn, also consider convergence as a crucial issue, specially regarding developing countries or regions. If the convergence property is present, the poorest areas will be able (at least on a theoretical basis) to catch up with the richest and therefore improve their relative levels of per capita income.

Although empirical results are far from conclusive, there is a certain consensus on the existence of the so-called conditional convergence for selected samples of countries and regions (for a recent survey, see De la Fuente, 2000). However, Quah (1996, 1997) has proposed and used a different methodology that casts some doubts on these results. He claims that the likelihood of a smooth trend towards convergence should be replaced by polarisation of countries in two or more groups (the convergence clubs) that do not seem to reduce the gap between them over time. By stating that countries are not automatically headed towards a common level of per capita income, this approach challenges the neo-classical prediction. According to Quah, countries are breaking down into two categories: the low-income countries, on one side, and the developed nations, on the other. This has been christened the 'Twin Peaks' property.

For obvious reasons, the topic of convergence has gained importance in Europe after the implementation of EMU. At this stage it is not easy to predict whether the single currency will foster or jeopardise the convergence process among European countries and regions. As for the Spanish economy, there are some concerns about the potential effects of the single currency upon the reduction of spatial inequalities. Although a large amount of literature has been devoted to this topic in recent years (for example, Cuadrado *et al.*, 1998, and Villaverde, 1999), there is no doubt that some questions related to it have not been answered so far.

The structure of the chapter – the main goal of which is to try to shed new light on this issue – is as follows: Section 2 makes some brief remarks about the main characteristics of the regional dynamics of the Spanish economy. Section 3 surveys the literature on polarisation and convergence clubs. Section 4 provides some basic ideas regarding the theoretical background employed in Section 5, which describes the data, implements the computations and presents the most interesting results. Finally, the main conclusions are summarised in Section 6.

2. SPATIAL DISPARITIES IN SPAIN: WHAT HAVE WE LEARNT?

According to the empirical research that has been carried out on spatial inequalities in Spain, the main conclusions regarding the behaviour of provincial disparities may be expressed in the following two points.

1. Spanish provinces have experienced conditional β-convergence. In particular, this kind of convergence has been enhanced by variables such as public capital, technological catching up and reallocation of inputs among sectors.[2]

This result implies that Spanish provinces are headed towards different steady states, meaning that they are not expected to attain a common level of per capita income automatically, by the sole action of traditional convergence mechanisms such as the diminishing marginal productivity of capital.

In addition, part of the provincial inequality in Spain may also be attributed to the behaviour of unemployment rates, whose dispersion has increased during the 1980s. This fact, in turn, may be related to severe rigidities in the labour market and in the bargaining process, ending up in quite uniform rates of growth of wages across the nation despite provincial differentials in productivity dynamics and unemployment rates.

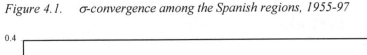

Figure 4.1.   σ-convergence among the Spanish regions, 1955-97

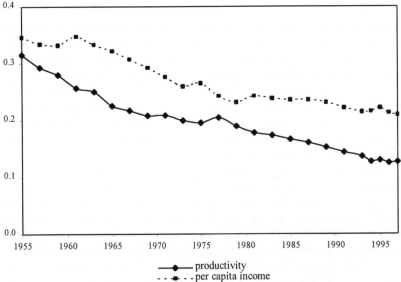

2. Generally speaking, σ-convergence has been observed (Figure 4.1) during the period under consideration. However, the reduction of disparities has not followed a regular trend but seems to have stagnated from the early 1980s onwards.

As has been pointed out several times (see for example, Sala-i-Martin, 1996), β-convergence is a necessary but not sufficient condition for σ-convergence. In addition, its analysis does not provide a full description of the pattern of reduction of spatial disparities, if it exists; furthermore, it has also been claimed (Quah, 1996) that the conventional analysis of β-convergence can easily be misleading if the time-series contain unit roots. Moreover, it is also true that σ-convergence analysis is not very informative on the mobility of the provinces within the distribution of regional income, or about their persistence in certain categories.

Therefore, it may be interesting to complement the traditional studies of β- and σ-convergence with alternative analyses that provide more specific tests of the intra-distribution dynamics of per capita income at the provincial level. In particular, we want to look at certain possible outcomes of the evolution of income per inhabitant, such as overtaking, relative regress or polarisation.

3. POLARISATION: A BRIEF REVIEW OF THE LITERATURE

The discussion on convergence has been abundantly covered by the literature of the last two decades. Nevertheless, the approach of looking at polarisation and, more precisely, at the existence of convergence clubs, is relatively new. A rationale for this fact is the idea that neo-classical growth models, generally speaking, do not predict multiple equilibria; according to these types of models, economies converge to a (unique) steady state in the long run. On the other hand, multiple steady states are indeed possible within the framework of endogenous models. This is the consequence of increasing returns, externalities or other non-convexities in the production function.

Some basic ideas underlying most models of economic growth may shed light on this issue. If the production function is of the neo-classical type $(y = f(k))$,[3] it can be shown that there is only one steady state to which the economy converges (Barro and Sala-i-Martin, 1998). This is the well-known property of the Solow (1956) model for a constant saving rate or of the Ramsey-Cass-Koopmans model (Ramsey, 1928; Cass, 1965; Koopmans, 1965).[4]

Focusing, for simplicity, on the Solow model (the basic results carry over, however, to the Ramsey-Cass-Koopmans model) the dynamics of the economy can be described by a very simple expression. Denoting the (constant) saving rate by s, the average product of capital by y/k, and allowing for constant rates of depreciation and population growth, δ and n, respectively, the rate of growth g is given by the following equation (all variables are expressed in per capita terms):

$$g = s\frac{f(k)}{k} - (\delta + n) \quad .\qquad(4.1)$$

This rate of growth may be positive, negative or zero. When it takes this last value it refers to the steady-state situation. Because of the aforementioned assumptions, marginal and average productivity of capital are monotonically decreasing, in which case there is a unique steady-state level of both output and capital per capita.

Several steady states are possible however if some assumptions concerning the production function are relaxed and, in particular, if average productivity is allowed to increase within a certain range. Notice that the increasing returns are only necessary in a limited interval of the domain of k, but not at all possible values of k (for a graphical analysis see Barro and Sala-i-Martin, 1998). Thus, conceivably, a country with a small level of per capita capital could end up in an abnormally low-level equilibrium state with respect to k, a (possibly) considerably higher amount of investment being required in order to reach the higher steady state. Since the corresponding increase in saving may be difficult to implement, the country may remain permanently in the so-called poverty trap represented by the low steady state.

If there were many countries in this steady state, in turn associated with smaller values of capital and income per capita, the world income distribution would display the so-called 'Twin Peaks' property.

Although one of the seminal contributions about polarisation and convergence clubs is Baumol (1986), discussed further by Baumol *et al.* (1989), perhaps Quah – in a well known series of papers – is an author who has given this topic most of its present popularity. Furthermore, he has forcefully stressed the point of using the Markov-chain approach as a suitable test for the existence of convergence clubs.

Quah (1993) analyses a sample of 118 nations during the period 1962-84 and does find some evidence of polarisation into two groups: a group of rich-income countries and a group of low-income countries. In subsequent papers (Quah, 1996, 1997), he extends his analysis to the USA, finding a larger degree of mobility among states and no tendency to polarisation. Lopez-Bazo *et al.* (1999) have also employed this technique in order to ascertain the dynamics of GDP per capita of European regions for the period 1980-92, their results suggesting a slight tendency to polarisation.

Regarding the Spanish case, there are a few papers that have dealt with this issue by employing the same methodology. Gardeazábal (1996) studies the provincial income per capita distribution over the period 1967-91 and does not find evidence of polarisation. Pérez (1999) addresses the same issue at the regional level concluding that, between 1955 and 1995, the degree of persistence in the distribution of GDP per capita and productivity is high, but the final long-run distribution seems to be unimodal. Lamo analyses the performance of the per capita income of Spanish provinces during the period 1955-91 and finds no evidence of convergence among them (Lamo, 2000).

There are other recent contributions that have covered this topic under alternative approaches for countries other than Spain. To quote just a few, Durlauf and Johnson (1992) use a regression tree analysis and suggest the existence of multiple equilibria among countries. Canova (1999) finds clubs within the distribution of per capita income of OECD countries, by means of employing a technique that applies some ideas from Bayesian statistics to the analysis of polarisation.

Finally, Chatterji (1992) has proposed an alternative technique used in order to test for the existence of convergence clubs. The basic idea is to focus in the pattern of convergence or divergence of income gaps with the leader. Using this technique, Chatterji and Dewhurst (1996) identified a high-income and a low-income group of regions for the UK in the period 1989-91. Villaverde and Sánchez-Robles (1999a) have also used this approach and identified some degree of divergence from the leader within the Spanish provinces during the last two decades.

4. MARKOV PROCESSES AND CONVERGENCE: SOME ELEMENTARY THEORETICAL CONSIDERATIONS

Markov processes can be considered as a special case of stochastic processes. They can be defined in continuous or discrete time and relate to a continuous or discrete set of states. Following Amemiya (1985), a Markov model can be characterised by the following two properties.

a) A sequence of binary random variables taking the values

$$y_j^i(t) = 1 \quad \text{if the } i^{\text{th}} \text{ unit is in the state } j \text{ at time } t \text{ and,}$$

$$y_j^i(t) = 0 \quad \text{otherwise.}$$

If, in a discrete-time context, for each unit i, the distribution of the vector $y^i(t)$ depends fully and only on $y^i(t-1)$, then the process is a first-order discrete-time Markov process.

b) A set of transition probabilities, in which $p_{jk}^i(t)$ denotes the probability of unit i being in state j at time $(t-1)$ and jumping to state k at time t. If the set of states is finite and denumerable then all the transition probabilities may be ordered in the form of the so-called Markov matrix $P^i = \{ p_{jk}^i(t) \}$, in which the sum of all the elements of a row will add up to one. Let $p(t)$ be the vector describing the distribution of the units over the different states at moment t. It holds of course that

$$p_j(t) = \frac{1}{n} \sum_{i=1}^{n} y_j^i(t) \quad ,$$

where n is the number of units. Such a model is called a Markov chain.

Furthermore, if the transition probabilities do not depend on time or on the unit, the model is called homogeneous and stationary. It can be shown (Amemiya, 1985) that, under fairly general conditions, there exists a uniquely defined long-run, or 'ergodic', matrix of transition probabilities P^∞ and a corresponding vector of equilibrium probabilities associated to a stationary

Markov chain. More formally, if we denote the transition matrix by $P = \{p_{jk}\}$, then the 'ergodic' equilibrium vector is π, verifying

$$\pi = P'\pi \ , \tag{4.2}$$

such that

$$\pi_j \geq 0 \quad \text{and} \quad \sum_{j \in E} \pi_j = 1 \ . \tag{4.3}$$

It follows that

$$\lim_{t \to \infty} p_j(t) = \pi_j \ . \tag{4.4}$$

In other words, in the long run the elements of the transition matrix will reach the state of nature j with probability π_j, irrespective of the starting position. These ideas are intuitively appealing for the study of spatial convergence or divergence, as Quah has shown in the papers mentioned above. If we consider a finite number of states (as determined, for example, by different levels of per capita income), the shift of the units among states can be easily traced and, therefore, the transition probability matrix may be obtained. This matrix will show the dynamic behaviour of the units, since the transition matrix expresses, roughly speaking, the probability of a unit starting off in a particular state and ending up in the same or in a different state. Notice that, by means of using first-order Markov chains, it is implicitly assumed that all the relevant information about the past behaviour of a particular region is embedded in its present value. This idea is in accord with the one expressed by Jones (1997), that the fundamentals underlying the steady state towards which a country or region converges are fairly stable over time.

We can apply – again following Amemiya – the rule that the maximum likelihood estimator of the transition probabilities can be computed as follows:

$$\hat{p}_{jk}^{ML} = \frac{\sum_t s_{jk}(t)}{\sum_t \sum_k s_{jk}(t)} = \frac{\sum_t \sum_i y_j^i(t-1) y_k^i(t)}{\sum_t \sum_k \sum_i y_j^i(t-1) y_k^i(t)} \ , \tag{4.5}$$

in which $s_{jk}(t)$ denotes the number of units that have changed from state j to state k in period t. The ergodic vector, which describes the income distribution of the units in the long run, is obtained by means of iterating the transition matrix. If the ergodic density vector has only one maximum, it suggests some degree of convergence. Instead, if it tends to a bimodal (or trimodal,...) structure it may be pointing to some degree of polarisation.

The nature of this analysis, however, suggests that results regarding the steady-state income distribution should be looked at with some caution. The computation of long-run probabilities implicitly implies that historic probabilities will somehow carry over in the future. In other words, there is no place for shocks to alter the course of this economy and change the current trend.[5] This surely is unrealistic: there is no reason to believe that institutions, the rate of technological progress, the nature of human capital and other crucial factors determining per capita income will remain constant over time.

5. DISTRIBUTION DYNAMICS ACROSS SPANISH PROVINCES

Data on provincial per capita Gross Added Value (GAV) in constant pesetas of 1986, as provided by *Renta Nacional de España y su Distribución Provincial*, Fundación Banco Bilbao Vizcaya (2000), have been used to test the existence of polarisation among Spanish provinces. The sample covers the period 1955-97. For the largest part of the period, that is until 1993, data are available every two years; from 1994 onwards they are available on a yearly basis. The number of total observations is, however, large enough to make the analysis reliable, since we have observations from 24 years.

Figures 4.2-4.5 highlight some basic features of the income distribution among Spanish provinces in selected years. The non-parametric densities have been computed using a Gaussian kernel, and with an optimal bandwidth selected for each case.

Figure 4.2 captures the income profile for the starting year (1955). It departs largely from the normal distribution, and the probability density is right-skewed. In particular, some back-of-the-envelope computations show that a large proportion of the provinces (almost half) did not even reach 75 percent of the average income. As time goes by, though, it is observed that the actual distribution starts to be closer to the Gaussian, albeit however that there are certain 'anomalies' in particular years. Figure 4.3 represents the situation in 1973. The progress experienced in the lowest part of the distribution is noticeable, since the probability mass has partly shifted to the right. Figure 4.4 exhibits the distribution in 1981. A local peak at the right of the mode is now dramatically high, suggesting some degree of polarisation for this specific year. Figure 4.5 represents the last year of the sample, 1997. The slope of the probability density changes remarkably little over the values 100 to 120 on the horizontal axis, displaying a small protuberance at the latter level. Finally, Figure 4.6 shows all densities in a more compact way by means of using a three-dimensional plot. It should be observed that the 'Twin Peaks' property is not apparent any more at the end of the period. However, it is also true that the densities are not entirely Gaussian in some years, having small *plateaux* that have led eventually to a bimodal distribution.

Figure 4.2. *Non-parametric density of real per capita income in the Spanish regions, 1955 (average over the regions = 100)*

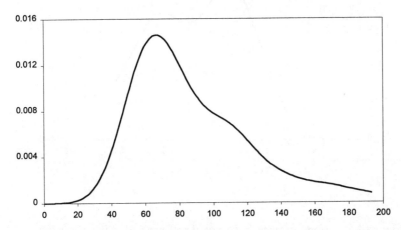

Figure 4.3. *Non-parametric density of real per capita income in the Spanish regions, 1973 (average over the regions = 100)*

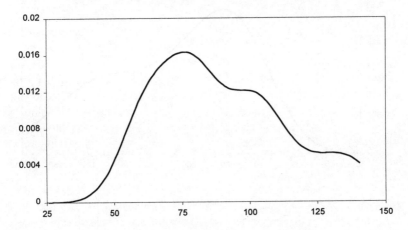

*Figure 4.4.   Non-parametric density of real per capita income in the
                Spanish regions, 1981 (average over the regions = 100)*

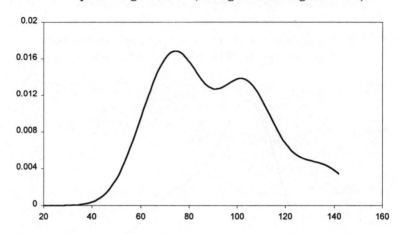

*Figure 4.5.   Non-parametric density of real per capita income in the
                Spanish regions, 1997 (average over the regions = 100)*

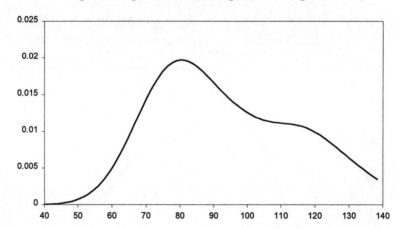

Figure 4.6.   *Real per capita income distribution of Spanish regions, 1955-97 (average per capita income over the regions = 1)*

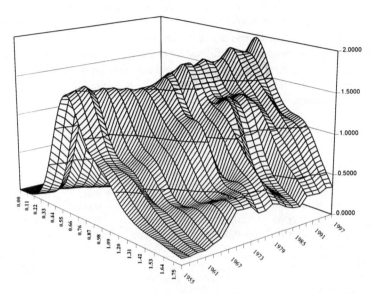

Although this particular issue deserves further research, a first interpretation of the 'Twin Peaks' phenomenon that takes place in 1981 can be linked to the recession that the Spanish economy experienced in the early 1980s: the crisis led in the short run to the exacerbation of the internal economic cleavages between regions (richer regions getting relatively richer and poorer regions poorer). The subsequent expansion from the mid 1980s onwards, following the entry of Spain and Portugal in the EC, had the opposite effect, that is the reduction of the disparities among the regions.

After the graphical analysis, attention is shifted to a quantitative approach. Following other similar studies, among which Quah's, the entire distribution has been defined in terms of five states, state 1 representing the group of provinces with the lowest levels of per capita income: for computational reasons the analysis has been carried out in a discrete-state fashion.[6] It has indeed been a complex task to choose the appropriate grid in order to make the income distribution discrete and establish the different classes. In the end, a common practice in regional studies has been applied, defining classes in terms of a specific percentage of average per capita income at the national level. In this case, the first class comprises provinces earning an income less than 75 percent of the average. The second class refers to those placed between 75 percent and 90 percent, the third corresponds to the interval 90-110 percent and the fourth to 110-125 percent. Provinces exceeding the 125 percent of the national average are included in the fifth class.[7]

Next, Amemiya's methodology for estimating Markov chains (expression 4.5) has been applied. This is the first step. In a second step, the *P*-matrix that was obtained has been iterated for successive times in order to get the ergodic matrix. This procedure has been carried out not only for the whole period but also for some sub-periods. The main results are displayed in Table 4.1 for the whole period and two particular sub-periods.

Table 4.1.   *Transition matrices for the Spanish provinces, 1955-97*

1955-97 states	1	2	3	4	5
1	0.9177	0.0823	0.0000	0.0000	0.0000
2	0.0560	0.8955	0.0485	0.0000	0.0000
3	0.0000	0.0258	0.9188	0.0554	0.0000
4	0.0000	0.0000	0.0977	0.8647	0.0376
5	0.0000	0.0000	0.0000	0.0593	0.9407
ergodic vector	0.1283	0.1886	0.3545	0.2010	0.1275

1955-79 states	1	2	3	4	5
1	0.9143	0.0857	0.0000	0.0000	0.0000
2	0.0692	0.8615	0.0692	0.0000	0.0000
3	0.0000	0.0270	0.9189	0.0541	0.0000
4	0.0000	0.0000	0.1250	0.8214	0.0536
5	0.0000	0.0000	0.0000	0.0610	0.9390
ergodic vector	0.1243	0.1539	0.3950	0.1710	0.1503

1979-97 states	1	2	3	4	5
1	0.9236	0.0764	0.0000	0.0000	0.0000
2	0.0435	0.9275	0.0290	0.0000	0.0000
3	0.0000	0.0250	0.9188	0.0563	0.0000
4	0.0000	0.0000	0.0779	0.8961	0.0260
5	0.0000	0.0000	0.0000	0.0566	0.9434
ergodic vector	0.1455	0.2557	0.2972	0.2147	0.0986

The first part of Table 4.1 shows the results for the period 1955-97. It conveys a few interesting messages. First, the degree of persistence in the relative position of the provinces is high, as shown by the large values in the main diagonal of the matrix. This persistence attains its highest value for states 1, 3 and 5. The high persistence in the lowest state of provinces should, no doubt, be a matter of concern for both academics and policy-makers: it may be hiding some kind of poverty trap. The economic conditions for growth could be linked, in turn, to a particular level of human capital, infrastructure endowments or availability of financial services.[8] Second, jumps are only observed to the adjacent state. There are evidently no visible jumps from state 1 to 3 or 2 to 4 (or vice versa) – there are no *growth miracles* in this sample – and thus the degree of mobility is limited to the next category.[9] The highest degree of mobility is found in state 4.

The long-run equilibrium of the regional income distribution is, not entirely surprisingly, characterised by a distribution that has a maximum in state 3. The likelihood of belonging to states 2 and 4 is smaller, and the minimum correspond to the extremes of the distribution, states 1 and 5.

The results agree with the intuitions obtained from the visual inspection of the graphs above, since they do not predict polarisation among Spanish provinces in the years 1955-97 but, rather, some kind of concentration around the average values. Nevertheless, these results may also suggest some sort of geographical externality, along the lines of Krugman (1991). Lopez-Bazo *et al.* (1998) and Goicolea *et al.* (1998) have indeed found evidence of these kinds of spillovers among neighbouring regions for the Spanish economy, whereby fast growth in one region may foster the development of the contiguous areas. In particular, when examining the provinces in the highest states in 1955 and 1997, a shift of the most prosperous provinces to the Northeast of the country can be observed, while in 1955 some well-off provinces were located in other areas of Spain, such as the Cantabrian range or even Andalucia.

Therefore, the final distribution of provinces in groups (or states) may suggest externalities associated to location – either their relative closeness to dynamic provinces or their proximity to the centre of Europe – since the richest provinces tend to concentrate over time in the North-east part of the country.[10] The case of the provinces surrounding Madrid is remarkable. One possible explanation, apart from the spillover effect of capital, is related to the spatial distribution of activities (Iranzo and Izquierdo, 1999), whereby some industries prefer to establish themselves in nearby provinces that have lower costs of real estate.

In order to explore the main determinants of intra-state mobility, an ANOVA analysis has been carried out. The main results are displayed in Table 4.2. The sample has been split into three categories on the basis of a comparison between the situation in 1955 and 1997: the first one is made up of provinces jumping to a higher class (48 percent of the total); the second category comprises the provinces moving to a lower state (15 percent); finally, the third category includes the provinces remaining in the same state (37 percent) (a detailed list of the provinces comprising each group may be found in the Appendix).

The left part of the table displays the value of the F-statistic, computed for different variables, while the right part shows the average value of every indicator for each of the categories mentioned above.

The main messages conveyed by the table can be summarised as follows:

1. Productivity growth appears as a crucial factor explaining the change in the relative position of the provinces. This is not the case, however, for the occupation rate.

2. The impact of externalities exerted by the contiguity to rich provinces (defined as those pertaining to class 4 and 5) has been captured by means of a dummy. This variable, called location (level effect), is significant at the 95 percent level. However, if the two Basque provinces of Vizcaya and Guipuzcoa are excluded from the sample (they may be regarded as outliers), the value of the F-statistic increases remarkably. The impact of externalities has also been measured through the potential gains from the vicinity of a province exhibiting a faster growth than the Spanish average. This variable, called location (growth effect), is not significant. Nonetheless, the value of the F-statistic is certainly higher when Vizcaya and Guipuzcoa are not included in the sample.

3. The role of sectoral structure has been explored next. The growth of the relative contribution to GDP[11] of the services sector does not seem very relevant. The opposite is true, however, for the relative contribution of industry (again, if we exclude Vizcaya and Guipuzcoa). This is not a surprise since, as Cuñado and Sánchez-Robles (2000) have pointed out, this is the sector in which gains in productivity have been larger in the last few decades. Simple observation of the Spanish recent history also suggests that those provinces whose industrial sector has declined (such as Asturias and Cantabria) are also worse off in terms of their position in the per capita income ranking. The opposite is true for the provinces with increasingly dynamic industrial sectors (such as Navarra and La Rioja). The exceptions are the two archipelagos, Canarias and Baleares that have in part based their development in the tourism sector. It can therefore be concluded that the strength of the industrial sector in recent decades has been crucial for the development of the Spanish provinces.[12]

Relative contributions of construction and agriculture also seem to have played an important role. The figure regarding agriculture should be considered carefully, though. The number of provinces descending in the ranking is higher than the number of provinces going up in the ranking, and hence the message is that a smaller growth of the relative contribution of agriculture increases the probability of jumping to a higher state.[13]

Table 4.2.   Variables influencing provincial mobility in Spain, 1955-97

	F Statistic	degrees of freedom	Average values of provinces		
			going up (48%)	moving down (15%)	staying (37%)
Productivity growth	12.77[b]	2, 49	0.0541	0.0423	0.043
Employment rate	0.2884	2, 49	0.3636	0.3658	0.354
Location (level effect)	3.4224[a]	2, 49	0.6800	0.6250	0.579
Location (level effect)[c]	23.0158[b]	2, 47	0.5600	0.3333	0.421
Location (growth effect)	1.7351	2, 49	0.8800	0.6250	0.682
Location (growth effect)[c]	2.3291	2, 47	0.9200	0.6667	0.682
Growth of GAV in services as a share of the overall GAV	0.1617	2, 49	0.0464	0.0466	0.045
Growth of GAV in industry as a share of the overall GAV	2.1281	2, 49	0.0248	0.0237	0.023
Growth of GAV in industry as a share of the overall GAV	4.4781[a]	2, 47	0.0248	0.0175	0.023
Growth of GAV in construction as a share of the overall GAV	4.9432[a]	2, 49	0.0286	0.0249	0.029
Growth of GAV in services as a share of the overall GAV	7.6018[b]	2, 49	0.0108	0.0142	0.019

Notes: $F_{critical}(2, 49)$ at 95% = 3.19; at 99% = 5.08;
            $F_{critical}(2, 47)$ at 95% = 3.20; at 99% = 5.10;
            (a) : significant at 95%; (b) : significant at 99%.; (c) : excluding Guipuzcoa and Vizcaya.
Source: Fundación BBVA, and own computations.

The second part of Table 4.1 displays the results for some relevant sub-periods. The main conclusions stated continue to hold for the 1955-79 sub-period. The long-run matrix predicts convergence, similarly to the one computed for the sub-period 1979-97, albeit convergence seems more intense in 1955-79, according to the higher level of the long-run probability of the third class. In fact, as was stated above, σ-convergence was faster in those years.

6. PRELIMINARY CONCLUSIONS

In this chapter Quah's methodology has been employed in order to analyse the pattern of regional GDP per capita dynamics of Spanish provinces over the period 1955-97. After some visual inspection of the non-parametric densities of per capita income distribution, the transition probability matrices were computed and an ANOVA exercise was carried out in order to ascertain the factors behind the success of some provinces. The results are consistent with others obtained in previous contributions. They can be summarised as follows.

- There is a large degree of persistence in the relative position of Spanish provinces over the period examined. However, some slight mobility among classes that shifts the position of some provinces in the ranking can be observed.
- There is some evidence of convergence towards the centre of the probability distribution for the whole period 1955-97, and for the subperiods 1955-79 and 1979-97.
- A tendency is visible whereby the richest provinces tend to progressively concentrate in the North-east of the country. This result can possibly be attributed to some sort of geographical externality linking economic development in one area to that experienced by nearby zones (through technological spillovers, for example), or simply to the proximity to the most prosperous areas of Europe.
- There is also some connection between the sectoral reallocation of industrial sectors and a good performance of the per capita income in a particular area. The specialisation in this specific kind of activities seems crucial in order to achieve high levels of income and welfare. This idea is consistent with the preliminary evidence of geographical externalities mentioned above.

APPENDIX

provinces that jump to a higher class	provinces that move to a lower class	provinces that remain in the same class
Córdoba	Sevilla	Almería
Huelva	Huesca	Cádiz
Jaén	Asturias	Granada
Teruel	Madrid	Málaga
Palmas (las)	Guipúzcoa	Baleares
Sta. Cruz de Tenerife	Vizcaya	Cantabria
Ávila	Alicante	Valladolid
Burgos	Valencia	Albacete
Palencia	*total: 8*	Barcelona
Segovia		Girona
Soria		Castellón
Zamora		Badajoz
Ciudad Real		Navarra
Cuenca		Álava
Guadalajara		Ceuta
Toledo		Melilla
Lleida		Zaragoza
Tarragona		León
Cáceres		Salamanca
A Coruña		*total: 19*
Lugo		
Ourense		
Pontevedra		
Murcia		
Rioja		
total: 25		

Note: The table compares positions in 1955 with positions in 1997. The performance in the intermediate stages is not considered here.

NOTES

1. The authors are both at the Department of Economics of the Universidad de Cantabria. They appreciate the comments and useful discussions on previous versions of this chapter made by X. Sala-i-Martin, P. Pérez and participants in the 2000 APDR meeting. The usual disclaimer applies.
2. For a more thorough comment on the relevant variables for β-convergence and the correspondent references, see Villaverde and Sánchez-Robles, 1999b.
3. That is, with constant returns to scale, concave in each of them and fulfilling the Inada conditions.
4. A caveat is in order here. As is well known, the Ramsey model displays in fact three steady states. Nevertheless, only one (with positive levels of capital and consumption per capita) is relevant from the economic viewpoint and fulfils the transversality condition.
5. The authors are grateful to X. Sala-i-Martin for stressing this point.
6. We do not dismiss the possibility of carrying out the exercise using a continuous Markov chain approach in the future. However, based on the visual inspection of the non-parametric densities graphs, we think that results will not vary substantially.
7. We have also tried some alternative approaches in order to construct the grid but the results obtained by these cast doubts upon their appropriateness.
8. This idea is closely related to that of 'social capacity' (Abramovitz, 1986).
9. These results are common to other similar studies, such as Quah, 1996.
10. This argument may be valid in order to explain the case of La Rioja and Navarre, whereas the rise of Guadalajara and other provinces of Castilla-La Mancha may be interpreted as a consequence of a geographical externality (their proximity to Madrid). Instead, Andalucia has fallen behind dramatically in relative terms, and the same happens – to a lesser extent – with the provinces belonging to the Cantabrian range.
11. Computed as GAV in the services sector over total GAV.
12. We do not share the opinion, therefore, that the higher levels of development are necessarily associated with a higher size of the services sector.
13. The role of the relative weight of each sector in total GDP has also been analysed, but the results are not very convincing.

REFERENCES

Abramovitz, M. (1986), 'Catching Up, Forging Ahead and Falling Behind', *Journal of Economic History*, **46**, 385-406.

Amemiya, T. (1985), *Advanced Econometrics*, Oxford: Basil Blackwell.

Barro, R. and X. Sala-i-Martin (1998), *Economic Growth*, second edition, Cambridge, Mass: The MIT Press.

Baumol, W.J. (1986), 'Productivity Growth, Convergence and Welfare: what the long run data show', *American Economic Review*, **76**, 1072-1085.

Baumol, W.J., S. Blackman, A. Batey and E. Wolff (1989), *Productivity and American Leadership: the Long View*, Cambridge, Mass: The MIT Press.

Canova, F. (1999), 'Testing for Convergence Clubs in Income Per-capita: a predictive approach', CEPR Working paper No. 2201, London.

Cass, D. (1965), 'Optimum Growth in an Aggregative Model of Capital Accumulation', *Review of Economic Studies*, **32**, 233-240.

Chatterji, M. (1992), 'Convergence Clubs and Endogenous Growth', *Oxford Review of Economic Policy*, **8**, 67-69.

Chatterji, M. and J.L. Dewhurst (1996), 'Convergence Clubs and Relative Economic Performance in Great Britain: 1977-1991', *Regional Studies*, **30**, 31-40.

Cuadrado, J.R., T. Mancha and R. Garrido (1998), *Convergencia Regional en España. Hechos, Tendencias y Perspectivas*, Madrid: Fundación Argentaria.

Cuñado, J. and B. Sánchez-Robles (2000), 'Sectoral Structure and Real Convergence among Spanish Regions', *International Advances in Economic Research*, **6**, 259-270.

De La Fuente, A. (2000), 'Convergence across Countries and Regions: theory and empirics', Working Paper No. 447.00, Instituto de Análisis Económico, Barcelona.

Durlauf, S. and P. Johnson (1992), 'Local versus Global Convergence across National Economies', NBER Working Paper No. 3996, Cambridge, Mass.

Fundación Banco Bilbao Vizcaya (2000), *Renta Nacional de España y su Distribución Provincial*, Bilbao.

Gardeazábal, J. (1996), 'Provincial Income Distribution Dynamics: Spain 1967-1991', *Investigaciones Económicas*, **XX**, 263-269.

Goicolea, A., J.A. Herce and J.J. Lucio (1998), 'Regional Integration and Growth: the Spanish case', Working paper No. 98-14, FEDEA, Madrid.

Iranzo, J. and G. Izquierdo (1999), 'El Efecto Frontera en la Comunidad de Madrid: ¿Desbordamiento Industrial o Competencia Desleal?', *Papeles de Economía Española, Economía de las Comunidades Autónomas*, **18**, 189-199.

Jones, C. (1997), 'Convergence Revisited', *Journal of Economic Growth*, **2**, 131-153.

Koopmans, T. (1965), 'On the Concept of Optimal Economic Growth', in *The Economic Approach to Development Planning*, Amsterdam: North Holland.

Krugman, P. (1991), 'Increasing Returns and Economic Geography', *Journal of Political Economy,* **99**, 483-499.

Lamo, A. (2000), 'On Convergence Empirics: some evidence for Spanish regions', *Investigaciones Económicas*, **3**, 681-707.

Lopez-Bazo, E., E. Vayá, J. Mora and J. Suriñach (1998), 'Grow, Neighbour, Grow, Grow, ...Neighbour be Good', *I Encuentro de Economía Aplicada*, Barcelona, 4-6 June 1998.

Lopez-Bazo, E., E. Vayá, J. Mora and J. Suriñach (1999), 'Regional Economic Dynamics and Convergence in the European Union', *Annals of Regional Science*, **33**, 343-370.

Pérez, P. (1999), 'Dinámica de las Regiones en España: 1955-1995', *Revista de Economía Aplicada* 22, **VIII**, 155-173.

Quah, D. (1993), 'Empirical Cross-section Dynamics in Economic Growth', *European Economic Review*, **37**, 426-434.

Quah, D. (1996), 'Empirics for Economic Growth and Convergence', *European Economic Review*, **40**, 1353-1375.

Quah, D. (1997), 'Empirics for Growth and Distribution: stratification, polarization and convergence clubs', *Journal of Economic Growth*, **2**, 27-59.

Ramsey, F. (1928), 'A Mathematical Theory of Saving', *Economic Journal*, **38**, 543-559.

Sala-i-Martin, X. (1996), 'Regional Cohesion: evidence and theories of regional growth and convergence', *European Economic Review*, **40**, 1325-1353.

Solow, R. (1956), 'A Contribution to the Theory of Economic Growth', *Quarterly Journal of Economics*, **70**, 65-94.

Villaverde, J. (1999), *Diferencias Regionales en España y Unión Monetaria Europea*, Madrid: Pirámide.

Villaverde, J. and B. Sánchez-Robles (1999a), 'Convergence Clubs in Spanish Regions, 1955-95', Actas do V Encontro Nacional da APDR, Coimbra.

Villaverde, J. and B. Sánchez-Robles (1999b), 'Spain in the European Union : a new approach to regional convergence', in W. Meeusen (ed.), *Economic Policy in the European Union*, Cheltenham, UK and Northampton MA, USA: Edward Elgar, pp. 67-83.

5. The Impact of European Structural Funds on Economic Convergence in European Countries and Regions

**José García Solanes and
Ramón María-Dolores[1]**

1. INTRODUCTION

According to the standard postulates of economic integration theory, the process of commercial and financial integration in the European Union (EU) will increase GDP growth and real income per capita in the member states and regions. The catalyst elements of that result would be augmented competition and bigger and more efficient enterprises operating in the enlarged markets.[2]

However, opinions about the distribution of these effects are not unanimous. Two major strands of thought may be discerned, supported by very different models of international trade and economic growth. On the one hand, the agglomeration theory developed by Krugman (1991) and the endogenous growth models of Romer (1986 and 1990) leave open the possibility that economic integration may widen economic discrepancies between countries and regions.[3] The reason is that increasing returns to scale and externalities may lead production factors to concentrate on the more developed areas. On the other hand, the theoretical frameworks based upon neo-classical growth and comparative advantage models predict economic convergence, provided that mobility of factors and diffusion of technological knowledge are not restricted. According to the second approach, if persistent differences in income per capita and labour productivity are observed between countries and regions, this should be attributed not to different endowments of aggregate capital stocks, but to the fact that the production factors are somehow immobile and/or prices are not flexible.

The two theoretical approaches discussed above lead to two alternative types of prescriptions for European regional policy. The first casts doubts on the ability of free-playing market forces to erode regional inequalities, and, consequently, supports a system of European transfers towards the lagging countries and regions (see, for example, European Commission (1999) and the works cited there). The second relies on automatic convergence and, as a result, considers that a system of financial assistance by the EU is useless or even harmful since it reduces factor mobility and precludes economic adjustment (see, for instance, Obstfeld and Peri (1998), and Boldrin and Canova (2000)).

The thesis of non-automatic convergence supports the EU Regional Policy, and its focal principle of social and economic cohesion. Not surprisingly, this principle has received renewed impulses at key stages in the EU economic integration processes. In fact, it was introduced in 1986 when the creation of the Single Market was approved, and it received an important stimulus a few years later with the signature of the Maastricht Treaty and the creation of the Cohesion Fund.

Given that current economic discrepancies in both income per head and unemployment are very strong between European countries and regions, any effort to understand better the contribution of European transfers in smoothing out disparities in regional economic developments is fully justified.[4] Correspondingly, the main concern of this work is to assess the impact of the structural interventions on regional convergence by the EU in recent years. The start of our time sample is set in 1989, since this is the first year in which official series on European assistance became currently available. Furthermore, 1989 coincides with one of the last reforms of the structural policies and is also the start of a very important process of European economic integration.

We do not intend to judge the validity of the theoretical approaches on economic growth and convergence discussed above, but rather to test their main implications for the European Regional Policy.

Our analysis will firstly focus on member states, and then on regions. With respect to European countries we will use data of the two programming periods 1989-93, and 1994-99. In the case of the regions, availability of data limits our time scope to the period 1989-96.

We now discuss the not completely conclusive empirical evidence currently available in this field. Let us first review the works that report positive impacts. Boscá *et al.* (1999) obtained favourable results applying a growth model with exogenous technological progress. They found that EU transfers have contributed decisively (mainly by increasing the public capital stock) to reduce the differences between income per head in the Union. The European Commission (1997) analysed the allocation of Structural Funds and their main impacts on each assisted region and country by broad categories of funds. Its general conclusion was that the Funds have had a significant effect on reducing disparities in economic performance across the Union.

Finally, the European Commission (1999) reported quantified evidence using simulations with four macroeconomic models. According to the results, EU structural assistance had increased GDP, on average, by 0.4 to 0.9 percentage points in Greece, Portugal and Ireland, and by 0.3 to 0.5 percentage points in Spain.[5]

On the side of non-positive effects Boldrin and Canova (2000) should be mentioned. These authors examined changes in the statistical distributions of several kinds of factor productivities and income per head of the EU regions during the period 1980-92, and found that the economic performance of the assisted regions was not very different from the rest of the Union.[6] The important implication is that the European regional and structural policies are based on political (as opposed to economic) motivations.

In this chapter we look for new evidence on the economic effects of the structural EU transfers following an econometric methodology which to our knowledge has not been applied so far in this domain. After proving that absolute convergence has taken place, we perform two types of dynamic β-convergence tests that somehow incorporate the amounts transferred during the two programming periods, and apply them both to member states and individual European regions using the NUTS2 classification. The first test consists of estimating the β-convergence equation with fixed effects in order to ascertain whether the GDP per head converges towards particular stationary states in each country or region. If this is the case, we will further investigate the extent to which the stationary levels and convergence towards them have been influenced by Structural Funds.

The second test consists of β-convergence regressions conditioned by the amounts of funds distributed to countries and regions during the two programming periods. Here the crucial point is to try to answer the question whether European structural assistance has contributed to the increase in global convergence and/or whether it has reinforced the growth rate of individual economies. Our general conclusion is that Structural Funds have had a significant effect on narrowing the gap in GDP per head between European countries and regions. This result seems to be robust since the two methodological approaches point in the same direction and deliver very similar results.

The remainder of this chapter is organised as follows. In Section 2 we examine the flows of Structural Funds distributed to member states and regions during each of the two programming periods, and we investigate the fiscal progressive nature of the European Regional Policy. For the latter task, we look at the relationship between the distribution of funds and GDP per head of each economy. In Section 3 we apply our econometric tests to the European Member States and to the European NUTS regions. Finally, Section 4 summarises the main results and discusses some policy implications.

2. REGIONAL DISTRIBUTION OF THE STRUCTURAL FUNDS

The first part of this section concentrates on the financial assistance to the EU-12 Member States. We exclude the remaining three EU countries (Austria, Sweden and Finland) because we lack information concerning the European transfers granted to their regions. Figure 5.1 shows the flows per head, in ECU at 1990 prices, distributed by all the European funds to each of the EU-12 countries. The information refers both to single programming periods and the whole time period. Inspection of this figure draws our attention to two features. First, the best-assisted inhabitants were namely those of Ireland, Portugal, Spain, Italy and Greece. Second, that the amounts of funds per head increased in the second period with respect to the first one in each country except in the case of Portugal.

Figure 5.1.   *Structural Funds distributed to EU-12 countries in ECU per capita (1990 prices). Programming periods 1989-93, 1994-99 and the whole period 1989-99*

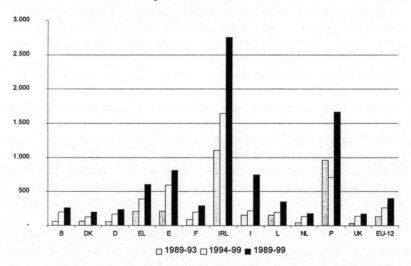

Figure 5.2 gives the same kind of information as the preceding one, but is restricted to the financial aids distributed by the European Regional Devel-

opment Fund (ERDF). As can be seen, the distribution is quite similar to the preceding one in relative terms, except for Luxembourg and Portugal. The time profile indicates that in the second period financial assistance decreased in Luxembourg with respect to the first period and that it increased in Portugal. The explanation is that whereas Luxembourg does not have Objective 1 eligible regions (that absorb the bulk of ERDF assistance), all the Portuguese regions are wholly eligible for this objective in the two programming periods. The ranking and situations of some regions may of course change in the coming years as their economic indicators evolve in time.

Figure 5.2.   Funds distributed to EU-12 countries through the ERDF, per capita, in ECU (1990 prices)

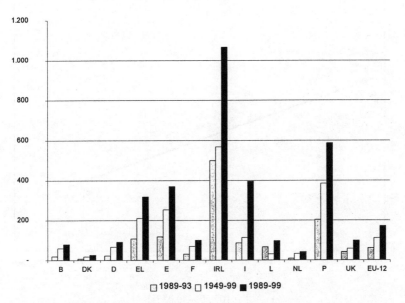

Given that the distributive effects of the European budget take place on the expenditure side, it seems interesting to analyse whether structural expenditures have or have not been progressive from the fiscal point of view. This issue is relevant to the extent that fiscal progressiveness is frequently interpreted as a symptom of social and economic cohesion or even a necessary condition for economic convergence between the member countries. For that purpose, in Figures 5.3 to 5.5 we represent, for each country, the relationship between GDP per head and the amount of structural financial aid per head received during each time span. In each figure, the set of points implies a negatively sloped regression line, which reveals that, in general, the distributed funds are inversely related to the degree of development of the country (measured by GDP per head).

Figure 5.3.   *Structural Funds per capita (X) and relative GDP per capita (1989, PPP units, EU-12=100)(Y) in EU-12 countries. Programming period 1989-93*

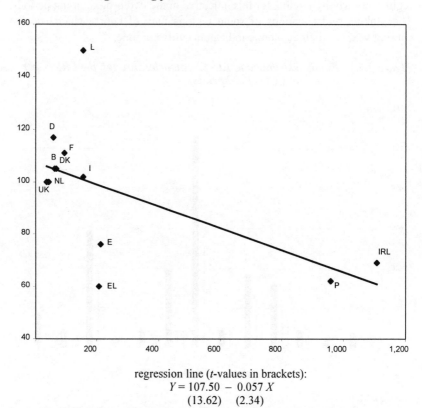

regression line (*t*-values in brackets):
$$Y = 107.50 - 0.057\,X$$
(13.62)   (2.34)

The fact that the line of the first period is steeper than that of the second period indicates that progressiveness has increased in recent years. Further-more, the information of these figures allows us to make judgements about the financial treatment that countries have received in comparison with their wealth level. Thus, taking as a benchmark the adjusted relationships, the best relative positions (represented by the horizontal distances between the coun-try points and the adjusted line) correspond, in this order, to Luxembourg and Ireland in both periods. The worst positions are those of Greece and Spain in the first period, and Greece and Portugal in the second period.

Figure 5.4. Structural Funds per capita (X) and relative GDP per capita
(1994, PPP units, EU-12=100)(Y) in EU-12 countries.
Programming period 1994-99

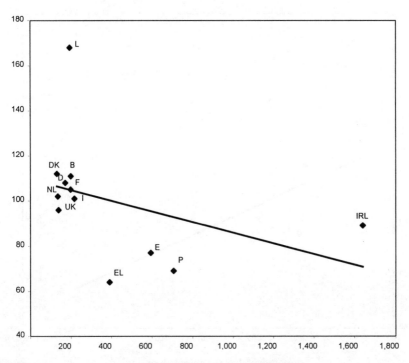

regression line (*t*-values in brackets):
$$Y = 111.41 - 0.062\,X$$
(10.47)   (1.68)

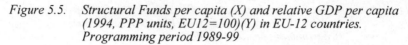

*Figure 5.5.   Structural Funds per capita (X) and relative GDP per capita
(1994, PPP units, EU12=100)(Y) in EU-12 countries.
Programming period 1989-99*

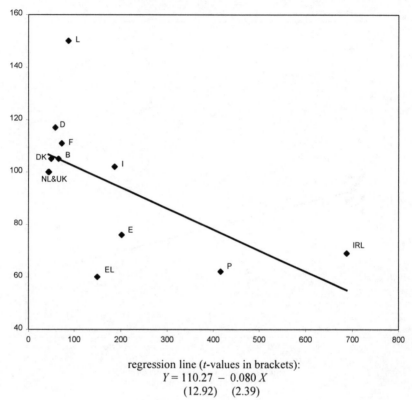

regression line (*t*-values in brackets):
$$Y = 110.27 - 0.080 \, X$$
(12.92)   (2.39)

Let us now consider the case of the European regions. Before explaining
how funds have been distributed, some preliminary remarks should be made.
First of all, the data that we use for the funds transferred to regions cover the
amounts under the Objectives 1, 2, 5b and 6 and exclude the rest of the transfers. The reason is that the latter are not explicitly broken down on a regional
basis in European Commission (1997) (our main source for the Structural
Funds data) since they are not centred on regions as such, but instead on specific problems. In fact, Objective 3 is concerned with helping to alleviate
unemployment across the EU, Objective 4 assists in the adaptation of workers to industrial change, and Objective 5a promotes structural adjustment in
agriculture and fisheries. In any case, the figures that we include in the analysis represent a large proportion (some 79 percent) of the total European
Structural Funds distributed to European regions during the two program-

ming periods, and cover the transfers which have the highest potential effects on both economic convergence and structural adjustment.[7]

Second, since the regional series of European GDP per head, reported in Eurostat, end in 1996, the analysis that we undertake here, referring to regions, focuses on the period 1989-96.

Third, the Greek regions are excluded because our source on EU transfers does not provide regional information for Greece.

Figure 5.6 relates GDP per capita to Structural Funds per capita distributed to each region during the period 1989-96. As can be seen, the regression line adjusted to the set of points has a negative slope as well, but is more pronounced than in the country case.

Figure 5.6.   *Structural Funds per capita (X) and relative GDP per capita (1989, PPP units, EU-12=100) (Y) in EU-12 regions. Programming period 1989-96*

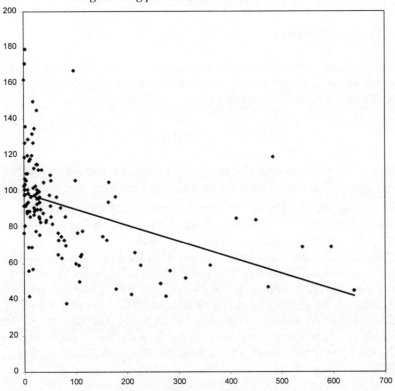

regression line (*t*-values in brackets):
$$Y = 101.74 - 0.120\,X$$
$$(43.30) \quad (7.79)$$

From the above general analysis it seems clear that Structural Funds have been distributed progressively between EU countries and regions. In the case of countries, their relative positions and the slope of the adjusted line indicate that progressiveness increased from one programming period to the next. These findings fully corroborate the results of De la Fuente and Doménech (2000b), according to whom the distributive regional impact of the EU budget has increased throughout time, thanks to the implementation of the structural programmes. Consequently, an important – and probably necessary – condition has been fulfilled for the Structural Funds to enhance regional economic convergence in the EU during the last few years.

In the next section we undertake several econometric tests to ascertain the likelihood of this outcome during the two periods considered.

3. DYNAMIC CONVERGENCE

3.1. European countries

Table 5.1 reports the results of the traditional β-convergence test following the well-known approach of Barro and Sala-i-Martin (1991, 1992). It consists of estimating the following equation:

$$\Delta \log(y_t^i) = \alpha - \beta \log(y_{t-T}^i) + \varepsilon_t^i \quad , \tag{5.1}$$

where y_t^i is GDP per head of country i (in purchasing power parity units), in the year t; T is the length of the period, α is a constant, β is the annual convergence rate of GDP per head to the common stationary state, and ε_t^i is the error term. The left side of the equation represents the rate of growth of GDP per head rate, of country i, between $t-1$ and t.

The regression has been carried out, assuming for the time being that, as a result of a common knowledge base and technology, the twelve EU countries share the same GDP-per-head stationary state, and that therefore the relationship between the growth rate of that variable and its initial value is not conditioned by other parameters (absolute convergence). Our data source for national GDP series and population sizes has been Eurostat. Data on the distribution of Structural Funds comes from the European Commission (EC, 1997).

As can be seen in Table 5.1, β has a significant and positive value, which indicates that GDP per head of the EU-12 countries has converged at the annual 8.6 percent rate along the whole sample period. This speed of convergence is considerably higher than the stylised value that Barro and Sala-i-

Martin (1991 and 1992) obtained for a large variety of less homogeneous (and less integrated) groups of countries and regions. The important difference in these results, apart from the degree of homogeneity of the countries analysed, might perhaps be explained by the fact that our sample includes some recent years where improvements in convergence have been intense.

Table 5.1.   *Unconditional convergence in GDP per head among EU-12 countries (equation 5.1), 1989-99*

β	α	R^2
0.086*	9.22*	0.87
(45.16)	(31.30)	

Note: *t*-ratio in parentheses; * = 95% significant.

Although, according to the preceding results, the EU-12 countries would seem to converge to a unique and common stationary state with respect to GDP per head, we should not overlook the possibility that in actual fact national values of that variable might tend to different levels in the long run. This possibility is implicit in the neo-classical model of economic growth when countries have different structural parameters concerning preferences, technology and the population growth rate. To test whether convergence is guided by this situation, we have estimated the following fixed-effects panel equation:

$$\frac{1}{T}\log(y_t^i / y_{t-T}^i) = \alpha^i - \beta\log(y_{t-T}^i) + \varepsilon_t^i \quad . \tag{5.2}$$

α^i stands for the fixed effects defined by the structural parameters of country *i.* The national stationary levels of GDP per head will then be given by:

$$\log y_*^i = \frac{\alpha^i}{\beta} \quad . \tag{5.3}$$

The currently available evidence indicates that if diversity of long-run stationary levels is relevant, the introduction of fixed effects in the convergence equation increases the estimated value of the speed at which each zone converges to its own stationary state. The estimation of equation (5.2) for the EU-12 countries confirms this result. In effect, as can be seen in Table 5.2, where the estimated values of the relevant parameters are presented, the new annual rate of convergence has the expected sign and is more significant and considerably higher (16.9 percent) than in the case where fixed effects were ruled out.

Table 5.2.   Unconditional convergence with fixed effects (equation 5.2), 1989-99

	α^i	β	R^2
		0.1691*	0.98
		(10.72)	
Belgium	18.62		
Denmark	19.09		
Germany	18.70		
Greece	10.71		
Spain	13.40		
France	18.08		
Ireland	15.26		
Italy	17.20		
Luxembourg	28.36		
the Netherlands	17.91		
Portugal	11.62		
UK	16.78		

Notes: t-ratio in parentheses; * = 95% significant.

Table 5.3.   Relative stationary steady-states and Structural Funds per capita relative to the European average.

	(1) Structural Funds per head relative to the EU average	(2) GDP per capita relative to the EU average in 1989	(3) Estimated steady-state	(4) GDP gap (3)-(2)
Belgium	66	105	110	5
Denmark	50	105	113	8
Germany	59	117	111	-6
Greece	150	60	63	3
Spain	202	76	79	3
France	73	111	107	-4
Ireland	688	69	90	21
Italy	187	102	102	0
Luxembourg	88	150	168	18
the Netherlands	45	100	106	6
Portugal	416	62	69	7
UK	44	100	99	-1

Notes: Standard deviation of 1989-GDP per head (column(2)): 26.88; standard deviation of stationary states (column(3)): 25.92; correlation between (1) and (4): - 0.5803.

The new regression suggests that the EU-12 countries have different stationary states in GDP per head.[8] As can be seen in the fourth column of Table 5.3 the relative values of these long-run states differ considerably among countries. Giving 100 to the average EU value, the highest level corresponds to Luxembourg (168) and the lowest one to Greece (63). However, comparison of these values with the levels of GDP per head in 1989 (column 3), reveals that the initially poorest countries (Greece, Portugal, Ireland and Spain) improve their relative position. Ireland shows the most important progress.

The following step of our analysis consists in looking for evidence of the contribution of Structural Funds to economic convergence in the EU-12 countries. It is well known that an important part of the structural grants and/or subsidies has been used to increase the capital intensity of production and/or to replace existing plant and equipment with more modern machinery in the lagging countries and regions. Other parts of the funds have been devoted to raise the skills of the local workforce.[9] Either way implies improvements in productivity and structural changes.[10] Consequently, it is reasonable to think that Structural Funds contribute both to bringing countries nearer to their own stationary states and to changing progressively these long-run levels in a convergent manner.

An indirect proof of these effects is given by the following considerations. First, the fact that structural financial assistance is positively correlated with differences between GDP stationary states and initial values of this variable (called 'GDP gaps' in Table 5.3), indicates that the distribution of funds does help the lagging countries to achieve their own stationary states. Second, the last row in Table 5.3 shows that the standard deviation of stationary GDP levels (25.92) has decreased compared to that of the 1998 GDP values (26.88).

Finally, an alternative and more direct way to assess the contribution of structural policies to economic convergence consists in performing β-convergence tests conditioned by structural assistance. In the definition of Barro and Sala-i-Martin (1991; 1992) and Sala-i-Martin (1994), there is conditional convergence between a group of economies when by including certain additional control-variables in the convergence equation we obtain a significant and negative value for the β-coefficient.

Table 5.4 shows the results of the regressions when convergence is conditioned, alternatively, by the total amounts of funds per inhabitant distributed to member states during the whole period, and by each of their individual categories separately. The estimates of the first regression indicate that the newly estimated value for the speed of convergence almost doubles the value of the non-conditioned rate (cf. Table 5.1). Furthermore, the policy variable is significant at the 95 percent level and has a positive sign, indicating that

Structural Funds, whatever their specificity, contribute to increase the average rate of growth of EU-12 countries.

Table 5.4.   Conditional convergence in GDP per head among EU-12 countries, 1989-99

	α	β	Structural Funds per inhabitant	R^2
Total Structural Funds	16.28* (12.25)	0.1518* (23.92)	0.002* (3.56)	0.95
ERDF	16.60* (9.69)	0.1525* (26.81)	0.007* (4.18)	0.94
ESF	16.68* (34.24)	0.1529* (15.31)	0.006* (5.65)	0.97
EAGGF	15.93* (10.71)	0.1498* (15.59)	0.012* (4.23)	0.98

Notes: Estimated equation: $(1/T)(Y_{it}/Y_{i,t-T}) = \alpha - \beta(Y_{i,t-T}) +$ Structural Funds term $+ u_{i,t-T}$; t-ratios in parentheses.* = 95% significant.

Looking at the impacts of individual funds, we find that each one causes β to increase similarly. However, the effects on the average rate of growth vary from one fund to another, those of the European Agricultural Guidance and Guarantee Fund (EAGGF) seemingly being the most relevant.

The econometric results fully corroborate the fact that convergence takes place towards particular stationary states, and shows that the latter are influenced by Structural Funds. To the extent that this process coincides with a general motion towards a common stationary state (absolute β-convergence), the implication is that Structural Funds have had a positive impact on economic convergence of EU countries.

3.2. European regions

Table 5.5 reports the results of the unconditional β-convergence test applied to EU regions. Here, the convergence rate is lower than in the case of countries, but it has the expected sign and is statistically significant at the 95 percent level.

Table 5.5. *Unconditional convergence in GDP per head among EU-12 regions, 1989-96*

α	β	R^2
2.56*	0.025*	0.18
(7.73)	(7.44)	

In order to assess whether European regions converge to different stationary states we have estimated the equation (5.2) with regional data, and obtained the results presented in Table 5.6. As can be seen, after introducing different stationary states we obtain statistically better estimates and an annual rate of convergence close to 18 percent. Table 5.6 also suggests that there are sharp differences between the regional stationary levels. The highest one (Brussels) is more than four times the lowest ones, the French overseas islands Guadeloupe and Réunion. However, disparities in this long-run position seem to be smaller to the extent that dispersion of the stationary states is lower than that of the initial 1989 values.

Table 5.6. *Unconditional convergence with fixed effects, 1989-96*

	α	β	steady-state	R^2
		0.179		0.98
		(65.76)		
Bruxelles	30.76		171	
Antwerpen	24.66		137	
Limburg	19.73		110	
Oost-Vlaanderen	18.80		105	
Vlaams Brabant	17.24		96	
West-Vlaanderen	21.07		117	
Brabant Wallon	15.92		89	
Hainaut	14.49		81	
Liège	17.72		99	
Luxembourg Belge	17.30		96	
Namur	15.45		86	
Denmark	22.71		126	
Baden-Wurttemberg	21.01		117	
Bayern	22.75		127	
Berlin	18.57		103	
Brandenburg	11.65		65	
Bremen	27.42		153	
Hamburg	35.01		195	
Hessen	26.86		150	
Mecklenburg-Vorpommern	10.70		60	
Niedersachsen	18.71		104	

Table 5.6 (continued)

Nordrhein-Westfalen	20.20	113
Rheinland-Pfalz	17.57	98
Saarland	19.37	108
Sachsen	11.19	62
Sachsen-Anhalt	10.69	60
Schleswig-Holstein	18.86	105
Thüringen	10.55	59
Galicia	11.25	63
Asturias	13.26	74
Cantabria	13.82	77
Pais Vasco	16.60	92
Navarra	17.58	98
La Rioja	15.95	89
Aragón	15.93	89
Madrid	17.67	101
Castilla León	13.46	75
Castilla La Mancha	11.74	65
Extremadura	9.73	54
Cataluña	17.71	99
Comunidad Valenciana	13.32	74
Baleares	17.51	98
Andalucía	10.25	57
Murcia	12.17	68
Ceuta y Melilla	13.00	72
Canarias	13.38	75
Île de France	29.16	162
Champagne-Ardennes	17.19	96
Picardie	15.51	86
Haute-Normandie	19.35	108
France-Centre	16.89	94
Basse-Normandie	16.15	90
Bourgogne	16.60	92
Nord-Pas-de-Calais	15.65	87
Lorraine	16.20	90
Alsace	19.17	107
Franche-Comté	16.93	94
Pays de la Loire	16.49	92
Bretagne	15.63	87
Poitou-Charentes	15.13	84
Aquitaine	16.78	93
Midi-Pyrénées	15.86	88
Limousin	14.74	82
Rhône-Alpes	18.49	103
Auvergne	15.21	85
Languedoc-Rousillon	14.33	80
Provence-Alpes-Coté d'Azur	16.89	94

Table 5.6 (continued)

Corse	14.93	83
Guadaloupe	6.94	39
Martinique	9.32	52
Guyane	8.23	46
Réunion	7.86	44
Piemonte	21.10	118
Valle D'Aosta	23.43	130
Liguria	21.32	119
Lombardia	23.81	133
Trentino-Alto Adige	22.70	126
Veneto	22.16	123
Friuli-Venezia Giulia	22.53	125
Emilia Romagna	23.63	132
Toscana	19.82	110
Umbria	17.59	98
Marche	19.07	106
Lazio	20.37	113
Abruzzo	16.15	90
Molise	13.98	78
Campania	11.89	66
Puglia	12.76	71
Basilicata	12.31	69
Calabria	10.66	59
Sicilia	11.86	66
Sardegna	13.19	73
Luxembourg (GD)	30.27	169
Groningen	23.48	131
Friesland	15.76	88
Drenthe	15.88	88
Overijssel	16.81	94
Gelderland	17.04	95
Flevoland	13.66	76
Utrecht	21.38	119
Noord-Holland	21.55	120
Zuid-Holland	19.87	111
Zeeland	18.72	104
Noord-Brabant	19.10	106
Limburg	17.60	98
Portugal Norte	11.11	62
Portugal Centro	10.73	60
Lisboa e Vale do Tejo	15.89	88
Alentejo	10.58	59
Algarve	12.61	70
Açores	8.92	50
Madeira	9.72	54
UK North East	14.99	83

Table 5.6 (continued)

UK North West	15.99	89
Yorkshire and the Humber	15.98	89
East Midlands	16.72	93
West Midlands	16.51	92
UK Eastern	17.07	95
London	25.13	140
UK South East	18.38	102
UK South West	16.79	94
Wales	14.74	82
Scotland	17.44	97
Northern Ireland	14.30	80

Table 5.7.   *Conditional convergence in GDP per head among EU-12 regions, 1989-96*

	α	β	Structural Funds per inhabitant	R^2
Total Structural Funds	3.69* (6.65)	0.038* (7.48)	0.0003° (1.75)	0.35
ERDF	3.74* (6.61)	0.039* (7.44)	0.0005° (1.83)	0.34
ESF	3.56* (6.63)	0.037* (7.44)	0.0002 (1.15)	0.34
EAGGF	3.69* (6.65)	0.038* (7.48)	0.0003° (1.75)	0.35

Notes: Estimated equation: $(1/T)(Y_{it}/Y_{i,t-T}) = \alpha - \beta(Y_{i,t-T})$ + Structural Funds term + $u_{i,t-T}$; t-ratio in parentheses. ° = 90% significant, * = 95% significant.

As in the case of countries, a rapid convergence to different stationary states is not at odds with the hypothesis of convergence to a unique and common long-run equilibrium level, provided that there are convergent changes in individual stationary states. Here, again, we find that structural transfers have an important potential role in financing efficient investment projects and raising the stock levels of public and human capital in the lagging regions. The European Commission (1997) confirms and explains these effects in the regions of each of the EU-12 countries.

We also find indirect evidence that the transferred funds help European regions to achieve their own stationary states, in the sense that financial assistance is positively correlated with the gap between the GDP per head stationary states and the initial levels (0.15).

Here again, a more explicit and direct proof of the impact of Structural Funds on regional convergence is obtained by estimating the β-convergence equation conditioned by the distribution of those funds. The results are presented in Table 5.7. It is apparent that Structural Funds (either the total amount of them or their individual sub-categories) contribute to increase the speed of convergence with respect to the unconditional case. Their effect on the average regional growth rate is, on average, also positive, but weaker and less significant (we do not find any effect for ESF funds) than in the case of EU countries. The more pronounced effects on regional growth are due to ERDF funds.

4. CONCLUDING REMARKS

Our main concern in this chapter has been to assess the impact of Structural Funds on GDP-per-capita convergence of both EU member states and EU regions during the two programming periods 1989-93 and 1994-99. The issue is important because European transfers (as well as the number of European inhabitants affected) have grown considerably in recent years, and academic opinion about the final effects of these financial aids is not unanimous.

After verifying, in general terms, that European transfers have been distributed regionally in a progressive manner, we have applied β-convergence tests that take into account the quantities of funds distributed to countries and regions. Our results may be summarised as follows.

First, absolute convergence tests indicate that countries and regions converge to a unique and common stationary state of income per capita, at the annual rates of 8.6 percent and 2.5 percent, respectively. Since the existence of different stationary states is also confirmed for both countries and regions (convergence with fixed effects), both results jointly imply that individual stationary states also converge progressively along time. In this process Structural Funds play an important role by gradually modifying the structural parameters which define individual stationary states. Indeed, there are clear signs that structural policies have had a major effect on productivity by improving infrastructures, raising the skills of the workforce and strengthening local business.

Second, to assess more directly the impact of Structural Funds on economic convergence, we have tested whether European financial assistance might be a relevant conditioning variable in the convergence equation. The estimated β-coefficient turns out to be 15.2 percent, and to 3.8 percent percent in the equation referring to countries, and to regions respectively. In any case, the influence of transfers is clearly positive on both the speeds of convergence and the average growth rate of GDP per head. The biggest impact on growth, by categories of funds, corresponds to those given in the context of the European Regional Development Fund and the European Agricultural Guidance and Guarantee Fund.

To interpret correctly those results we should bear in mind the fact that, since the period of our analysis is relatively short (10 years in the case of countries, and 7 years in the case of regions), our estimates capture only part of the economic impact of the European structural programmes. In fact, many of the programmes and measures introduced are of a long-term nature and produce their full effect on the economy only after a lengthier period.

However, one general implication seems unavoidable: structural programmes should be maintained in the Community budget, not only because they satisfy political interests (which are always present), but fundamentally also because they improve regional equilibrium and economic welfare. Of course, the distribution of funds needs to be regularly adjusted according to new relevant economic indicators of countries and regions. Furthermore, official surveillance will be necessary for the funds to be correctly administered and invested on highly efficient projects.

NOTES

1. J. García Solanes is at the Department of Economics of the Universidad de Murcia, and R. María-Dolores is at the Department of Economics of the Universidad de Murcia and currently visiting professor at the Department of Economics of the Universidad Carlos III de Madrid. The research was supported by a grant from the Séneca Foundation, Project PL/8/FS/00. The authors are grateful to Andrea Mairate (DG XVI's Evaluation Unit of the European Commission) for his assistance with the data on European transfers that were used in this work.
2. Estimates of Cecchini (1988) and Smith and Venables (1991), for instance, indicate that the Single Market will increase the GDP of Member States by more than 5 percent. On the other hand, the Maastricht Treaty predicts that GDP will tend to grow several tenths faster in countries that participate in the EMU.
3. A weaker version of this thesis is the idea that groups of countries tend to converge to a limited number of different stationary states with respect to GDP per capita. See, for example, the idea of 'clusters' or convergence clubs developed, among others, by Canova (1998) and Canova and Marcet (1995).
4. According to the recent data provided by the European Commission (see also Villaverde, 2000), the GDP per head is five times higher in the richest European region (Inner London) than in the poorest ones (Ipeiros, Greece). Furthermore, the levels of GDP per head of the Objective 1 regions are equivalent only to some 68 percent of the EU average. Inequalities remain surprisingly strong even inside individual European countries.
5. Furthermore, the accumulated increase of GDP during the whole sample period was 10 percent in Greece, Ireland and Portugal, and 4 percent in Spain. The macroeconomic models mentioned are those of Pereira (1999), Bradley *et al.* (1995), and those of Christodoulakis and Kalvitys cited by Bradley *et al.*
6. The authors did not find clear symptoms of either convergence or divergence, since the rates of GDP growth per capita were very similar between regions independently of their initial conditions.

7. The 2000 Agenda, which was approved in 1999, and which covers the period until 2006, reduces the number of objectives to three, and simplifies their content and goals. The Community Initiatives have also been reduced from thirteen to four.
8. There is positive empirical evidence of this thesis in some works applied to the Spanish regions (Raymond and García, 1994) and provinces (Pérez and Serrano, 2000).
9. With respect to Spanish regions, Más *et al.* (1994) and Gorostiaga (1999) found that investments in public capital had a positive impact on GDP-per-head convergence. De la Fuente and Da Rocha (1996) and De la Fuente and Doménech (2000a) stress the importance for convergence of investment in human capital.
10. The European Commission (EC, 1999) provides abundant evidence on the fact that structural policies have had a major effect on increasing productivity and competitiveness in the lagging EU countries and regions.

REFERENCES

Barro, R. and X. Sala-i-Martin (1991), 'Convergence Across States and Regions', *Brooking Papers on Economic Activity*, **1991**(1), 107-182.

Barro, R. and X. Sala-i-Martin (1992), 'Convergence', *Journal of Political Economy*, **100**, 223-251.

Boldrin, M. and F. Canova (2000), 'Inequality and Convergence: reconsidering European regional policies', *Economic Policy*, **32**, 207-253.

Boscá, J., R. Doménech and D. Taguas (1999), 'La Política Fiscal en la Unión Económica y Monetaria', *Moneda y Crédito*, nr. 206, 267-324.

Bradley, J. *et al.* (1995), *Regional and Convergence: Evaluation of the Impact of Structural Funds on the European Periphery*, Aldershot: Avebury.

Canova, F. (1998), 'Testing for Convergence Clubs: a predictive density approach', mimeo, Universitat Pompeu Fabra.

Canova, F. and A. Marcet (1995), 'The Poor Stay Poor: non-convergence across countries and regions', CEPR Discussion Paper nr. 1265.

Cecchini, P. (1998), *Europa 1992: Una Apuesta de Futuro*, Madrid: Alianza Editorial.

De la Fuente, A. and J.M. Da Rocha (1996), 'Capital Humano y Crecimiento: una panorámica de la evidencia empírica y algunos resultados para la OCDE', *Moneda y Crédito*, nr. 203, 43-84.

De la Fuente, A. and R. Doménech (2000a), 'Human Capital in Growth Regressions: how much difference does data quality make?', OECD Working Paper 262, Economics Department.

De la Fuente, A. and R. Doménech (2000b), 'The Redistributive Effect of the EU Budget: an analysis and a proposal for reform', Documentos de Economía/3. Fundación Caixa Galicia, Centro de Investigación Económica y Financiera.

European Commission (1997), *The Impact of Structural Policies on Economic and Social Cohesion in the Union 1989-99*, Brussels: Commission of the European Union.

European Commission (1999*)*, *Sixth Periodic Report on the Social and Economic Situation and Development of the Regions of the Community*, Brussels: Commission of the European Union.

Gorostiaga, A. (1999), '¿Cómo Afectan el Capital Público y Humano al Crecimiento?: un análisis para las regiones Españolas en el marco neoclásico', *Investigaciones Económicas*, **23**, 95-114.

Krugman, P. (1991), 'Increasing Returns and Economic Geography', *Journal of Political Economy*, **99**, 483-499.

Más, M., J. Maudos, F. Pérez and E. Uriel (1994), 'Disparidades Regionales y Convergencia en las Comunidades Autónomas', *Revista de Economía Aplicada*, **4**, 129-148.

Obstfeld, M. and G. Peri (1998), 'Regional Non-adjustment and Fiscal Policy', *Economic Policy*, **26**, 207-247.

Pereira, A.M. (1999), 'International Public Transfers and Convergence in the European Union', *Public Finance Review*, **27**, 194-219.

Pérez, F. and L. Serrano (2000), 'Capital Humano y Patrón de Crecimiento Sectorial y Territorial: España (1964-1998)', *Papeles de Economía Española*, **86**, 20-41.

Raymond, J.L. and B. García (1994), 'Las Disparidades en el PIB per Cápita entre Comunidades Autónomas, y la Hipótesis de Convergencia', *Papeles de Economía Española*, **59**, 37-58.

Romer, P. (1986), 'Increasing Returns and Endogenous Growth', *Journal of Political Economy*, **94**, 1002-1037.

Romer, P. (1990), 'Endogenous Technical Change', *Journal of Political Economy*, **98**, S71-S102.

Sala-i-Martin, X. (1994), 'La Riqueza de las Regiones. Evidencia y Teorías sobre el Crecimiento Regional y Convergencia', *Moneda y Crédito*, nr. 198, 13-54.

Smith, A. and A. Venables (1991), 'Economic Integration and Market Access', *European Economic Review*, **35**, 388-395.

Villaverde, J. (2000), 'Los Desequilibrios Regionales en Europa y España: Nuevas Estimaciones, ¿Viejos Problemas?', *Cuadernos de Información Económica*, nr. 155, 107-115.

6. Optimum Currency Area Theory and Monetary Integration as a Gradual Process

Philippe De Lombaerde[1]

1. INTRODUCTION

The concept of (regional) economic integration refers both to a state of affairs and a process (Balassa, 1961).[2] In this contribution we will refer to integration seen as a gradual process. Both in terms of the agenda of the negotiations, as in terms of the number of countries taking part in the integration treaties, post-war regional integration can indeed be perceived and observed as a cumulative and partly irreversible (or, at least, costly-to-reverse) process. Integration in the European Union context and in other geographical areas can easily be modelled as a process of both 'deepening' and geographical expansion.

In this theoretical contribution, we analyse the phenomenon of monetary integration seen as a gradual process, and evaluate the usefulness of optimum currency area (OCA) theory – essentially a static theory – in order to predict the path of integration. More specifically, the following aspects are studied:

- Is the idea of a monetary union with an incremental number of participating countries consistent with Kenen's thesis about interindustry labour mobility, for given industrial structures?
- Does the theory of optimum currency areas, according to Mundell and Kenen, yield time-consistent (and politically feasible) recommendations about the suitability of monetary integration for a group of economies characterised by divergent industrial development patterns?
- Given the fact that the theoretical literature on OCAs suggests different criteria for testing the suitability of forming currency unions, are

the rankings of countries according to their suitability to enter a
monetary union sufficiently independent from the choice of the criteria? And, by extension, how robust are the results of the empirical
methods that are used?

Before addressing these questions however, we present a brief review of
basic OCA theory,[3] and some recent contributions that are also relevant for
our dynamic perspective on OCA theory (Frankel and Rose, 1997, 1998;
Gros and Steinherr, 1997).

2. THE THEORY OF OPTIMUM CURRENCY AREAS: A BRIEF REVIEW

2.1. Mundell's OCA theory

2.1.1. Mundell's central ideas

According to Mundell, the choice of an exchange rate regime should be the
result of a cost-benefit analysis (Mundell, 1961).[4] He considers the traditional
argument of macroeconomic stabilisation (the central argument in his article)
as an argument in favour of flexible rates. But he also stresses that this should
be evaluated in the light of other (mainly microeconomic) arguments in favour of fixed rates: the reduction of transaction and valorisation costs (the
efficiency argument), the elimination of the risk of currency speculation and
the absence of money illusion. This last aspect refers to the fact that it is im-
probable that wage earners will accept a reduction in their real income in the
form of a devaluation, but not in the form of a reduction in their nominal
wages in open economies or in small monetary unions. Mundell adds other
conditions of efficiency and effectiveness to the case for flexible rates: the
dynamic stability of international prices, the limited cost of structural adjustments provoked by changes in the exchange rate, the existence of instruments
to cover exchange rate risk, the absence of speculation by the central banks, a
sustainable monetary discipline in conditions of depreciation and political
instability, and the absence of a significant negative effect of exchange rate
variability on long-run capital flows.

The importance and originality of Mundell's contribution consists, among
other things, in the fact that he explains the necessity to distinguish between
the concepts of 'region' and 'country'. The region is defined as a zone within
which factor mobility exists, but not between the zone and the rest of the
world. Using the words of Kenen (1969, p. 42),

> Mundell's notion of a region is functional, not literal. You will not find his regions
> on an ordinary map but must instead use an input-output table. As I understand the

substance of his argument, a region is defined as a homogeneous collection of pro-
ducers that use the same technology, face the same demand curve, and suffer or
prosper together as circumstances change.

According to Mundell, the region is, at least theoretically, the adequate
level to define the exchange rate policy. The countries in the real world might
coincide with the region, might count various regions within their borders, or
might be smaller than the region. Mundell shows, using some simple examples, that the exchange rate regime can be ill-defined from the perspective of
macroeconomic equilibrium when the country and the region do not coincide.

Incorporating the dimension of the extension of the currency areas in the
analysis, the arguments in favour of floating and fixed exchange rates can
also be interpreted as arguments in favour of smaller or bigger areas, respectively. In other words, Mundell reoriented the academic debate on exchange
rates. Today, the debate is not only about whether countries should adopt a
fixed or flexible rate, but also about the level from which geographical aggregation exchange rates should be flexible. Or, which is the same, from what
level of geographical desegregation should exchange rates be fixed.

It is well known that Mundell recommended that exchange rates be fixed
between different geographical entities when factor mobility exists between
them, and that they should be flexible when the factors are not mobile. However, in the same article, Mundell also argues that the exclusive use of this
criterion would imply an exaggerated number of currency unions, characterised by specific dominant economic activities, given the fact that only this
type of region would not face the problem of interindustry factor immobility.
But in this case, however, the transaction and efficiency costs would obviously be too high.[5]

2.1.2. Asymmetries in Mundell's theory

In Mundell's reasoning about the stabilisation argument, two types of asymmetries appear: (i) the asymmetries related to the vulnerability towards (internal or external) shocks between different entities (countries or regions), (ii)
the asymmetries related to the preferences of the economic (monetary)
authorities of the different entities.

Mundell states that the arguments in favour of flexible exchange rates
between geographical entities are valid:

• when the latter come close (or, ideally, coincide) with 'regions', as defined above, and,
• when the possibility exists that asymmetric shocks occur, without co-
  ordination (or coincidence of preferences) between the respective
  monetary authorities.

The asymmetric shocks in Mundell's first example (1961) are a direct consequence of the structural differences between the different economies. Any shock, in these circumstances, is necessarily asymmetric.

With the previous assumptions, suppose now that there is an asymmetric shock (regardless of its origin) that changes the relative demand and/or supply of the goods in the distinct zones, and suppose that the shock occurs under initial conditions of full employment and trade balance equilibrium. With the additional (realistic) assumptions of (downward) rigidity of prices and nominal wages, and monetary authorities controlling the rate of inflation, one country would suffer unemployment whereas the other would suffer inflationary pressures. The adjustment of the exchange rates permits the distribution of the burden of macroeconomic adjustment between both countries. However, a restrictive monetary policy in the country(ies) with inflationary pressures ('favoured' by the demand shock) places the adjustment in the hands of the country(ies) with the unemployment problem. With (downward) rigid prices, this necessarily implies a reduction in production and employment levels.

The implication is the recessive impact of the adoption of anti-inflationary policies in countries with (initial) surpluses in their trade balance. Only an asymmetric supra-national institutional mechanism, compromising the surplus countries to inflate, could reduce the world unemployment level.

In Mundell's second example, the economic zones share a currency (or fix their exchange rates 'forever'), but they still have the same characteristics as presented before. A similar shock initially has similar effects on the relative demands, the employment levels, prices, and 'inter-zone' trade balances as in the previous case. The monetary authorities can only induce full employment when they relax the monetary policy, worsening the inflation problem in the zones with inflationary pressures.

Mundell juxtaposed the two examples to show that the existence of an adjustment cost in terms of unemployment or inflation, caused by a shock, is independent from the choice of the exchange rate policy.

2.2. McKinnon's openness criteria

McKinnon argues that in open economies – characterised by a high rate of imports to GDP or a high proportion of tradables to non-tradables – with a flexible exchange rate regime, the domestic currency loses 'utility' as a value of deposit, because it loses stability in terms of purchasing power and future transactions (McKinnon, 1963). Additionally, the exchange rate volatility is directly reflected in domestic prices. Devaluation automatically produces inflation and may signify a loss of export competitiveness when the exportables have a high import content. McKinnon recommends fixed exchange rates for small, open economies, and flexible rates for large, closed economies. In closed economies, the flexible exchange rates facilitate balance-of-payments adjustment and the restoration of internal and external equilibrium, without causing inflation.

Mundell anticipated McKinnon's vision and agrees with the latter that in very open economies – with a high proportion of imports to total consumption – monetary illusion, one of the central assumptions behind the argument in favour of flexible rates, is less probable and less realistic (Mundell, 1961). In this case, a vicious circle might be expected: a devaluation that initially improves export competitiveness causes an almost immediate adjustment of salaries and prices; this effect neutralises the competitiveness gain and requires a new devaluation, starting a new cycle...

McKinnon supposes that the shocks are internal. However, this is not obvious; the source of volatility might be found abroad, which would invalidate McKinnon's proposition. According to the author, it would make sense to fix the bilateral exchange rate when the country is more sensitive to shocks than its commercial partner. This would be the case if the country's economy were smaller, more open and less diversified than the economy of its partners. The logic of McKinnon's argument leads to an impossibility: with two countries, it is impossible for both to find, in monetary integration, a solution to fix their currency in terms of the currency of a 'more stable' partner.

2.3. Kenen's diversification criteria

Kenen proposed an alternative criterion to define OCAs. He argues that the diversification of the productive structure – the number of regions with homogeneous production within a country – is more relevant than Mundell's criteria of labour mobility. According to Kenen, (i) very diversified national economies with, consequently, a diversified export supply, do not need to adjust their terms of trade as frequently as non-diversified economies, and (ii) when they suffer specific negative shocks, the effect on the unemployment level is not as drastic (Kenen, 1969). Fixed exchange rates are thus more adequate for diversified economies.[6]

Kenen also showed that the links between external and domestic demand, especially the link between exports and investment, are weaker in diversified economies, so that the 'imported' variations in domestic employment are not strengthened by the respective variations in investment (Kenen, 1969).[7]

3. A DYNAMIC PERSPECTIVE

3.1. The validity and endogeneity of the OCA criteria

3.1.1. The contribution of Gros and Steinherr

McKinnon (1963) established that the costs of participating in a monetary union, and losing the exchange rate as an instrument of adjustment, diminish with higher degrees of openness. In a context of globalisation and increasing openness and interdependence of the world economy, this assertion, if true, would offer support for a scenario of monetary integration as a continuing process. Taking the Mundell-Fleming model as a starting point, Gros and Steinherr (1997) question this generally accepted proposition. The authors reach the conclusion that the cost of fixing the exchange rate increases with higher openness ratios in the case of external shocks, given the fact that the cost of an inadequate exchange rate is higher when the external sector is more important. But given that openness diminishes the impact of an internal shock on domestic demand or production, the cost of fixing the exchange rate, in this case, diminishes with openness. The implication of this conclusion for policy formulation is that in order to evaluate the cost of abandoning flexible exchange rates, it is not sufficient to analyse the degree of openness of an economy: the importance of external shocks should also be considered. In other words, the cost of losing the exchange rate as a policy instrument for macroeconomic adjustment would be greater for an economy with a high degree of openness and industrial and export structures that are very different from those of the rest of the region, than for a country that also possesses a different export structure but that is relatively closed. From a dynamic perspective, this suggests that it is not only relevant to monitor the degrees of openness, but also the degrees of structural convergence/divergence between countries.[8]

3.1.2. The contributions of Frankel and Rose

The trade intensity and the correlation of the economic cycles are important criteria for establishing the convenience of the formation of a monetary union, according to the OCA theory. Nevertheless, although the values of these parameters can offer indications, *ex ante*, on the desirability of a monetary union, it is important to understand that, in turn, these parameters are also a function of the chosen exchange rate regime. That is, the trade intensity and the (non-)synchronisation of the economic cycles are cause and consequence. It is very probable, for example, that trade is stimulated within a monetary union because of the lower transaction costs. In the same way, it is theoretically possible that the conditions for monetary union are not achieved *ex ante*, but rather *ex post*. This phenomenon is referred to as 'the endogeneity of the OCA criteria'. Frankel and Rose (1997, 1998) published a number of important contributions on this topic. The authors start from the theoretical observation that when the higher mentioned parameters are endogenous, the effect of greater trade interdependence on the correlation of the economic cycles between countries is ambiguous. As is well established in the theory of international trade, the elimination of trade barriers is able to produce more inter-industry trade or more intra-industry trade, or what amounts to the same, more or less specialisation. In the first case, the integration results *ex post* in a lesser correlation in the respective cyclical movements (asymmetric shocks). Theoretically, this raises a difficult problem. It means that the effects of a decision of economic policy – here, monetary integration – change the values of the variables that were used to justify the same decision, in the sense that the pre-established conditions are not satisfied *ex post*. Frankel and Rose showed, nevertheless, that this problem is more theoretical than empirical. Based on an econometric exercise with a panel of data on 20 countries and for a period of 30 years, they showed the existence of a clear positive relationship between bilateral trade intensity and the correlation of the business cycles. The consequence of this is that a simple analysis of historical data might not be sufficient to establish the desirability of forming monetary unions.[9]

3.2. Labour mobility and monetary integration as a process

3.2.1. Labour mobility and OCA theory
Both international (interregional) and interindustry labour mobility are relevant criteria in the OCA theory. Mundell referred to both forms of labour mobility, applied to the regions that were defined as single-product regions with homogeneous production. Labour mobility was thus, by definition, both of the interregional and interindustry type. Kenen clarified that when the regions are defined in terms of their economic activities, the perfect interregional mobility of labour requires a perfect mobility between jobs. This is only possible when labour is homogeneous or when the different regions of the currency area have very similar requirements in terms of labour qualifications. In practice, the OCA coincides then with the homogeneous production or single-product region (Kenen, 1969). Kenen shared with Mundell (1961) and McKinnon a view on the reasons why the number of monetary unions that would follow from this logic is not realistic.

In relation to interindustry labour mobility, Kenen made the important observation that stability of export income will normally be greater when the shocks are mutually independent, and this, in turn, is more probable when the produced goods are not substitutes. As a consequence, as goods differentiated

by their final use are generally also differentiated by their method of production, this might reduce interindustry labour mobility. In this way, export diversification assures external equilibrium but not internal stabilisation. If, on
the contrary, related goods are being exported, the shocks are not independent
and the law of large numbers does not hold, although interindustry factor
mobility may increase. According to Kenen, however, this anyway does not
question the fact that a diversified economy that produces a *continuum* of
goods, will have higher labour mobility because it widens the labour opportunities for specific qualifications. Kenen reaches the conclusion that fixed
exchange rates are more adequate for highly diversified national economies.
We note that this proposition is not necessarily incompatible with Mundell's
criteria of internal labour mobility.

Although the contributions of Kenen and McKinnon are generally considered as complementary to Mundell's proposition, Kindleberger (1986) emphasised the fact that the Mundell and McKinnon criteria do not necessarily
lead to the same conclusions. The case of Canada, for example, shows that
countries may have low levels of interregional factor mobility, which pleads
against fixing the exchange rates. But at the same time, they can show a high
degree of openness and the dominance of a particular trade partner, which are
characteristics in favour of fixed exchange rates.[10]

3.2.2. Labour immobility and capital mobility
Inspired by the situation in the European Union, Krugman and Obstfeld
(2000) consider the case of a combination of capital mobility and labour immobility as an application of second best theory. According to these authors,
the possibility exists that the non-satisfaction of one condition – labour mobility – out of all those indicated by basic OCA theory in order to reach an
economic optimum (free trade, capital mobility, labour mobility, fixed exchange rate) might lead, on the contrary, to a greater loss of macroeconomic
stability and welfare. For example, an unfavourable shift in the demand of a
country's products might, in these circumstances, lead to a capital outflow,
worsening even more the employment situation in this country, compared
with the alternative of flexible exchange rates and internationally immobile
production factors.[11]

3.2.3. Labour mobility and monetary integration as a process
Returning to standard OCA theory, it has been established that labour mobility might increase with the degree of diversification of the economies
(Kenen, 1969). The reason is that with a larger number of industries it will be
more feasible and probable to find industries with similar demands for different labour qualifications.[12]

Consider now a situation with a heterogeneous workforce, and let us classify the industries from lower to higher degrees of 'sophistication' or from less to more 'demanding' tasks. Suppose further that there exists limited upward labour mobility, consisting of the fact that a worker employed in industry i can only be employed at most in industry $i+1$, and suppose that there are no limitations to 'downward mobility'. This might seem obvious from the perspective of capacities; however, in reality there might also be downward rigidities (limits to mobility) for sociological, cultural or psychological reasons.

It can be shown then that the choice for monetary integration as a gradual process might not be a valid one. Whereas a monetary union with a given number of members might have a high degree of internal labour mobility (Mundell's criterion), paths of monetary integration that include stages with monetary unions with a smaller number of countries might have lower levels of interindustry labour mobility. This has to do with the fact that the existence of a continuous chain of industries in the planned monetary union (that is, the presence of industries 1, 2,..., $i-1$, i, $i+1$,... in the sense explained above) is a necessary condition for (upward) labour mobility. This is of course more likely to be the case within a large set of countries. With few countries, the chain might be discontinuous (e.g., a chain of industries like 1, 2,... ,$i-d$, i, $i+d'$,... with d and $d' > 1$ for one or more values of i), thus reducing labour mobility. In other words, if the criterion of Mundell combined with Kenen's criterion is valid for a given number of countries, this does not imply necessarily that it is valid for a smaller set of countries and, vice versa, if it is not for a given set of countries it may well be for an enlarged set.

3.3. Convergence and divergence in the industrial development paths in the light of OCA theory

One of the logical implications of the combined use of Mundell and Kenen's criteria is the instability of the exchange rate regime in the process of economic development characterised by structural changes. It can be shown that the application of the OCA criteria of Mundell and Kenen might lead to different conclusions about the long-run desirability of forming a monetary union, depending on the development phase in which the countries find themselves.

We will illustrate our point in a 2-country model.[13] Consider first a base scenario with time-consistent results. Initially, the two countries find themselves in the first stage of development characterised by the existence of a dominant economic activity (mono-crop economies). If they have similar activities (cases A and B in Table 6.1), they could form a monetary union, although in this case the efficiency gains (related to the greater liquidity of money) would normally be small, due to the low transaction levels. If they are not characterised by similar activities (cases C and D), they should not form a monetary union. Now, if both countries initiate a parallel process of economic development, characterised first by a moderate degree of diversification of their activities, in order to finally reach a high level of diversification, the criteria that point to maintaining fixed exchange rates will continue to be valid with initially similar activities (case A). With initially dissimilar activities, there will come a moment in this development process, in which the degree of diversification and the reduction of the potential impact of specific shocks will be such that, following Kenen, it is justified to fix the exchange rates 'forever' (case C).

Table 6.1.   *Time-consistency of policy recommendations in a 2-country model*

	Phase II: convergence	Phase II: divergence
Phase I: similar activities	*Case A*: countries form a monetary union from phase I on (time-consistent result)	*Case B*: countries form a monetary union in phase I, not in phase II, but again in phase III (time-inconsistent result)
Phase I: dissimilar activities	*Case C*: countries form a monetary union from phase II on (time-consistent result)	*Case D*: countries form a monetary union from phase III on (time-consistent result)

However, when starting from the initial situation with a similar dominant activity but following a different path of industrial development, different conclusions are reached. If the development paths and the diversification patterns do not show structural convergence, the OCA theory would imply the formation of a currency area in the first phase, to leave the exchange rate flexible in the second phase, and then again form a currency union (case B). The inconsistency of these results has to do with the partially irreversible character of the formation of monetary unions. On the one hand, the cost of disintegration in a monetary union is likely to be high, and on the other hand, the apparent collapse of the arrangement after the first stage might make it difficult to revive and reinstall a similar arrangement after the second stage. An implication of this might be that for countries that find themselves in the early stages of development, the formation of a monetary union might be counterproductive. Finally, when countries are characterised by different dominant activities in phase I and divergent development paths in phase II, they should consider fixing the exchange rate and forming a monetary union

only when both of them reach high levels of diversification (case D). Monetary integration would be justified, in this case, because of the fact that specific asymmetric shocks would lose much of their importance and because of
the (expected) high transaction levels.

3.4. Monetary integration as a process, the choice of the OCA criteria, and the choice of the empirical methods: the predictive power of OCA theory

The literature on OCAs offers a range of criteria that are empirically measur-
able, in order to establish the desirability of monetary integration between a
set of countries. The relative degree of compliance with the different criteria
establishes a ranking of countries, showing the theoretically optimal sequence
of accession to a monetary union (viewed as a process).

Theoretically, most of the criteria are interchangeable. Factor mobility,
intra-industry trade, diversified industrial structures, synchronicity of the
business cycles, synchronicity of external shocks, and so on, are all supposed
to measure the same: the absence of harmful country-specific shocks or the
symmetry of the economic shocks between countries.[14]

Empirically, however, there is sufficient evidence to conclude that the
utilisation of different criteria and different empirical methods may lead to
inconsistent results in terms of the extension of monetary union and the
ranking of countries according to the optimal moment of entry.

In the case of the European Union, several empirical studies of the *ex ante*
type about the synchronisation of business cycles, the convergence of macroeconomic variables and the degree of symmetry of external shocks have been
published in the years leading up to monetary unification. The importance of
these studies is related to the fact that the adequate functioning of the unified
monetary system depends on the nature of the shocks and how they can be
absorbed in the absence of an independent exchange rate and monetary instruments. The conclusions of these *ex ante* studies on convergence were not
unanimous. Westbrook (1998) established convergence in the inflation rates
but not in monetary policy. Bai, Hall and Shepherd (1997) identified common patterns in the time series of GDP, exchange rates and nominal interest
rates – short-term convergence – for the large countries in the EU. The series
of real interest rates did not show convergence.[15]

Many studies reached the conclusion that the optimal size of the EMU
was/is in fact different (smaller) than its actual size. Classifying the European
counties in a 'core', an intermediate group and a peripheral group, these
studies also suggested a scenario of monetary integration in a process of
gradual inclusion.[16] Table 6.2 presents the results of a number of studies that

tried to define empirically the extent of a European OCA around Germany (the 'core'), and to indicate its path of expansion (through the incorporation of the countries belonging to the intermediate group and the peripheral group, respectively).[17] The countries that formed part of the intermediate group showed asymmetries for some of the variables.

Table 6.2.   Optimal composition of the EMU according to the (a)symmetrical character of the shocks: review of empirical results

Reference	Method	Core (≈ OCA)	Periphery	Intermediate
Von Hagen & Neumann (1994)	Variability of the real exchange rate	Germany, Austria, Belgium, the Netherlands, France		Italy, Denmark, UK
DeSerres & Lalonde (1995)	Variability of the exchange rate	Germany, Belgium, the Netherlands	Sweden, France, Italy	UK, Spain
Helg *et al.* (1995)	Sector data, VAR cointegrated	Germany, Belgium, the Netherlands, Denmark, France, UK	Italy, Spain	Greece, Ireland, Portugal
Bayoumi & Eichengreen (1992)	Structural VAR	Germany, Belgium, the Netherlands, Denmark, France		UK, Italy, Spain, Ireland, Portugal, Greece
Artis & Zhang (1995)	Correlation between cyclical components	Germany, Belgium, the Netherlands, France, Spain, Portugal, Italy	Ireland	UK
Boone (1997)	VAR and dynamic correlation	Germany, Belgium, the Netherlands, France	UK, Greece	Italy, Spain, Ireland, Denmark
Beine & Hecq (1997)	Co-dependence	Germany, Belgium, the Netherlands, Italy	Spain, Portugal	France, UK, Denmark

Sources: Beine and Hecq (1997), Boone (1997).

In a recent analysis of the conditions of monetary integration in the Andean region, similar conclusions were reached (De Lombaerde *et al.*, 2002). The utilisation of different criteria, all inspired by the OCA literature, produced inconsistent paths for gradual monetary integration among CAN member countries. The Colombian economy was taken as the central economy (the 'core'), because of its size, the structure of its trade relations, and the leadership role it has played in regional integration.[18] The other member countries (Bolivia, Ecuador, Peru and Venezuela) were classified according to their compliance with the OCA criteria, or, their 'probabilities' of forming a monetary union with the central country.

The first criterion that was used was the Mundell criterion, referring to factor mobility, as proposed by Mundell in his original article (Mundell, 1961).[19] The next two indicators are based on Kenen's bilateral similarity arguments: one based on the production structure ('Kenen 1'), another on the export composition ('Kenen 2').[20] The fourth criterion, based on the same logic as the previous ones, takes the importance of intra-industry trade in the bilateral economic relations as an indicator of the desirability of monetary integration. This criterion is called the 'European Commission criterion' as it was suggested in European Commission (1990).[21] Finally, consistent with the recent tendencies in the empirical analysis of OCAs, two criteria were used that directly show the (a)symmetry of the external shocks: the correlation between the GDP growth rates, and the correlation between the inflation rates (index of consumer prices, CIP).[22]

The results of the calculations are presented in Table 6.3. It can easily be observed that there are clear inconsistencies in the different country classifications (showing, for each country, the relative desirability of forming a monetary union with Colombia), using different criteria. This shows the limited predictive capacity of OCA theory in relation to gradual processes of monetary integration. The results are very sensitive to the choice of the criteria, and there are no obvious ways available for weighting them. There is a need for additional econometric research capable of establishing a hierarchy among the criteria, according to their respective relevance, enhancing in this way the predictive capacity of OCA theory.

Table 6.3.   Appropriateness of forming a monetary union with Colombia:
classification of countries according to the different criteria

Criterion	Bolivia	Ecuador	Peru	Venezuela
Mundell	4	2	3	1
Kenen 1	1	2	3	4
Kenen 2	1	2	3	4
European Commission	4	2	3	1
GDP correlation	3	4	1	2
CIP correlation	1	2	3	4

Source: De Lombaerde *et al.* (2002).

4. CONCLUSION

In this contribution, we analysed the phenomenon of gradual monetary integration, and evaluated the usefulness of optimum currency area (OCA) theory in order to predict the path of integration.

We found that the idea of a monetary union with an incremental number of participating countries is not a logical outcome of OCA theory. Consistent with Kenen's thesis, a gradual process of monetary integration among economies with given industrial structures might not be optimal because currency areas may require a minimum scale (a minimum number of members) in order to guarantee interindustry labour mobility.

We also found that for a group of economies characterised by divergent industrial development patterns, the theory of optimum currency areas does not yield time-consistent recommendations about the suitability of monetary integration.

Finally, we established that the OCA theory weakly predicts gradual processes of monetary integration. The empirical tests on the optimality of currency areas seem to be very sensitive to the choice of criteria. Taking into account that OCA theory suggests various valid criteria, there is a need for additional econometric research capable of establishing a hierarchy among them, according to their relevance.

NOTES

1. Associate Professor at the Department of Economic Theory and Policy, Universidad Nacional de Colombia and Lecturer at the Institute of Development Policy and Management, Universiteit Antwerpen.
2. See also De Lombaerde (1996).
3. See also, Mundell (1997) and De Lombaerde (2000).
4. Mundell's original article was reproduced in: Mundell (1968), Krauss (1973) and Blejer *et al.* (1997, 17-27).
5. Kenen agrees with Mundell (1961) that the logical implication of the application of the factor mobility criteria is an exaggerated and unrealistic number of currency areas. Kenen clarifies that when the regions are defined in terms of their activities, the perfect interregional mobility of labour requires a perfect mobility between occupations. And this is only possible when labour is homogeneous or when the different regions of a monetary union have very similar requirements in terms of labour qualifications. In practice, the OCA coincides with a region of homogeneous production or single-product region (Kenen, 1969). Kenen shares with Mundell and also McKinnon the (efficiency) reasons for which the high number of monetary unions that would result from this logic is not adequate.
6. Kenen stresses further the necessity to have effective internal policies to accompany the fixed exchange rates: nominal wage controls and regional fiscal policies.
7. This argument is not valid when the 'imported' shocks affect the whole range of exports; for example shocks related to the economic cycles abroad.
8. It should be noted, however, that the classification in external and internal shocks is perhaps not satisfactory. For the purpose of the debate on monetary integration it might be more adequate to consider three categories: internal shocks, external shocks originating within the (prospective) monetary union, and external shocks originating outside the (prospective) monetary union.
9. Herz, in a previous publication, studied the relationship between exchange rate stabilisation in the framework of the EMS and trade and financial integration (Herz, 1995). His point of departure is the observation that the main effect of the EMS has been the reduction of the real and nominal exchange rate volatility in the short run; the effect in the long run is not observable. His results confirm those of previous studies: it is not possible to establish empirically a significant relationship between the reduction of the exchange rate volatility and the integration of the markets of goods, services and capital.
10. Kindleberger (1986) stressed also that it is important to consider the sociological and cultural factors to explain the degree of labour mobility, and that the mobility also depends on the receptivity of non-mobile labour.
11. The situation might even be worse when a limited labour mobility would lead to an emigration of the most qualified persons, which is not an unrealistic assumption.
12. According to Kenen (1969), the labour mobility issue should also be related to the interindustry differences in labour intensities.
13. Including more countries in the model does not invalidate our thesis. The model becomes just more complex and the probability of finding time-inconsistencies simply increases.
14. Although it might make sense, as suggested by the European Commission (1990), to take the growing importance of intra-industry trade as an indicator of the symmetry of external shocks, one should beware of inverting the logic of the argument and considering the existence of important levels of intra-industry trade as a necessary condition for shock symmetry. As shown by the case of the Caribbean, the absence of intra-industry trade does not mean that the economic structures are not similar. In the Caribbean, the flows of intra-regional trade are marginal, and therefore, they are bad indicators of the underlying structures. On the other hand, the flows of extra-regional trade are indeed important and the analysis of their composition does reveal a great similarity between the economic activities of the different countries (De Lombaerde, 1999; see also Griffith, 1998).

15. Following Frankel and Rose, these findings may tell little about *ex post* convergence, due to the endogenous character of the criteria.
16. Former Belgian Prime Minister Marc Eyskens proposed the formation of a 'pre-monetary union' within Benelux. See Eyskens (1996) and De Lombaerde (1997).
17. Other empirical studies about the EMU or about larger sets of European countries, using Mundell's conceptual framework, include: Karras (1996), Bayoumi and Eichengreen (1997), Dibooglu and Horvath (1997), Sörensen and Yosha (1998).
18. CAN stands for 'Comunidad Andina de Naciones'.
19. For data reasons, this criterion was only applied to capital flows.
20. Additionally Hirschmann-Herfindahl index numbers were calculated for production and exports. The results showed relatively high degrees of diversification of the production structures (values close to the minimum value $1/n$, n being the number of industries or categories) for all countries; and a relatively low variation around the mean for the CAN countries.
21. The Grubel-Lloyd index was used (Grubel and Lloyd, 1975), using data from Pombo (2000).
22. The correlation was calculated between the deviations from the trend in the original series for the period 1970-99.

REFERENCES

Artis, M. and W. Zhang (1995), 'International Business Cycles and the ERM: is there a European business cycle?', CEPR Discussion Paper, No.1191.

Bai, H., S. Hall and D. Shepherd (1997), 'Convergence and Common Cycles in the European Union', *Economic Issues*, **2**, 59-71.

Balassa, B. (1961), *The Theory of Economic Integration*, Homewood, Ill.: Richard D. Irwin.

Bayoumi, T. and B. Eichengreen (1992), 'Shocking Aspects of European Monetary Unification', CEPR Discussion Paper, No. 968.

Bayoumi, T. and B. Eichengreen (1997), 'Ever Closer to Heaven? An Optimum-Currency-Area Index for European Countries', *European Economic Review*, **41**, 761-770.

Beine, M. and A. Hecq (1997), 'Asymmetric Shocks Inside Future EMU', *Journal of Economic Integration*, **12**, 131-140.

Blejer, M., J.A. Frenkel, L. Leiderman, A. Razin and D. Cheney (eds) (1997), *Optimum Currency Areas. New Analytical and Policy Developments*, Washington DC: International Monetary Fund.

Boone, L. (1997), 'Symétrie des Chocs en Union Européenne: une analyse dynamique', *Économie Internationale*, **70**, 7-34.

De Lombaerde, P. (1996), 'Integración Internacional: un marco conceptual y teórico', *Colombia Internacional*, **33**, 12-18.

De Lombaerde, P. (1997), 'El Papel de la Benelux en el Proceso de Integración Europea en la Posguerra: lecciones para terceros países frente a los bloques comerciales', *Memoria y Sociedad*, **2**, 137-145.

De Lombaerde, P. (1999), 'Integración Monetaria Caribeña, Choques Simétricos y Comercio Intraindustrial', *Innovar. Revista de Ciencias Administrativas y Sociales*, **13**, 176-177.

De Lombaerde, P. (2000), 'Robert A. Mundell y la Teoría de las Areas Monetarias Optimas', *Cuadernos de Economía*, **18**, 39-64.

De Lombaerde, P., G. Carrillo and A.M. Reyes (2002), 'Integración Monetaria Gradual en la CAN y Teoría de las Areas Monetarias Optimas', in P. De Lombaerde (ed.), *Integración Asimétrica y Convergencia Económica en las Américas*, Bogotá: Universidad Nacional de Colombia, pp. 293-300.

Deserres, A. and R. Lalonde (1995), 'Les Sources des Fluctuations des Taux de Change et leurs Implications pour l'Union Monétaire', *Recherches Économiques de Louvain*, **61**, 3-42.

Dibooglu, S. and J. Horvath (1997), 'Optimum Currency Areas and European Monetary Unification', *Contemporary Economic Policy*, **15**, 37-49.

European Commission (1990), 'One Market, One Money', *European Economy*, **44**.

Eyskens, M. (1996), 'Europa tussen Verdieping en Uitbreiding', in K. Malfliet (ed.), *Wie is bang voor Oost-Europa?*, Leuven-Apeldoorn: Garant, pp. 23-31.

Frankel, J.A. and A. Rose (1997), 'The Endogeneity of the Optimum Currency Area Criteria', in M. Blejer, J.A. Frenkel, L. Leiderman, A. Razin and D. Cheney (eds), *Optimum Currency Areas. New Analytical and Policy Developments*, Washington DC: International Monetary Fund, pp. 67-68.

Frankel, J.A. and A. Rose (1998), 'The Endogeneity of the Optimum Currency Area Criteria', *Economic Journal*, **108**, 1009-1025.

Griffith, W. (1998), 'Integración Monetaria en el Caricom', *Innovar. Revista de Ciencias Administrativas y Sociales*, **12**, 135-151.

Gros, D. and A. Steinherr (1997), 'Openness and the Cost of Fixing Exchange Rates in a Mundell-Fleming World', in M. Blejer, J.A. Frenkel, L. Leiderman, A. Razin and D. Cheney (eds), *Optimum Currency Areas. New Analytical and Policy Developments,* Washington DC: International Monetary Fund, pp. 69-71.

Grubel, H.G. and P.J. Lloyd (1975), *Intra-Industry Trade*, London: Macmillan.

Helg, R., P. Manassa, T. Monacelli and R. Rovelli (1995), 'How Much Asymmetry in Europe? Evidence from Industrial Sectors', *European Economic Review*, **39**, 1017-1041.

Herz, B. (1995), 'Promoting Economic Integration by the EMS?', in F.P. Lang and R. Ohr (eds), *International Economic Integration*, Berlin: Physica-Verlag, pp. 67-89.

Karras, G. (1996), 'Is Europe an Optimum Currency Area? Evidence on the Magnitude and Asymmetry of Common and Country-specific Shocks in 20 European Countries', *Journal of Economic Integration*, **11**, 366-384.

Kenen, P.B. (1969), 'The Theory of Optimum Currency Areas: an eclectic view', in R.A. Mundell and A. Swoboda (eds), *Monetary Problems of the International Economy*, Chicago: University of Chicago Press, pp. 41-60 (reprinted in P.B. Kenen (1994), *Exchange Rates and the Monetary System. Selected Essays of Peter B. Kenen*, Aldershot, UK and Brookfield, USA: Edward Elgar, pp. 3-22).

Kindleberger, C. (1986), 'International Public Goods Without International Government', *American Economic Review*, **76**, 1-13.

Krauss, M. (ed.) (1973), *The Economics of Integration*, London: George Allen & Unwin Ltd.

Krugman, P. and M. Obstfeld (2000), *International Economics. Theory and Policy*, 5th edn., Reading, Mass.: Addison Wesley.

McKinnon, R. (1963), 'Optimum Currency Areas', *American Economic Review*, **53**, 717-725.

Mundell, R.A. (1961), 'A Theory of Optimum Currency Areas', *American Economic Review*, **51**, 509-517.

Mundell, R.A. (1968), *International Economics*, New York: Macmillan.

Mundell, R.A. (1997), 'Updating the Agenda For Monetary Union', in M. Blejer, J.A. Frenkel, L. Leiderman, A. Razin and D. Cheney (eds), *Optimum Currency Areas. New Analytical and Policy Developments*, Washington DC: International Monetary Fund, pp. 29-48.

Pombo, C. (2000), 'Comercio Intraindustrial e Innovación en Colombia', in R. Rocha and M. Olarreaga (eds), *Las Exportaciones Colombianas en la Apertura. Instituto del Banco Mundial*, Bogotá: Universidad del Rosario, pp. 246-289.

Sörensen, B.E. and O. Yosha (1998), 'International Risk Sharing and European Monetary Unification', *Journal of International Economics*, **45**, 211-238.

Von Hagen, J. and M. Neumann (1994), 'Real Exchange Rates Within and Between Currency Areas: how far away is EMU?', *Review of Economics and Statistics*, **76**, 236-244.

Westbrook, J. (1998), 'Monetary Integration, Inflation Convergence and Output Shocks in the European Monetary System', *Economic Inquiry*, **36**, 138-144.

PART II

Convergence in the EU: Fiscal and
Monetary Issues

7. The Impact of EU Membership on Tax Revenue Structures

John Ashworth and Bruno Heyndels[1]

1. INTRODUCTION

A country's tax structure reflects how the government decides to distribute the budgetary burden among its population. Given the budgetary importance of most governments, changing revenue structures is a major political act. It also reflects the scope of the country's discretion. This discretion is subject to several constraints. These typically refer to the internal economic and political context. However, the globalisation of the world economy has added external constraints. In the present chapter we concentrate on one such constraint: EU membership. We analyse whether and to what extent formal EU membership affects the individual countries' discretion in tax matters. To do so, we construct a measure for tax structure turbulence (Ashworth and Heyndels, 2001). This measures the degree of tax structure change within a given country. Using data for the period 1965-95, we analyse whether and how this turbulence is affected by EU membership (section 2).

Membership to the EU may not only influence the *amount* of fiscal activity as measured by our turbulence index. It may also affect the *nature* of tax policy (which taxes are increased/decreased?). In section 3 we analyse these structural evolutions in more detail. Taking the tax structures of the founding members as a point of reference, we analyse how revenue structures evolved in countries that became a member since 1973. More specifically, we analyse whether any convergence of revenue structures took place and, if so, we try to identify which countries set the pace.

2. TAX STRUCTURE TURBULENCE

2.1. Introduction

In their seminal work *Taxation by Political Inertia* Rose and Karran (1987) show how tax policy in a democratic setting is constrained by electoral responses. They predict that non-decision-making will be the dominating force in real-world tax policy. Still, revenue structures do change. This is the case for two sets of reasons. First, exogenous changes in the economic environment may affect tax revenues from different sources. Second, politicians may opt for deliberate changes in the revenue structure if they consider that political benefits outweigh the costs referred to by Rose and Karran. Controlling for the exogenous influences, the degree to which revenue structures change is thus an indicator for the discretionary power of governments.

Using a measure of tax structure turbulence as introduced in Ashworth and Heyndels (2000), we investigate to what extent this discretionary power (or rather: its expression) is affected by a country's membership to the EU. Section 2.2 introduces the measure of tax structure turbulence and discusses how this may be affected by – among others – membership to the EU. In section 2.3 we discuss the main results of our empirical analysis. Section 2.4 gives a short discussion.

2.2. Measuring and explaining tax structure turbulence

2.2.1. The index

The index for *tax structure turbulence* introduced in Ashworth and Heyndels (2001) measures the extent to which the ith country tax structure in year t differs from the structure in the previous year. The tax structure reflects the distribution of tax revenues among different sources. Considering n different taxes, the tax structure of country i in year t R_t^i is given by:

$$R_t^i = (R_{1t}^i, R_{2t}^i, ..., R_{jt}^i, ..., R_{nt}^i) \quad ,$$

with

$$\sum_{j=1}^{n} R_{jt}^i = 1 \quad \text{and}$$

$$0 \leq R_{jt}^i \leq 1 \quad ,$$

where R_{jt}^i is the share of tax j in i's total tax revenue in year t. The turbulence index is then:[2]

$$\Delta R_t^i = \sum_{j=1}^{n} \left| R_{jt}^i - R_{jt-1}^i \right| \quad \text{with} \quad 0 \le \Delta R_t^i \le 2 \quad .$$

The turbulence index takes a value of 0 if tax structures in $t-1$ and t are identical; it takes its maximum value of 2 if the tax structure has changed completely: any tax raised in year $t-1$ is non-existent in year t and vice versa.

We calculated tax structure turbulence for the 15 EU countries over the period 1965-95. The OECD publishes yearly data on national tax structures of its member countries. This information is very detailed, giving revenues from over 60 different sources. These are grouped under six main headings (codes ending in '000', where the categories are: taxes on income, profits and capital gains; social security contributions; taxes on payroll and workforce; taxes on property; taxes on goods and services and other taxes) and 19 sub-headings (ending in '00'). Thus, the shares of 19 different tax sources are used for each country to calculate the turbulence index ('turbulence-19').[3] However, for completeness, and to investigate the effect of the degree of aggregation, consideration will also be given to the main headings with a re-calculated turbulence index ('turbulence-6').

Ashworth and Heyndels (2001) show that important differences exist among countries with respect to their average turbulence. Countries like Austria, Switzerland and France are identified as 'fiscal conservatives' in the sense that their tax structure remains relatively stable from year to year. At the other extreme, the Southern European countries (Italy, Spain and Portugal) together with the UK and Luxembourg are characterised by larger annual changes to their tax structure. As an illustration – also of the difference between the two indicators – Figure 7.1 gives the evolution of tax structure turbulence in the UK. The two series of data are plotted, giving turbulence using information on the 19 sub-headings (upper line) and the six main headings (lower line) respectively.

Whereas, in general, turbulence as measured by the main and by the sub-headings give a similar picture, there are some years for which we observe important differences. By far the most important divergence between sub- and main headings is seen for the UK in 1975: while the information using main headings suggests this was a 'modal' year in terms of tax changes, the series using sub-headings suggests high turbulence.[4] The reason for this divergence is that within the category of income taxation (main heading 1000) a substitution took place with an increase in the share of individual income taxation (sub-heading 1100) and a decrease in the corporate income taxation (sub-heading 1200). Such divergences are rather exceptional (see previous endnote). Still their presence at some instances warrants that in our further analysis we consider both the main and the sub-headings. The 'general' pattern of turbulence in the UK is 'flat'. Only in the early 1990s do we see higher values. Most clear is the increase in turbulence in 1990, which can be attributed to the introduction of the poll tax.

Figure 7.1.   Tax structure turbulence in the UK, 1965-95

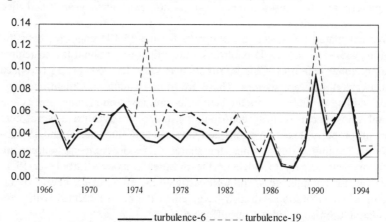

2.2.2. Explaining turbulence in a closed economy

Since Adam Smith introduced his 'canons of taxation', stability – lack of turbulence – has been considered a major characteristic of a good tax system. This idea also underlies Barro's tax-smoothing model (Barro, 1979) and Mankiw's (1987) version of this model for the *structure* of taxation. Only under very restrictive conditions does the tax smoothing approach allow for systematic turbulence (see Ashworth and Heyndels, 2000).

The prescriptive value of the tax-smoothing model – also in a context of multiple tax instruments – is not doubted. Its descriptive value is less clear (Roubini and Sachs, 1989). To understand why and under what conditions turbulence occurs, we need a positive model. Politico-economics does not offer a fully developed model of revenue structure manipulation. Still, a number of hypotheses have been put forward. For empirical purposes, these should be embedded into a structural model that accounts for other determinants of tax structure turbulence. Such a model is provided by the tax choice literature. Here, revenue structures are considered as equilibrium outcomes of a collective choice process that is constrained by political and economic forces. Hettich and Winer (1999a,b) argue that probabilistic voting offers the most appropriate framework. Politicians choose a tax structure that minimises the political costs for given total revenues. In equilibrium, the marginal political costs of all taxes are equalised. As such, the model shows how tax structure determination not only depends on dead-weight losses from taxation but also on the relative political influence of individual voters. The Hettich and Winer model predicts substantive turbulence: 'Because there is no respite from political competition, the government is forced continually to readjust tax structure in response to changes in (...) economic, political, and administrative determinants' (Hettich and Winer, 1999b, p. 196). The Hettich and Winer model predicts 'systematic' turbulence which, more importantly, is expected to be country-specific, reflecting differences in political and institutional contexts among countries. The Hettich and Winer model considers the tax choice process for given total tax revenues. When the total tax revenue changes, this may additionally lead to tax structure changes.

Against these structural backgrounds, tax structure turbulence varies on a year-to-year basis following changes in the economic and/or political environment. A first determinant of tax structure turbulence follows directly from the previous discussion. Changes in the tax burden relative to GDP are a first potential determinant of tax structure turbulence. Increasing as well as decreasing taxes can lead to changes in the tax structure. So, it is the *absolute* value of the change in tax burden that has to be considered as a first possible determinant of turbulence.

Turbulence can have an *economic* origin. Real economic growth as well as inflation can induce tax structure turbulence. A different responsiveness (elasticity) of tax bases to economic growth changes the relative importance of individual taxes, and thus increases tax structure turbulence. Inflation has a similar effect (Messere, 1993; Steinmo, 1993; Volkerink and De Haan, 1999). Again, the effect depends on absolute values of growth and inflation. The argument is similar to that for the changes in the tax burden. Only zero-growth and constant price levels are expected to leave the tax structure unaffected.

Turbulence can be *politically* induced. Opportunistic manipulation of the tax structure may be carried out by incumbents who try to secure re-election. Two extremes are possible (likely to be combined in practice). First, government can lower taxes in general. As discussed, this may have an (indirect) effect on tax structure turbulence. Second, government can change the tax structure. Electoral manipulation that takes the form of budget-neutral swaps among tax sources in election years will by definition lead to positive tax structure turbulence. A theoretical rationale for such opportunistic manipulation is given in Rogoff's signalling model (Rogoff, 1990). There, politicians signal their competence by temporary distortion of policy prior to elections (in non-election years, voters' preferences are followed).[5]

Ideological manipulation is a second political source of turbulence. If politicians have partisan preferences for tax structures (as in Pommerehne and Schneider, 1983), they may change the tax system accordingly when they are in power. Such changes are most likely to occur when the re-election constraint is not binding (Frey and Schneider, 1978), for instance immediately after elections have taken place. As a result of partisan preferences, regime shifts are expected to enhance tax structure turbulence: a partisan cycle occurs, following successive regime shifts.[6]

A third possible political determinant is the potentially high fixed cost of reform. This refers to Rose and Karran's ideas that changes to the tax system, even lowering the burden, induce considerable fixed electoral costs (see also Rose, 1985). The reason is that changes create uncertainty and direct media attention to the taxes that citizens already pay (Peters, 1991, p. 10). Also, the 'fixed' cost may reflect the prospect-theoretical idea that losers from a tax reform are more likely to be resentful of changes than the winners are grateful (Messere, 1993, p. 52). To the extent that politicians are more sensitive to the inertia-argument in election years, we expect a negative effect on tax structure turbulence in such years.

Dispersion of political power may affect turbulence. The political budget cycle literature has shown that political fragmentation obstructs budgetary adjustments to economic shocks, resulting in larger public debt (Roubini and Sachs, 1989; De Haan and Sturm, 1997 offer counter-evidence). If fragmentation leads to political indecisiveness, then we expect that dispersed political power lowers tax structure turbulence in all years. Fragmented governments will be less able to introduce changes. Moreover, when they do succeed in adapting the level of tax revenue, fragmented governments will more likely use different tax instruments simultaneously (to serve the different interests of government parties). Thus, fragmented government leads to fragmented tax reform and lower turbulence. Following the same reasoning, the lack of decisiveness of fragmented government may interact with the capacity to change the tax system for electoral or ideological reasons. Thus, government fragmentation may lower the electoral or ideological impact on turbulence.

2.2.3. Turbulence and internationalisation

The determinants of turbulence discussed above are internal to the country. However, the last century has been characterised by a strong globalisation of political and economic life. This evolution may also affect national tax policies. Internationalisation offers opportunities for individual countries but it also imposes new constraints. These can be formal or informal in nature. The latter refer to the existence of *fiscal externalities*. Decisions on tax policy by any given country may affect the welfare elsewhere. For example, lowering corporate taxes in country A may attract industries from neighbouring countries. This relocation has obvious welfare implications for the latter countries. Two 'behavioural' reactions are possible: tax competition and tax harmonisation (see Table 7.1).

Given the presence of fiscal externalities, tax competition arises if countries neglect any effects of their (tax) decisions on other countries. It is not a priori clear whether the presence of fiscal externalities will increase or decrease tax structure turbulence. In a context of tax competition, countries may decide on additional changes to the tax structure or they may *not* make changes that they would have made in the absence of externalities. For example, a decision to increase corporate taxation may not be taken in order to avoid the effects on international competitiveness. Therefore, whether internationalisation (as measured by the openness of individual countries) has a positive or negative effect on tax structure turbulence is to be considered an empirical matter. The question then boils down to whether tax competition paralyses or stimulates fiscal 'activity' (turbulence).

Table 7.1.   Positive (+) and negative (–) effects on turbulence

	Tax competition	Tax harmonisation
+	• Country A lowers tax as this attracts tax base from country B • Country B lowers tax as a reaction to decision in A	• Country A brings tax in line with B ('tacit collusion' by follower or forced to by formal agreements)
–	• Country A does not increase tax as it fears exodus of tax base	• Country A does not increase tax in order to avoid detrimental effects on B ('tacit collusion' by leader)

Alternatively, given the presence of fiscal externalities countries may respond co-operatively and harmonise their tax systems. Co-operative action is facilitated when formal interdependencies are constructed. The EU is a clear example. For example, members of the EU stimulate international trade among each other and recognise the benefits from this. This creates a context that may facilitate explicit co-operative action, also in the field of taxation. The demand for tax harmonisation is a logical and explicit consequence of the formation of an economic and political union. Still, it should be recognised that success in terms of explicit harmonisation among EU countries is limited. Deheja and Genschel (1999) argue – and illustrate – that this failure of collective action in the field of taxation can to a large extent be attributed to the fact that benefits from co-operation are *not* mutual. In particular, smaller states may well gain from tax competition (see also Kanbur and Keen, 1993).

As a general rule, however, benefits for smaller countries do not outweigh costs for larger countries so that harmonisation is beneficial from a general EU perspective. As such, and even though the process of harmonisation may be a slow one, it is fair to say that there is a general awareness of the need for such harmonisation. It should be observed that the incentive might be towards 'informal harmonisation': countries may take effects on each other into account, even without formal agreement to do so. This may, for example, be the case when the country wants to avoid detrimental effects on mutual goodwill in international trade and other non-fiscal domains. As a result we observe a form of unspoken or *tacit collusion* where countries recognise the interdependencies and the costs which may be involved if rivalry becomes too intense.

The effects of tax policy on other EU countries may thus be seen as an additional constraint on national policies. This may affect tax structure turbulence. Countries may not be able to realise specific changes to their tax systems because of (expected) negative externalities on EU partners. As a consequence tax structure turbulence will be lowered. If tacit collusion takes the form of 'tax leadership' (in analogy to 'price leadership' under 'tacit collusion' in oligopolistic firms), then a move by a leading country may increase turbulence in followers. Finally, it is possible that the EU – formally –imposes additional tax structure changes (thereby increasing turbulence). In general, again, the direction of the effect on turbulence is an empirical matter.

Apart from the effects through fiscal externalities, EU membership may also affect responses to macroeconomic policy. To the extent that member countries lose degrees of freedom in responding to changes in economic activity and/or inflation, we expect a positive effect on turbulence as measures to offset the effects on tax structures can not be taken as easily as before. In the extreme case, countries are not able to take any deliberate action, and growth and inflation effects on tax structure will be very strong. This prediction is based on the view that EU membership serves as a constraint on deliberate policy action. One may argue, however, that membership will impose a constraint, not on action, but on the degree to which countries can allow for automatic changes to their tax structure. From this perspective, EU members may be obliged more than other countries to offset the effects from macroeconomic fluctuations.

2.2.4. Estimation
In order to examine this further, the analysis of Ashworth and Heyndels (2001) is expanded to see if there are direct effects from the EU. This corresponds with the estimation of the following equation, explaining tax structure turbulence in country i for year t:[7]

$$\Delta R_t^i = \alpha_t^i + \alpha_1 TB_{t,t-1}^i + \alpha_2 y_{t,t-1}^i + \alpha_3 p_{t,t-1}^i + \alpha_4 OP_{t,t-1}^i + \alpha_5 EL_t^i +$$
$$\alpha_6 RE_{t-1}^i + \alpha_7 RS_{t-1}^i + \alpha'_5 RS_{t-1}^i EL_t^i + \alpha'_6 RS_t^i RE_{t-1}^i + \alpha_8 EU_{t-1}^i +$$
$$\alpha_9 y_{t,t-1}^i EU_t^i + \alpha_{10} p_{t,t-1}^i EU_t^i + \varepsilon_t^i \quad .$$

$TB_{t,t-1}^i$ is the absolute change in tax burden; $y_{t,t-1}^i$ is the absolute value of the real growth rate; $p_{t,t-1}^i$ is the absolute value of the inflation rate (CPI) and OP is a vector of the level of change in a country's openness (proportion of exports and imports to GDP). Openness is used as a proxy for the fiscal externalities (with possibly resulting tax competition or harmonisation). Following the discussion above, we expect α_1, α_2 and α_3 to be positive. The sign on α_4 is unclear a priori and so must be determined empirically.

EL_t^i and RE_{t-1}^i are two political dummies. The first equals 1 in election years and 0 in other years. The sign of α_5 depends on whether opportunistic manipulation of the tax structure or high fixed political costs of taxation dominate. The second measures regime shifts. It equals 1 in $t-1$ when the political orientation of the incumbent government changed in the first half of $t-1$ or in the second half of $t-2$.[8] The idea is that a new government which comes into power in the first half of a year can adapt the tax code in the second half of that year, changing tax revenues the year after. α_6 is expected to be positive: partisan preferences imply that a new government adapts the tax system to its wishes.

RS_t^i is a variant of the Roubini and Sachs measure of government fragmentation as proposed by Edin and Ohlsson (1991). It actually consists of three separate dummy variables with their respective coefficients (the corresponding α's are therefore vectors). $RS1$ equals 1 for governments consisting of 2 or 3 parties (and 0 if not); $RS2$ equals 1 for 4-party governments (and 0 for other); $RS3$ equals 1 for minority governments (values taken from De Haan and Sturm, 1997).[9] α_7 is expected to be negative: the more fragmented the government is, the less it will be able to change the relative importance of different tax instruments.

α'_5 and α'_6 capture the interaction effects of the Roubini-Sachs indicator with the election and regime shift indicators. Political dispersion is expected to weaken the effects of election years and regime shifts. The corresponding coefficients are therefore expected to be negative if the electoral or ideological coefficients are positive. If the electoral coefficient is negative, revealing the dominance of a fixed cost-effect, then the interaction coefficient is expected to be negative. This would indicate that passivity with respect to tax policy is further enhanced by the dispersion of political power.

Table 7.2.   Panel estimation of tax turbulence, 1965-95

Independent Variables	Turbulence-19		Turbulence-6	
	Fixed Effects	Random Effects	Fixed Effects	Random Effects
Intercept	0.043	0.041	0.037	0.032
	(0.008)	(0.009)	(0.005)	(0.005)
$TB^i_{t,t-1}$	0.434	0.482	0.394	0.434
	(0.135)	(0.133)	(0.106)	(0.105)
$y^j_{t,t-1}$	-0.018	-0.018	-0.020	-0.015
	(0.091)	(0.086)	(0.018)	(0.012)
$p^j_{t,t-1}$	0.030	0.035	0.043	0.084
	(0.081)	(0.071)	(0.022)	(0.031)
EL^i_t	-0.004	-0.004	-0.004	-0.003
	(0.002)	(0.002)	(0.002)	(0.001)
$RS2^i_{t-1}$	-0.016	-0.014		
	(0.004)	(0.004)		
$RS1^i_{t-1}EL^i_t$			0.008	0.006
			(0.004)	(0.003)
$RS3^i_{t-1}EL^i_t$	0.014	0.014	0.012	0.010
	(0.006)	(0.006)	(0.005)	(0.004)
$y^j_{t,t-1}EU^i_t$	0.185	0.187	0.032	0.034
	(0.090)	(0.092)	(0.014)	(0.013)
$p^j_{t,t-1}EU^i_t$	0.180	0.163		
	(0.070)	(0.070)		
EU^i_{t-1}	-0.019	-0.019	-0.015	-0.015
	(0.008)	(0.008)	(0.005)	(0.005)
R^2	0.849	0.782	0.412	0.221
Omission	12.441 (1		11.455 (	
M2 vs M1	38.908 (1		17.255 (	
M3 vs M2	69.606 (2		73.876 (	
M3 vs M1	108.514 (4		91.131 (	
LM		21.843 (		12.711 (2)
HS		8.581 (		13.994 (8)

Notes: (1) Values in parentheses below the coefficients are estimated standard errors. (2) The three basic fixed-effects models examined are denoted by M1 (the standard regression equation where the variable of interest is explained by the corresponding explanatory variables); M2 (fixed country effects are also included); M3 (time specific effects to accommodate shocks are added). The fixed effect model is compared with the random effects model (REM). The fixed effects model includes country and time effects. 'MA vs MB' indicates the likelihood ratio test statistic between the versions A and B of the model. The values in parentheses are the degrees of freedom for the χ^2 test. (3) To distinguish between the REM and the fixed effects model, there are two test statistics of relevance: the Breusch and Pagan (1980) Lagrange Multiplier (LM) test statistic, and the Hausman (HS) test statistic (see Hausman, 1978). Large values of LM reject the Classical regression model, in favour of the Random Effects Model. Large values of HS imply a larger variance of the GLS estimator relative to the LSDV estimator and a greater efficiency of the LSDV (least squares dummy variables) estimator. Thus a rejection of the null hypothesis confirms the preference for the fixed estimator to the REM alternative. For the REM to be preferred to the fixed effect model the Hausman test must not be rejected. The numbers in parentheses after the HS statistic and the fixed effects are the numbers of degrees of freedom. (4) The regression for turbulence amongst the sub-divisions includes a dummy for the re-classification of social security in Italy. (5) 'Omission' is the likelihood ratio test statistic for the omission of the variables from the general model outlined in the text and the restricted models presented here. It should be noted that there is no significant difference for the omission of countries from the original. (6) Stability across the original and new members: 0.898 (Turbulence-19), 1.001 (Turbulence-6).

The additional variables examine the effect of EU membership on turbulence; the idea being in line with those outlined above in that membership – through tax competition or harmonisation – may or may not stimulate activity in tax movements (see Table 7.1). Further, the effects of external 'shocks' which may be absorbed in an economy operating on its own may be constrained by membership of a union. Thus the anticipation of the signs on these variables are that α_8 will be indeterminate whilst α_9 and α_{10} will be positive if EU membership serves as a constraint on deliberate action, whereas they will be negative if membership brings in incentives to offset the consequences of macroeconomic changes.

The equations are estimated following standard panel data estimation (see Greene, 1999) with the results presented in Table 7.2. The data set consists of 13 EU countries (Portugal and Spain were left out because of data availability) for the period 1965-95. A number of factors are worth noting. The random effect model is the preferred model. It was possible to remove a number of variables from the model in order to give a more efficient final estimating equation. For ease, the table gives the preferred results after the omission of insignificant variables.

The general tenor of the main results is in line with those of the original work by the authors (Ashworth and Heyndels, 2001). In particular, the effects of the political variables remain as before. Further, the effect of openness remains insignificant. Turning to the effects of the re-specification, it can be seen that there is a clear effect of membership of the European Union. Membership dampens tax revenue turbulence significantly. Furthermore, the effect is of a similar magnitude for the main categorisation of tax structure or for the sub-categories. The dampening effect from EU membership may be taken to suggest that countries that become members do not take fiscal decisions that they would have taken without formal membership. In line with Table 7.1, this could mean two things. Turbulence could be lowered as a consequence of increased tax competition or as a consequence of 'tacit collusion'. If the former were the case, then we would expect openness to be a clear determinant of turbulence. After all, the degree of openness is a measure of fiscal externalities and therefore of possible gains/losses of tax competition. The insignificance of the openness variable in our regression may thus be taken to indicate that the significant EU-membership variable reflects the presence of 'orderly competition' among countries behaving like 'good competitors' (Porter, 1985).

The effect of the other variables is less consistent among the turbulence-6 and turbulence-19 regressions. The effect of inflation on turbulence in the main categories is unaffected by membership whilst there is an effect on the sub-category definition. Furthermore, whilst there is a significant effect of membership on the effect of growth on the turbulence, this effect is much less marked in the main categorisation. Overall, it would appear that countries are less able to absorb a shock when they are members of the union. The main effect of this only manifests itself in the sub-divisions (turbulence-19) suggesting that the turbulence comes from the detail and is submerged in the aggregation. However, this inability to react is considerably offset by membership of the Union, which imposes its own discipline.[10]

3. TAX STRUCTURE CONVERGENCE

EU membership may systematically affect the *nature* of a country's tax policy. The formal and informal forces of membership may induce countries to converge to a uniform – or at least analogous – tax structure. Ashworth and Heyndels (2000) observed a general convergence of tax structures among OECD countries over the period 1965-95. This process was such that differences among tax structures – tax structure heterogeneity – fell over time, but there is no prospect of full convergence. Indeed, they find that tax structures move together, but that in equilibrium international differences are expected to remain.

In what follows, we analyse the evolution of tax structures among EU members. More precisely, we analyse how tax structures of new member countries evolved compared to the revenue structures of the six founding EU members.

To do so, we first take a look at how revenue structures within the 'nucleus' group of the six founding countries, denoted as EU6, have evolved. We then calculate the index of tax structure heterogeneity as introduced by Rose (1985) (see also Ashworth and Heyndels, 2000). This index is formally identical to the one used to measure tax structure turbulence, with this provision that we now compare the revenue structure among countries (in given years), rather than among years (in given countries). Considering the EU6 countries, we calculate for each the following series:

$$D_t^{i,EU6-i} = \sum_{j=1}^{n} \left| R_{jt}^i - R_{jt}^{EU6-i} \right| \quad with \quad 0 \le D_t^{i,EU6-i} \le 2 \quad ,$$

where $D_t^{i,EU6-i}$ gives a measure of the 'distance' between the tax structure in country i and that in the set of six initial EU countries excluding i. The latter 'European-6 tax structure' for country i corresponds with the unweighted structure in the other five member countries. To calculate the tax distance index we use data on each country's tax revenues allocated over six headings. We calculated yearly values over the period 1965-95. Figure 7.2

summarises the distances for the year 1995 for the main headings. It is observed that Germany and the Netherlands have a tax structure that most closely resembles the 'European' structure in the other five founding member countries. France and Luxembourg, on the other hand, have most atypical revenue structures.

Figure 7.2. 	*Tax structure heterogeneity among the 6 initial EU members (main headings), 1995*

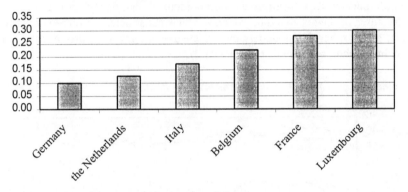

The average value of the distance index for any given year gives an indication of tax structure heterogeneity among EU6 countries:

$$H_t^{EU6} = \frac{1}{6}\sum_{i=1}^{6} D_t^{i,EU6-i} \quad .$$

For 1995, this value amounts to 0.202 for the EU6 countries. This means that tax structures differed by 10.1 percent on average. Of course, this value as such does not give us much information, if only because the heterogeneity measure depends on the number of taxes that are considered (just as in the case of turbulence where turbulence-19 was systematically higher than turbulence-6). However, the value of the heterogeneity index does reveal important information when compared to the value in alternative subgroups and/or by its evolution over time. For example, a similar heterogeneity measure using the same subdivision of tax revenues for 20 OECD countries (each time comparing to the unweighted average in the other 19 countries) amounts to 0.274; for 17 European countries (EU15 countries including Switzerland and Norway) the value is 0.254. The lower value obtained for EU6 gives a clear indication that there is 'familiarity' in tax structures among the EU6 countries.

What is – in the context of the present convergence-analysis – of most relevance, is how heterogeneity evolves over time. The evolution of the index over time gives an image of patterns of fiscal convergence or divergence. This evolution, calculated over the period 1965-95 is plotted in Figure 7.3. Two lines are given. The lower line in Figure 7.3 gives the evolution of tax distances between the six founding members. The upper line gives the average distances between EU6 on the one hand and the other nine EU members. From Figure 7.3, it is clear that the latter line is considerably higher over the whole period. This confirms the observation of 'familiarity' in the revenue structures of the six founding countries (their tax structure is more similar to that of the other five founders than is the average tax structure in non-EU6 countries compared to this EU6 standard).

Figure 7.3.   Tax structure heterogeneity (main headings), 1965-95

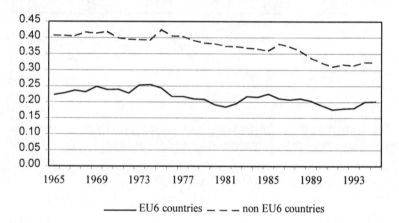

——— EU6 countries — — — non EU6 countries

The study of the time pattern amounts to analyse the presence of so-called σ-convergence, that is the 'moving together' of tax structures.[11] Considering first the heterogeneity among the EU6 countries, Figure 7.3 shows that over time a very moderate convergence of tax structures has taken place. The average distance indicator in 1965 was 0.223, whereas in 1995 it was 0.202. The strongest convergence among the revenue structures in the six countries took place in the late 1970s. Actually, in 1981 the average distance indicator took its minimum value (0.185). What is more interesting, however, is the fact that the distance from non-EU6 members to the EU6 average has fallen considerably over the period (from 0.407 in 1965 to 0.323 in 1995). This gives clear evidence of the fact that revenue structures among EU countries have converged to the standard set by the six founding members.

Technically Figure 7.3 shows that EU15 countries have converged with the EU6 standard. This may mean that nine non-EU6 members have adapted their tax structure to bring it in line with EU6 *or* that the EU6 have adapted to the other 19 countries. In other words, it is unclear which set of countries has been setting the example. This brings us back to the 'tacit collusion' analogue mentioned earlier. Just as firms in an oligopolistic environment may choose price leadership as a form of tacit collusion, so may countries choose tax leadership, where the tax structure set by a leader is followed systematically by followers. The recent literature on tax mimicking offers several reasons why countries follow this model (Besley and Case, 1995).

3.1. Leaders and followers

To identify potential leaders in EU taxation, we first identify all countries that have converged pair-wise (Ashworth and Heyndels, 2000). This is done by comparing the distance index between any two countries (from the set of 15) calculated for 1965 and 1995 respectively (we use data for sub-headings). If the 1995 distance index takes the lower value, this indicates that countries have converged. The results are in column two of Table 7.3. For example, for Germany we observe convergence with 10 (out of 14) countries. More generally, it is immediately clear from column 2 that the evidence of convergence of tax structures is highlighted. Indeed, the number of converging couples is much higher than the number of diverging ones. More precisely, we observe that no less than 13 countries had eight or more countries with which they converged. Only the Netherlands and Denmark converged with less than half of the other countries.

Given the converging couples, we identify leaders by comparing 1995 tax structures in any given country to the 1965 tax structure in any of the countries with which it converged (again using the distance index). The underlying idea is simple: if country A has converged towards country B, then we expect that the 1995 revenue structure in A more closely resembles the 1965 structure in B than the other way round. The results are in column 3 of Table 7.2 where countries are ranked according to their 'degree of leadership', i.e. the percentage of time they were the leading country in each of the 'converging couples'. For example, we observe that Germany is a clear leader: all 10 countries that had a tax structure in 1995 that resembles the German structure more closely than in 1965 appear to have moved towards the 'German example'. Germany's degree of leadership is therefore 100 percent. Also Luxembourg, the Netherlands and Denmark are 'pure' leaders. Still it should be noted that the latter two countries converge to only five and three countries respectively. More generally, with the clear exception of Italy (which is a special case in the sub-division because of its 1973 tax re-organisation), there is evidence of the original EU members occupying leading positions.

Table 7.3.   Convergence and leaders/followers (sub-headings)

	Number of converging countries	Leadership
Germany	10	100.0 %
Luxembourg	8	100.0 %
the Netherlands	5	100.0 %
Denmark	3	100.0 %
Austria	8	87.5 %
Belgium	8	87.5 %
UK	9	66.6 %
France	10	60.0 %
Sweden	10	60.0 %
Spain	9	44.4 %
Finland	11	36.4 %
Ireland	13	23.1 %
Italy	14	14.3 %
Greece	12	8.3 %
Portugal	14	0.0 %

3.2. σ-convergence

Given this, the rest of the analysis considers the convergence to the tax structures of the original six and compares this with the previous evidence (Ash-worth and Heyndels, 2000) concerning overall convergence among the 15 EU countries. The results will indicate whether the driving force towards convergence are the original six countries as the table above would suggest or whether there is a greater move towards overall convergence.[12]

There are a number of possible approaches. The first considers the effective estimation of the diagrams above. The visual representation can also be summarised by examining a cross-section regression for the 15 countries of the change in the measure over the 30-year period, $D_{1995}^{i,EU6-i} - D_{1965}^{i,EU6-i}$ as a function of the initial levels $D_{1965}^{i,EU6-i}$ for EU6 members, and $D_{1995}^{i,EU6-i} - D_{1965}^{i,EU6}$ as a function of the initial levels $D_{1965}^{i,EU6}$ for non-EU6 members.

The significant negative sign of the slopes in the sub-category specification confirms the visual evidence of σ-convergence in Figure 7.3. Thus the summary concept of σ-convergence allows us to conclude that over the period 1965-95, tax structures in European countries have become more similar to those of the original six members, though there must be a note of caution given the evidence from the aggregated (main headings) definitions. There, indeed, no significant convergence is observed.

It is possible from Table 7.4 to solve for the implied values of β, the speed of convergence (see Tondl, 1999). This measure tells us how fast tax structures converge. Following the growth literature, the corresponding equation assumes a steady-state tax structure rate of change and a long-term steady-state tax structure index (which may be zero, although this is not a requirement). Convergence in the case being examined requires a movement towards the tax structure of a set of countries, and evidence of the movement only tentatively suggests dominant partners.[13]

Table 7.4.   *Cross-section convergence of tax structures to 6-country average, 1965-95*

Variable	Intercept	Slope	β	R^2	FF	JB	HET
Main	0.031	-0.297	0.011	0.167	0.004	0.661	5.921
	(0.064)	(0.183)					
Sub	0.206	-0.667	0.035	0.449	3.921	4.373	3.062
	(0.106)	(0.205)					
Sub[+]	0.127	-0.456	0.020	0.652	2.208	8.525	0.006
	(0.093)	(0.135)					

Notes: FF is the Ramsey RESET test of functional form; JB is the Jarque-Bera test for normality; HET is the Breusch-Pagan test for heteroscedasticity;
+ : this equation is adjusted with a dummy for Italy to accommodate the major alignment in the data set.

Table 7.4a.   *Cross-section convergence of tax structures of the newer 9 members to 6-country average, 1965-95*

Variable	Intercept	Slope	β	R^2	FF	JB	HET
Main	0.014	-0.260	0.010	0.078	0.233	0.433	2.581
	(0.144)	(0.337)					
Sub	0.147	-0.488	0.022	0.211	2.647	1.772	1.787
	(0.202)	(0.246)					

Notes: FF is the Ramsey RESET test of functional form; JB is the Jarque-Bera test for normality; HET is the Breusch-Pagan test for heteroscedasticity.
There is evidence at a 10 percent significance, but not at a 5 percent significance, that the patterns of convergence are different across the two groups; this disappears if we adjust for Italy.

The speed of adjustment is low: at most 3.5 percent, and once adjustment is made for the Italian re-alignment by a member country completely out of initial synchronisation, the rate falls to around 2 percent. Furthermore, the lack of clear evidence on convergence in the main headings suggests slow movements at this level. These results should be contrasted with the results for a movement to 'general' EU averages of over 9 percent per annum (4.5 percent after the adjustment for Italy) for the sub-categories and over 4 percent for the main categories (see Ashworth and Heyndels, 2000).

There is a clear case for estimating the regressions in Table 7.4 for the newer members only. These results are provided in Table 7.4a. The concern here must, however, be the lack of degrees of freedom.

Re-examining Figure 7.3, the original six countries are not showing much evidence of further convergence (that is, they have reached some form of internal equilibrium), whilst newer members do appear to be on some convergent path. Hence, whilst overall there may seem to be little effect, the effect of the six original members on the other countries may be much greater. However, cross-section results may be hiding the effects that can be identified by a panel. In the traditional convergence literature (Canova and Marcet, 1995 and Tondl, 1999) researchers find higher convergence rates when using panel data; a result mirrored in previous work in this area by the authors (Ashworth and Heyndels, 2000).

3.3. Panel estimation of convergence

Further investigation requires analysis using a full panel data set. To identify relevant determinants of tax structure convergence, we estimate a model based on the simple logic that differences in tax structures are determined by differences in determinants of tax structures. The idea is that a country with an economic environment (defined by GDP, openness, population, tax burden and other features) that is identical to the EU6 average will have a tax structure identical to this EU6 average. Thus the tax distance will be zero. The analysis again follows the growth literature and considers the index in terms of β-convergence, that is, it examines the dynamic pattern of the movement of the index (for fuller definitions, see Barro and Sala-i-Martin, 1991 and 1995). This leads us to the following model to investigate the panel regression, explaining tax distance indices DI_t^i :

$$\Delta DI_t^i = \alpha_t^i + \alpha_1 DGDP_t^i + \alpha_2 DTB_t^i + \alpha_3 DPOP_t^i + \alpha_4 OPEN_t^i + \alpha_5 EU_t^i + \alpha_6 DI_{t-1}^i + \varepsilon_t^i \quad ,$$

where *DGDP*, *DTB* and *DPOP* are administrative determinants of tax structure heterogeneity. The first corresponds with the difference between country *i*'s per capita GDP and the EU6 average. If a country has a GDP that is very different from the EU6 average, then we expect it to have a tax structure that is 'distant' from the EU6 tax structure. We expect negative GDP differences to have a similar effect as positive differences, so our explanatory variable is the absolute value. Similarly, *DTB* is the absolute value of the difference between a country's share of the tax burden in GDP and the EU6 average; *DPOP* is defined similarly for population. *OPEN* measures the openness of an economy. More precisely, it corresponds with the ratio of exports and imports to GDP. Finally, the country-specific political influences are captured by α_t^i, and EU_t^i. The latter variable captures the formal interdependency hypothesised for EU members. It is a dummy that takes a value 1 in those years that a country was a formal member of the EU, and 0 in other cases. Finally, the lagged variable DI_{t-1}^i is present to accommodate the time dynamic pattern of the tax structure.[14]

The difference term is used for the dependent variable to aid calculation of the speed of convergence. It is possible to model this effect using a time trend rather than an autoregressive term. The choice here is guided by being able to tie the work closely to the standard convergence literature. The general tenor of the result remains if the time trend is used; see Ashworth and Heyndels (2000) for a similar exercise.

The overall rationale for this formulation can be found in Ashworth and Heyndels (2000). There we estimated the model using a panel of OECD countries and relating all variables not to EU6 averages but to the OECD average. The re-estimation here is to identify the pull of the original EU members and to compare this with the results of all members identified in the previous work. The results of this exercise are found in Table 7.5. Results are given for two specifications of the dependent variable. Columns 2 and 3 refer to tax structure heterogeneity using the sub-heading definitions for the 15 EU members, while the last two columns give the results for the main headings.[15]

The presence of fixed country-effects means that countries are significantly different from one another and that this difference remains whatever convergence occurs. Thus *only conditional convergence will be achieved*. Furthermore, the results suggest a relatively high level of heterogeneity, though one must remember that the effects of the other independent variables are also country-specific and will have an effect. Overall, this first observation suggests that tax structure heterogeneity is to some extent a reflection of 'national culture' – a result that mirrors other results that have been found. This suggests that differences in tax structures among countries have to some extent historical origins, and as the history of any two countries is (almost) by definition different, one can expect tax structures to remain different.

Table 7.5.   *Convergence to the tax structure of the 6 original countries*
                 for 15 member states

	Unweighted sub-categories		Unweighted main categories	
	fixed effects	random effects	fixed effects	random effects
intercept[++]	0.134	0.098	0.147	0.006
	(0.074)	(0.131)	(0.058)	(0.009)
$DPOP^+$	-0.025	0.007	-0.038	0.004
	(0.034)	(0.005)	(0.024)	(0.003)
$DGDP^+$	-0.002	-0.011	-0.001	-0.001
	(0.001)	(0.008)	(0.001)	(0.0005)
DTB^+	0.042	0.077	-0.022	0.062
	(0.087)	(0.070)	(0.059)	(0.044)
OPEN	-0.026	-0.022	-0.012	-0.001
	(0.028)	(0.081)	(0.020)	(0.005)
EU	-0.015	-0.011	-0.006	0.006
	(0.007)	(0.005)	(0.005)	(0.035)
DI_{t-1}	-0.105	-0.050	-0.081	-0.022
	(0.022)	(0.014)	(0.024)	(0.010)
R^2	0.195	0.047	0.233	0.017
M2 vs M1	37.451 (14)		53.714 (14)	
M3 vs M2	42.630 (28)		53.037 (28)	
M3 vs M1	80.081 (42)		106.751 (42)	
LM(1)	5.712		9.564	
HS	17.921 (6)		36.963 (6)	
Stable	0.932		1.211	
Speed of adjustment	9.98 %	4.88 %	8.44 %	2.22 %

Notes: Estimated standard errors are in parentheses below coefficients.
+ : These variables are as defined in the text, that is, absolute deviations from the means. ++ : under the restriction that sum of the country-effects is zero.
The fixed effects include both country- and time-period effects.
The LM, HS and country effects terms are as outlined in Table 7.2.
'Stable' is a test of stability between the original 6 countries and the other 9 member states. As can be seen the test indicates stability; possibly because of the number of insignificant variables.
The relative (to the average) fixed effects are:
Sub-categories: Austria, Belgium, France, Germany, Italy, the Netherlands, **Spain**, Sweden (minus); **Denmark**, Finland, Greece, Ireland, Luxembourg, Portugal, UK (plus).
Main categories: Austria, Belgium, France, Germany, Italy, **the Netherlands**, Spain, Sweden (minus); **Denmark**, Finland, Greece, Ireland, Luxembourg, Portugal, UK (plus).
This gives an indication of those who will be more converged (minus) and those with a tendency to be less convergent (plus); the 'extreme' countries are those emboldened.

Table 7.5a.   *Convergence of 9 newer member states to tax structure of the 6 original countries*

	Unweighted sub-categories		Unweighted main categories	
	fixed effects	random effects	fixed effects	random effects
Intercept[++]	0.206	0.048	0.161	0.002
	(0.110)	(0.187)	(0.100)	(0.002)
$DPOP^+$	-0.047	0.020	-0.048	0.012
	(0.055)	(0.008)	(0.042)	(0.007)
$DGDP^+$	-0.003	-0.028	-0.001	-0.002
	(0.001)	(0.010)	(0.001)	(0.001)
DTB^+	0.257	0.274	0.037	0.098
	(0.111)	(0.092)	(0.084)	(0.066)
OPEN	-0.043	-0.035	-0.002	-0.011
	(0.032)	(0.022)	(0.003)	(0.019)
EU	-0.010	-0.009	-0.003	-0.006
	(0.007)	(0.007)	(0.002)	(0.005)
DI_{t-1}	-0.149	-0.082	-0.136	-0.071
	(0.035)	(0.014)	(0.031)	(0.010)
R^2	0.241	0.051	0.308	0.017
M2 vs M1	22.573 (8)		28.564 (8)	
M3 vs M2	29.266 (28)		55.343 (28)	
M3 vs M1	51.839 (36)		83.908 (36)	
LM (1)	4.221		8.683	
HS	11.192 (6)		11.362 (6)	
speed of adjustment	16.13 %	8.56 %	14.62 %	7.37 %

Notes: Estimated standard errors are in parentheses below coefficients.
     + : These variables are as defined in the text, that is, absolute deviations from the means. ++ : under the restriction that sum of the country-effects is zero.
     The fixed effects include both country and time period effects.
     The LM, HS and country effects terms are as outlined in Table 7.2.
     The relative (to the average) fixed effects are:
     Sub-categories: **Austria**, Spain, Sweden, UK (minus); **Denmark**, Finland, Greece, Ireland, Portugal (plus).
     Main categories: **Austria**, Spain, Sweden (minus); **Denmark**, Finland, Greece, **Ireland**, Portugal, UK (plus).
     This gives an indication of those who will be more converged (minus) and those with a tendency to be less convergent (plus); the 'extreme' countries are those emboldened.

Still, the national characteristics of tax structures may (slowly) disappear over time as we find clear evidence of autonomous convergence: the coefficient on the lagged dependent variables indicates that there is a movement towards the tax structure of the original EU countries. To be precise, we find that the speed of adjustment may be as high as 10 percent for the sub-categorisation and 8 percent for the main categories, though the random effect model suggests that this is smaller. These results are in line with those found with respect to convergence to an overall EU tax structure and give some weight to the notion that the leaders are 'forcing the pace' in tax changes. Crucially, this effect remains highest for the sub-categorisation rather than the main categorisation (where the fit of the equations is much weaker). Furthermore, it should be remembered that each country has a convergence to their own tax structure heterogeneity, given the different fixed effect intercepts, and may be converging even more quickly to their preferred point (see Canova and Marcet, 1995). Thus, while tax structures have an inherently national aspect, which distinguishes them from tax structures elsewhere, we find evidence that, over time, leaders are causing an effect, 'undermining' the national culture and explaining convergent tax structures.[16]

Evidence on non-autonomous convergence is mixed. It can be seen that the effect of the administrative determinants is patchy. The size of the tax burden has the anticipated effect but is insignificant. This is as anticipated in that as the tax burden rises, so there will be a greater 'invention' of taxes, which cannot occur in the main categorisation. For sub-categories we find some evidence in the random effects estimation that the more a country's per capita tax burden differs from the average, the more will its tax structure differ. Thus, similarity of per capita tax burdens among countries leads to similarity in tax structures in the sub-categories. The other two 'administrative' variables are not as anticipated. In the case of GDP per capita, it is insignificant for the main categories, and of the opposite sign in the sub-categories. In the case of population, this is of the opposite sign in the sub-categories and there is an insignificant effect in the main categories.

More important for our purposes, Table 7.5 illustrates that formal EU membership has a clear effect on countries' tax structures. More specifically, we see that being a member of the EU lowers the distance index from the founders' tax structures. There is evidence of a clear move towards the leaders' tax structures due to membership in the sub-categories. However, this effect is not present in the main categories; there is convergence to the (EU6) leaders' tax structures but there is weaker evidence of this being a formal operation. Overall, the result may be taken to indicate that the influence of certain members of the EU on tax policy is more important than others (supporting previous evidence of the authors of convergence but this time with dominant partners). To investigate this further, the equation was re-analysed for just the newer members (see Table 7.5a). The results are in line with those for all the members except for two vital considerations. Firstly, the distance of the tax base from the average slows down the convergence and second, whilst there is clear evidence of convergence to the tax structure of the original 'group of 6', there is no separate autonomous effect of EU membership. There is leadership but this does not appear to be enhanced by membership of the club.[17]

Overall, there is evidence of an effect of EU membership on the convergence of tax structures to the 'group of six'. Furthermore the convergence to the structures of the original members is continuing, as witnessed by a significant lagged dependent variable. However, there is a limit to this as there still remains evidence of significant country-specific effects. The latter mean that tax structures of countries will remain distinct from one another in the future.

4. CONCLUSION

This chapter has investigated two aspects of the evolution of tax structures within the EU. Firstly, it has considered how turbulence of tax structures is affected by EU membership and found that whilst membership itself lowers turbulence, the countries are less able to react to external shocks and so turbulence is increased. Second, the movement of the tax structures in the EU relative to those of the original founder countries has been examined. In this part, there is evidence that these countries are the leaders in that the tax structures of the other countries are moving towards those of the founders. Examination of this movement suggests that it is responsible for a considerable part of the increased uniformity of the EU tax base identified in previous work of the authors. However, what remains is that the convergence is limited, as country-specific effects will remain, and that the convergence (in a similar way to turbulence) shows itself at the second level of aggregation in the definition of taxes, not at the top level of aggregation.

NOTES

1. John Ashworth is at the Department of Economics of the University of Durham (UK), and Bruno Heyndels is at the Faculty of Economic, Social and Political Sciences of the Vrije Universiteit Brussel.
2. The index corresponds to Hymer and Pashigian's mobility index (Hymer and Pashigian, 1962). This index is used in industrial economics to measure the turbulence in the market

shares of individual firms. In political science, a turbulence measure has been used to analyse the volatility of political power (Pedersen, 1979).

3. It should be noted that detail has its cost in terms of the interpretation. Some changes in tax structure are 'technical' (for example, the tax is re-labelled although the identity of taxpayers and the tax burden has not changed, or only moderately). Our approach does not allow distinguishing such changes from 'genuine' tax reforms. We control for these influences by (also) analysing the data on the main headings (turbulence-6). Given the widely different nature of these categories 'technical' tax reforms in the sense discussed are most unlikely for turbulence-6.

4. It should be noted that such a divergence between both turbulence indicators is highly exceptional. For all other EU countries only Italy 1973 has a similar extreme divergence (as a consequence of the re-classification of social security contributions in the OECD statistics, see Ashworth and Heyndels, 2001).

5. Ben-Porath (1975), Tufte (1978), Mikesell (1978), Pack (1988), Bizer and Durlauf (1990), Poterba (1994), Yoo (1998) and Nelson (2000) give evidence for opportunistic manipulation of revenue structures for electoral purposes. Paldam (1979) and Alesina *et al.* (1993) analyse an international panel of OECD countries. Neither find a significant election year effect. However, Paldam (1979) finds some indications that taxes increase relatively little in the post-electoral year. All these authors' primary attention is on the level of taxation, not the structure. Ashworth and Heyndels (2000), finally, do find evidence of an electoral cycle: tax structure turbulence in OECD countries is significantly *lower* in election years. This result may be taken to support Rose and Karran's model.

6. It should be noted that regime shifts do not necessarily coincide with elections as intermediate changes of coalition are possible.

7. A variable examining the effect of leadership (interacted with openness of the economy) in terms of tax structures, $LEADOP^i_t$, (see also section 3) was also considered. As this variable was insignificant, it is omitted from the discussion of this section.

8. The regime changes were calculated on the basis of the CPG (ideological complexion of government) as given by Woldendorp *et al.* (1993) and updates. This variable ranges from 1 to 5, where 1 (5) corresponds with a government under right-wing (left-wing) dominance (share of seats in Government and their supporting parties in Parliament larger than 66.6 percent). The RE^i_{t-1} indicator is a 0/1 indicator that measures whether a regime change occurred or not. To capture the intensity of the ideological change, we also used an alternative indicator that gives the absolute value of the change in CPG (ranging between 0 and 4). This alternative did not affect our results in any significant way.

9. Conforming with the definitions of the electoral variables, the indicator in any year t takes the value of the first half of the year. Thus if a government changes in the second half of the year, this will affect the Roubini and Sachs indicator from $t+1$ on.

10. These results should be taken as an extension of the previous results of the authors. Given the preponderance of observations where there is membership, the results can be seen to be an investigation of the effects of membership and the reaction to shocks. Previously, these were all captured in the turbulence emanating from the shocks. As can be seen here that reaction can be subdivided. What is crucial is that the style of government and election political effects identified previously, remain.

11. The concept of σ-convergence is equivalent to the same notion in the literature on economic growth. There σ-convergence refers to the reduction in cross-country variation in per capita GDP (most often measured by the coefficient of variation of this variable).

12. It is possible for the countries to be all converging towards each other but not towards the average of a sub-group. This is not the case here and so the relative sizes of the convergence speed will indicate the greater strength.

13. The crucial issue here is that whilst in the previous work on convergence to an EU average, it was possible to presume a common steady state as the member countries could sign up for an agreement, here there is movement to a 'dictated' state laid down by the leaders.

14. The difference term is used for the dependent variable to aid calculation of the speed of convergence. It is possible to model this effect using a time trend rather than an autoregressive term. The choice here is guided by being able to tie the work closely to the standard convergence literature. The general tenor remains if the time trend is used, see Ashworth and Heyndels (2000) for details when considering the convergence to a EU norm.
15. The model operates with a variable intercept rather than a common intercept, which is the case in the cross-section analysis. There is a general preference for the fixed effects model as any omitted variable effect is systematically correlated with the explanatory variable under random effects. A full set of results are provided for completeness, though the preference is for the fixed effects (see Shroder, 1995). It should be noted that the estimations presented here contain a time component for ease of comparison across the estimations. As a comparison, the time-specific effect affecting all countries in period t was eliminated from the panel by considering the deviations of the variables from the period's mean, $DI_{it} - DI_t$, where DI_t is the period-specific mean, to minimise any effects of non-stationarity in the regressor, see Tondl (1999). The results were directly comparable, hence the presentation chosen. Naturally, other possibilities for estimating are possible (see for example, Canova and Marcet, 1995) where there are country-specific speeds of convergence. This and other issues on estimation are the subject of other work by the authors.
16. It should be remembered that there is a major difference between the work reported here and that on income. In the latter case, the ideal state is dynamic and so is akin to the changing steady-state position identified by Tondl (1999).
17. Of course, if the dominant partners are the 'group of six' and this has remained the case, as these results suggest, there will be clear multicollinearity between the (convergence) lagged dependent variable and the EU membership. One factor of real note is that the introduction of a dummy variable for the actual year of joining the EU proved to be insignificant in line with the turbulence non-effect identified earlier.

REFERENCES

Alesina, A., G.D. Cohen and N. Roubini (1993), 'Electoral Business Cycles in Industrial Democracies', *European Journal of Political Economy*, 9, 1-25.
Ashworth, J. and B. Heyndels (2000), 'The Evolution of National Tax Structures in View of the EMU', in H. Ooghe, F. Heylen, R. Vander Vennet and J. Vermaut (eds), *The Economic and Business Consequences of the EMU – A Challenge for Governments, Financial Institutions and Firms*, Boston: Kluwer Academic Publishers, pp. 155-180.
Ashworth, J. and B. Heyndels (2001), 'Political Budget Cycles in Tax Structures: an empirical analysis for OECD countries', *Public Choice* (forthcoming).
Barro, R.J. (1979), 'On the Determinants of Public Debt', *Journal of Political Economy*, **87**, 940-971.
Barro, R.J. and X. Sala-i-Martin (1991), 'Convergence across States and Regions', *Brookings Papers on Economic Activity*, **1991**(1), 107-182.
Barro, R. J. and X. Sala-i-Martin (1995), *Economic Growth*, New York: McGraw Hill.
Ben-Porath, Y. (1975), 'The Years of Plenty and the Years of Famine - A Political Business Cycle?', *Kyklos*, **28**, 400-403.
Besley, T. and A. Case (1995), 'Incumbent Behaviour, Vote Seeking , Tax Setting and Yardstick Competition', *American Economic Review*, **85**, 25-45.
Bizer, D.S. and S.N. Durlauf (1990), 'Testing the Positive Theory of Government Finance', *Journal of Monetary Economics*, **26**, 123-141.

Breusch, T. and A. Pagan (1980), 'The LM Test and its Application to Model Specification in Econometrics', *Review of Economic Studies*, **47**, 239-254.

Canova, F. and A. Marcet (1995), 'The Poor Stay Poor: non-convergence across countries and regions', CEPR Discussion Paper.

De Haan, J. and J.-E. Sturm (1997), 'Political and Economic Determinants of OECD Budget Deficits and Government Expenditures: a re-investigation', *European Journal of Political Economy*, **13**, 739-750.

Deheja, V.H. and P. Genschel (1999), 'Tax Competition in the European Union', *Politics and Society*, **27**, 403-430.

Edin, P. and H. Ohlsson (1991), 'Political Determinants of Budget Deficits: coalition effects versus minority effects', *European Economic Review*, **35**, 1597-1603.

Frey, B.S. and F. Schneider (1978), 'An Empirical Study of Politico-Economic Interaction in the United States', *Review of Economics and Statistics*, **60**, 174-183.

Greene, W. (1999), *Econometric Analysis*, 4th edition, New York: Macmillan.

Hausman, J. (1978), 'Specification Tests in Econometrics', *Econometrica*, **46**, 1251-1271.

Hettich, W. and S. Winer (1999a), 'Democratic Choice and the Political Economy of Taxation', in D.C. Mueller (ed.), *Perspectives on Public Choice*, Cambridge, UK: Cambridge University Press, pp. 481-505.

Hettich, W. and S. Winer (1999b), *Democratic Choice and Taxation, A Theoretical And Empirical Analysis*, Cambridge, UK: Cambridge University Press.

Hymer, S. and P. Pashigian (1962), 'Turnover of Firms as a Measure of Market Behavior', *Review of Economics and Statistics*, **44**, 82-87.

Kanbur, R. and M. Keen (1993), 'Jeux sans Frontières: Tax Competition and Tax Coordination when Countries Differ in Size', *American Economic Review*, **83**, 877-892.

Mankiw, N.G. (1987), 'The Optimal Collection of Seignorage, Theory and Evidence', *Journal of Monetary Economics*, **20**, 327-341.

Messere, K. (1993), *Tax Policy in OECD Countries*, Amsterdam: IBFD Publications BV.

Mikesell, J.L. (1978), 'Election Periods and State Tax Policy Cycles', *Public Choice*, **33**, 99-106.

Nelson, M.A. (2000), 'Electoral Cycles and the Politics of State Tax Policy', *Public Finance Review*, **28**, 540-560.

Pack, J.R. (1988), 'The Congress and Fiscal Policy', *Public Choice*, **58**, 101-122.

Paldam, M. (1979), 'Is there an Electional Cycle? A Comparative Study of National Accounts', *Scandinavian Journal of Economics*, **81**, 323-42.

Pedersen, M.N. (1979), 'The Dynamics of European Party Systems: changing patterns of electoral volatility', *European Journal of Political Research*, **7**, 1-26.

Peters, B.G. (1991), *The Politics of Taxation. A Comparative Perspective*, Cambridge: Blackwell.

Pommerehne, W.W. and W. Schneider (1983), 'Does Government in a Representative Democracy Follow a Majority of Voters' Preferences? - An Empirical Examination', in H. Hanush (ed.), *Anatomy of Government Deficiencies*, Berlin-Heidelberg: Springer Verlag, pp. 61-88.

Porter, M. (1985), *Competitive Advantage*, New York: Free Press.

Poterba, J.M. (1994), 'State Responses to Fiscal Crises: the effects of budgetary institutions and politics', *Journal of Political Economy*, **102**, 799-821.

Rogoff, K. (1990), 'Equilibrium Political Budget Cycles', *American Economic Review*, **80**, 21-36.
Rose, R. (1985), 'Maximising Tax Revenue While Minimising Political Costs', *Journal of Public Policy*, **5**, 289-320.
Rose, R. and T. Karran (1987), *Taxation by Political Inertia, Financing the Growth of Government in Britain*, London: Allen & Unwin.
Roubini, N. and J.D. Sachs (1989), 'Political and Economic Determinants of Budget Deficits in the Industrialised Democracies', *European Economic Review*, **33**, 903-938.
Shroder, M. (1995), 'Games the States don't Play: welfare benefits and the theory of fiscal federalism', *Review of Economics and Statistics*, **77**, 183-191.
Steinmo, S. (1993), *Taxation and Democracy*, New Haven: Yale University Press.
Tondl, G. (1999), 'The Changing Pattern of Regional Convergence in Europe', *Jahrbuch fur Regionalwissenschaft*, **19**, 1-33.
Tufte, E.R. (1978), *Political Control of the Economy*, Princeton, NJ: Princeton University Press.
Volkerink, B. and J. de Haan (1999), 'Political and Institutional Determinants of the Tax Mix: an empirical investigation for OECD countries', SOM research report 99E05.
Woldendorp, J., H. Keman and I. Budge (1993), 'Political Data 1945-1990. Party Government in 20 Democracies', *European Journal of Political Research*, **24**, 1-119.
Woldendorp, J., H. Keman and I. Budge (1998), 'Party Government in 20 Democracies: an update' (1990-1995), *European Journal of Political Research*, **33**, 125-164.
Yoo, K.R. (1998), 'Intervention Analysis of Electoral Tax Cycle: the case of Japan', *Public Choice*, **96**, 241-258.

8. The Propagation of Monetary Policy in Europe

Manuel Balmaseda and David Taguas[1]

1. INTRODUCTION

With the birth of the Economic and Monetary Union (EMU) in January 1999 the manner in which monetary policy is implemented in Europe has changed. European economies have voluntarily relinquished their sovereignty in monetary policy to the European Central Bank (ECB). Simultaneously, the introduction of the euro meant that they have also given up exchange rate policy, as national exchange rates have become irrevocably fixed to the euro. The design of monetary policy is now decided on the evolution of aggregate variables of the EMU, abandoning the national references of the past. The expectations about the dynamics of output growth and, specially, of inflation will determine the behaviour of the ECB. This has led to the development of new tools to assess the performance of the EMU, as well as econometric models to evaluate the impact of economic policies on economic activity (Ballabriga and Castillo, 1999, Coenen and Wieland, 2000, and Fagan et al., 2001). In particular, there has been ample work on the determination of monetary policy rules (Clarida et al., 1998, 1999, 2000, and Doménech et al., 2000).

However, the implantation of a unique monetary policy for the EMU as a whole does not necessarily change the way in which monetary policy shocks propagate through the economy. Furthermore, the monetary policy designed by the ECB, while being appropriate for the entirety of the EMU, may not suit each individual country within the Union. The states may be subject to locally asymmetric shocks, at different stages along the business cycle or they may be subject to a different fiscal policy. These factors make the mechanisms through which monetary policy affects each economy unique.

In this chapter we evaluate the response of each country's central bank to a tightening in German monetary policy and a rise in short-term interest rates in a pre-EMU setting as a way of elucidating the nature of these potential asymmetries. We also examine the impact of a rise in domestic short-term rates – a domestic monetary policy contraction – on the key variables of each European country. In particular, we examine the transmission of an increase in the domestic intervention rate on output, prices, interest rates and the exchange rate. The impact of monetary policy under a fixed exchange rate regime, that is, the introduction of the euro, is also evaluated.

We adopt a VAR methodology and use data to investigate the relationship between monetary policy and economic activity. We start by proposing and evaluating a scheme for identifying monetary policy that reflects the use of an interest rate targeting scheme by central banks and also takes into consideration the constraints of multilateral agreements that culminated with the introduction of the euro in January 1999. One advantage of our identification scheme is that it allows us to offer predictions for the response of each country's economy to innovations in monetary policy under the euro.

Our work is related to other research by Sims (1992), Bernanke and Blinder (1992), Christiano, Eichenbaum and Evans (1996) who use VARs to identify monetary policy for the US, Bernanke and Mihov (1997) for Germany, and Balmaseda and Braun (1998), Kim (1996, 1997) and Shioji (1997) for Spain. These authors also identify a set of restrictions that produce plausible responses of output, interest rates and prices to innovations in monetary policy. Identification in their analysis is achieved by directly imposing zero restrictions on the contemporaneous variance-covariance matrix of innovations.

The remainder of the chapter is divided into four sections. Section 2 describes the model and our identification scheme. Section 3 describes the empirical results, the response of output and prices to an innovation in monetary policy. Section 4 concludes.

2. THE MODEL

We use a vector autoregressive framework (VAR) to trace out the dynamic response of macroeconomic variables to innovations in monetary policy. For the USA, one of the findings of this research is that monetary policy tightens in advance of recessions and loosens in advance of expansions. These empirical results line up remarkably well with other more informal analyses of Federal Reserve policy (see, for example, Romer and Romer, 1989).

While there are good a priori reasons to believe that there is a strong link between monetary policy and economic activity, empirical efforts to quantify this connection have met with two problems. The first problem is how to identify monetary policy. Widely used proxies for monetary policy such as the growth rate of monetary aggregates or overnight lending rates such as the Federal Funds rate are endogenous variables that reflect the effects of both demand and supply. The VAR literature described above provides a solution to this problem.

The second problem is related to the formulation of expectations. To measure departures from the expectations model of interest rates one needs to describe how expectations are formed and then decompose candidate risk factors into expected and unexpected components. The VAR methodology in conjunction with the rational expectations hypothesis provides one such decomposition.

In this section we describe a VAR framework that represents the key dynamic relationships for each European economy and propose a strategy for identifying monetary policy.

2.1. The identification scheme

We use a linear approximation to the feedback rule followed by the monetary authority:

$$R_t = \Pi(L)Z_t + \sigma \varepsilon_t \quad , \tag{8.1}$$

where R_t, a scalar, is the policy instrument (the interest rate), $\Pi(L)$ is a matrix polynomial in the lag operator L, and Z_t, a vector, summarizes the state of the economy in period t. We will refer to ε_t as the innovation to monetary policy in period t. We assume that ε_t is serially uncorrelated with variance 1. This specification of the feedback rule decomposes monetary policy into an anticipated and an unanticipated component. In practice, the monetary authority responds to the state of the economy when implementing its policy decisions. This systematic component is captured in our specification by $\Pi(L)Z_t$. However, we assume that there is also an unanticipated idiosyncratic component to the policy-making process that is independent of all other disturbances to economic activity.[2]

Our objective is to identify this feedback rule from the coefficients of a reduced form VAR that can be easily estimated. Suppose that the reduced form VAR is given by

$$Z_t = B(L)Z_t + u_t \quad . \tag{8.2}$$

$B(L)$ is a matrix polynomial in the lag operator L, where L ranges from 1 to K, and u_t is serially uncorrelated with variance-covariance matrix Λ.

From a comparison of equations (8.1) and (8.2) it is clear that we will have to impose some assumptions in order to recover ε_t and $\Pi(L)$ from the coefficients of the reduced form VAR. For instance, the error terms in the reduced form VAR are contemporaneously correlated while ε_t is independent of all other economic disturbances. To facilitate the description of the mapping from the coefficients of the reduced form VAR to the coefficients of the monetary policy feedback rule it is convenient to start from a structural VAR of the following form:

$$[G_0 - G(L)]Z_t = v_t \ , \tag{8.3}$$

where $G(L)$ is a matrix polynomial in the lag operator L, G_0 is a lower triangular matrix with ones along the main diagonal, and v_t is a diagonal matrix of innovations with variance-covariance matrix Σ, where Σ is diagonal. Without loss of generality we can think of the monetary policy feedback rule as being the jth row in the system. However, it is important to note that the lower triangular structure of G_0 and the fact that Σ is diagonal do impose some restrictions on the structure of the system. Note that the first variable does not respond contemporaneously to innovations in any other variables, the second responds only to its own innovations and innovations in the first variable, and so on. That is, the system has a recursive structure. In Section 2.3 we will impose additional restrictions that allow us to specify which row in the system described by equation (8.3) corresponds to the monetary feedback rule. However, it should be clear already that the nature of the restrictions relates to which variables can and cannot respond contemporaneously to innovations in monetary policy.

To move from the reduced form VAR to the structural VAR we need to find a matrix A that has the following properties,

$$Au_t = v_t \ , \tag{8.4}$$

$$AB(L) = G(L) \ , \tag{8.5}$$

$$AI = G_0 \ . \tag{8.6}$$

Note that these restrictions imply that A will be lower triangular and that

$$E[Au_t u'_t A'] = \Sigma \ .$$

2.2. Specification of the VAR

We turn next to specify the list of variables that we include in our reduced form VAR and describe how we identify the monetary policy feedback rules. In general we select a sample period that runs from the first quarter of 1970 to the third quarter of 2000. However, data availability for some of the countries forces us to restrict the sample further. In particular, data for Spain, Italy, the Netherlands and Ireland are only available since 1977, and data for Portugal are only available since 1985. It must be noted that over the sample period most European economies have undergone very important structural changes that may affect the results. In particular, most central banks in Europe were not independent in the earlier part of our sample.

For our baseline specification we use gross domestic product (GDP) to measure output,[3] the GDP deflator to measure the aggregate price level,[4] the three-month interest rates as a measure of the policy instrument and the exchange rate with the Deutsche Mark. Additionally, we use the interest rate in Germany as an exogenous variable, in order to evaluate to what extent domestic policy follows the lead of the Bundesbank.[5]

In the previous section we left open the question of how to identify the feedback rules. That is, we did not explain which row of the structural VAR is the one that describes the feedback rule. We turn to discuss this matter now. Recall that we need to impose restrictions on the matrix A which appears in equations (8.4), (8.5) and (8.6). We assume that no other variables in this system, except the exchange rate, can respond contemporaneously to an innovation in monetary policy and that the instrument of monetary policy is the interest rate. Given the recursive structure of our specification this assumption also implies that monetary policy can respond contemporaneously to shocks from the goods market but not to innovations in the exchange rate. With respect to the goods market our assumptions are consistent with an environment in which firms in the goods market make their production and pricing decisions each quarter before seeing the current innovation to monetary policy. Ordering the exchange rate last implies that monetary policy either does not or cannot respond to current foreign exchange innovations using unsterilised interventions within the period. Finally, the German interest rate is ordered first, since it does not respond to any of the domestic variables contemporaneously.[6]

In practice these assumptions mean that the instrument of monetary policy is ordered second to last or that the interest rate appears in the fourth row of the structural VAR. In our baseline specification we order output before prices.[7]

3. EMPIRICAL RESULTS

In this section we report impulse response functions to innovations in monetary policy using the Cholesky decomposition for a VAR with five variables: German interest rates, domestic GDP, the implicit price deflator, the domestic interest rate and the exchange rate with the DM. We also examine the response of monetary policy in key European countries to innovations in German interest rates.

3.1. Response to German monetary policy

The introduction of the German interest rates within the dynamic specification of each country allows us to evaluate the interaction between European monetary policy over the last quarter of the 20th century. In particular, we would expect that the influence of German monetary policy should be greatest with the smaller countries of the European core, which are very much integrated with the German economy and are subject to symmetric shocks. On the other hand, the interaction should be smallest with larger economies, exposed to their own shocks, and it should diminish as we move towards the European periphery.

These intuitive results are fully confirmed by the outcome of the empirical analysis (see Table 8.1 and the different panels in Figure 8.1). A 100 basis point rise in German interest rates translates most rapidly to Austria, where rates rise by 91 basis points within the same quarter and have the largest impact one quarter after the shock. The German rise is also reflected quite vigorously in Belgium and the Netherlands, where the largest impact happens within two quarters. The contemporaneous response in these countries to the rise in German rates is 89 b.p. and 74 b.p. in Belgium and the Netherlands, respectively. The impact of the monetary policy tightening on the interest rates of other countries occurs with a significant lag, four quarters in Sweden, Portugal, Italy and Ireland, and five in Spain and France. Of these the largest contemporaneous response takes place in Spain, 52 b.p., and the smallest in Ireland, -5 b.p. It appears that Irish monetary policy is not conditioned by German policy. This result is consistent with the cyclical correlation of the Irish economy with the economies of the UK and the US. The response of the monetary authorities of France and Italy, the second and third largest economies within the Economic and Monetary Union, to a rise in the German interest rate is relatively small, 25 b.p. and 13 b.p. respectively. This reflects the existence of asymmetric shocks that have affected the main European economies over the last 30 years. For the Spanish economy, although it seems to react significantly to policy innovations in Germany, the response to interest rate rise by the Bundesbank is not very persistent and it takes over a year to reach its maximum impact. This result coincides with the response of the French economy. It appears as if the Spanish economy was affected not only by monetary policy in Germany but by its impact on the French economy, Spain's main trading partner.

With respect to the magnitude of the responses, some countries seem to overreact and tighten monetary policy more than the Bundesbank. This is the case of Sweden, Belgium and Austria. The Swedish Central Bank raises rates very little initially, 13 basis points in response to the 100 basis points tightening by the Bundesbank, but later it raises rates very aggressively, 50 percent more than the Bundesbank. Belgium and Austria also seem to adjust domestic rates in excess of the Bundesbank tightening. The Netherlands and Portugal match the hike of the Bundesbank, although they do not coincide in the timing. The central banks of France, Italy and Spain tighten rates between 20 percent and 25 percent less than the Bundesbank. This may reflect that, while these countries are affected by symmetric shocks, the impact of the shock in each economy is different and, hence, it requires different degrees of policy action. Ireland, once again, is the least responsive, raising rates by less than the Bundesbank.

Table 8.1.   *Domestic interest rates response to 100 basis points monetary policy tightening in Germany*

	contemporaneous response	periods until maximum	maximum relative to Germany's
Austria	0.91	1	1.09
Belgium	0.89	2	1.25
France	0.25	5	0.80
Ireland	-0.05	4	0.67
Italy	0.13	4	0.86
the Netherlands	0.74	2	0.98
Portugal	0.44	4	1.00
Spain	0.52	5	0.85
Sweden	0.13	4	1.50

3.2. Response to domestic monetary policy

The sign of the response of domestic variables to a monetary policy innovation by its central bank coincide well with our *a priori* beliefs about the effect of a tightening of monetary policy on economic activity. First, the response of output to an interest rate rise is negative and persistent for all countries. In particular, GDP is significantly less than zero for a period of about two years for France, Italy, the Netherlands, Sweden, Portugal and Ireland and significantly longer for Spain and Belgium (over five years). Second, prices fall in response to a tightening in monetary policy. In general, in the first few quarters following the innovation, prices do not change much. In subsequent periods they fall. Note however, that the magnitude of the decline is small and the response is, for the most part, insignificantly different from zero. From the price responses we see that there is a price 'puzzle' for Sweden, lasting somewhat less than a year, and for Belgium, lasting well over a year. In the United States researchers often have to include additional price variables in order to get prices to fall when monetary policy is tightened. While this might have worked here, we have opted not to include additional variables in order to evaluate homogeneous systems across countries.

The response of output and prices to a 100 basis point tightening in monetary policy is presented in Tables 8.2 and 8.3. The tables display the persistence of the shock, the span of time for which the response is significantly different from zero, as well as the magnitude and the timing of the maximum impact. The maximum output response to an innovation in monetary policy is smaller in Spain than in other countries. After two years, the cumulative deviation of output from steady state is larger in Italy and France, -0.0017, than in Spain, -0.0013. But, since the persistence in Spain is much greater, after four years the cumulative deviation in Spain becomes similar to that of France, -0.0016 and -0.0015 respectively, and greater than that of Italy, -0.0008.

Table 8.2.   Output response to a 100 basis points rise in domestic interest rates

	persistence	periods until maximum	maximum response
Belgium	20	15	-0.0028
France	7	5	-0.0034
Ireland	8	6	-0.0030
Italy	7	4	-0.0038
the Netherlands	8	6	-0.0116
Portugal	7	5	-0.0061
Spain	26	9	-0.0021
Sweden	10	5	-0.0060

Table 8.3.   *Inflation response to a 100 basis points rise in domestic interest rates*

	persistence	periods until maximum	maximum response
Belgium	?	?	?
France	0	4	-0.0016
Ireland	8	4	-0.0032
Italy	8-27	9	-0.0031
the Netherlands	24	6	-0.0158
Portugal	13	12	-0.0080
Spain	6-12	8	-0.0017
Sweden	0	19	-0.0073

The response to a tightening in monetary policy in France, Italy and Spain is also displayed in Figures 8.2, 8.3 and 8.4 respectively. The figures show the response of output, prices and the interest rate to an impulse in monetary policy. The solid line depicts the average response and the dotted lines show the one standard deviation error band.[8] Note that a positive impulse to monetary policy corresponds to a tightening of monetary policy: the interest rate rises.

The responses of output to a tightening of monetary policy in France and Spain are very persistent.[9] This may be for two reasons. On the one hand, most European countries underwent very important structural changes over the period that extends to 1985. In particular, Spain went through the transition from a very highly regulated economy to a market economy, in addition to fundamental political changes. This led to a decade of low growth and high interest rates. On the other hand, monetary policy over the period, as mentioned above, was not independent. Monetary policy was designed in combination with fiscal policy, so the estimated responses presented here capture the impact of the joint effects of both policies. This in turn produced very high interest rates in the 1980s and the subsequent impact on output. In order to isolate the interactions between the two policies, the sample period should be restricted to the period after which the central banks in Europe gained their independence.[10] Additionally, the estimated VAR should be augmented including the fiscal deficit. This would allow us to discriminate between monetary and fiscal shocks[11] and evaluate the impact that monetary policy has on fiscal decisions and the influence that fiscal policy has on the central banks' decision-making process.

The figures also report results from a *conditional* ('restricted') impulse response scheme that is designed to capture the effects of innovations in monetary policy on economic activity under the euro. With regards to monetary policy, the EMU has two principal properties. The interest rate continues to be the instrument of monetary policy, and the domestic exchange rates within the EMU are pegged to a particular value. By imposing these restrictions on our identification scheme, we can investigate how the economy is likely to respond to innovations in monetary policy under the euro. This is accomplished by retaining a Cholesky orthogonalisation structure for the sub-block of the first four variables, but imposing a different restriction on the exchange rate innovation. Now innovations in the exchange rate are constrained to adjust in a manner that leaves the exchange rate unchanged in response to innovations in monetary policy. Imposing this constraint produces impulse responses that are very similar to the unconstrained responses. This suggests that the monetary policy transmission mechanism should not have changed after the introduction of the euro (Canzoneri *et al.*, 1996); or, in other words, that the existing differences across countries in the propagation of monetary policy shocks will be maintained in the future. The interest rates, however, are now common to all countries in the EMU, so a 100 basis points rise by the ECB translates into a 100 basis points increase in domestic rates.

*Figure 8.1a. Impulse response of domestic interest rates to a 100 basis
          points monetary policy tightening by the Bundesbank: Belgium*

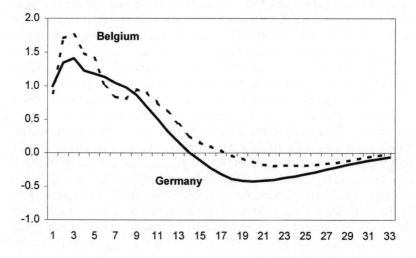

Figure 8.1b. Impulse response of domestic interest rates to a 100 basis points monetary policy tightening by the Bundesbank: Austria

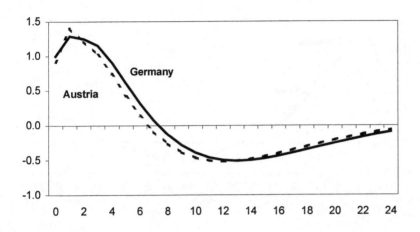

Figure 8.1c. Impulse response of domestic interest rates to a 100 basis points monetary policy tightening by the Bundesbank: the Netherlands

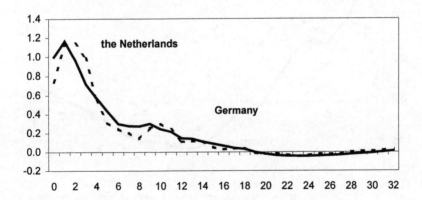

Figure 8.1d.   Impulse response of domestic interest rates to a 100 basis points monetary policy tightening by the Bundesbank: France

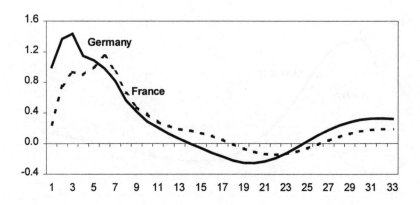

Figure 8.1e.   Impulse response of domestic interest rates to a 100 basis points monetary policy tightening by the Bundesbank: Italy

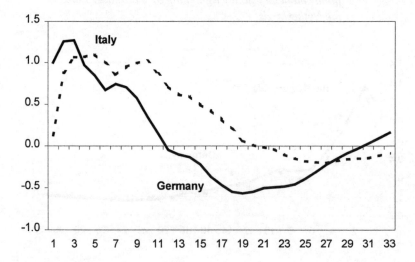

Figure 8.1f. *Impulse response of domestic interest rates to a 100 basis points monetary policy tightening by the Bundesbank: Spain*

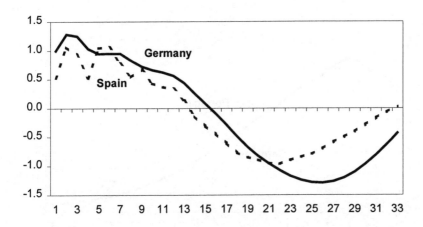

Figure 8.1g. *Impulse response of domestic interest rates to a 100 basis points monetary policy tightening by the Bundesbank: Sweden*

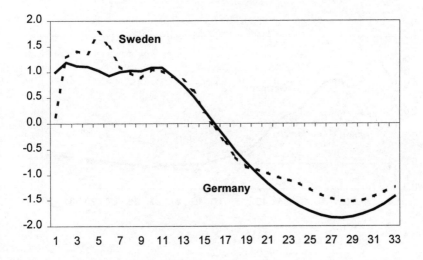

*Figure 8.1h. Impulse response of domestic interest rates to a 100 basis
points monetary policy tightening by the Bundesbank: Portugal*

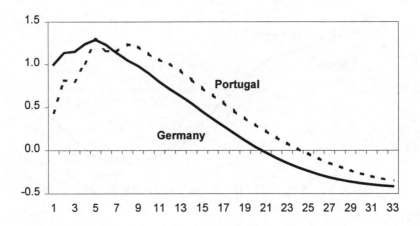

*Figure 8.1i. Impulse response of domestic interest rates to a 100 basis
points monetary policy tightening by the Bundesbank: Ireland*

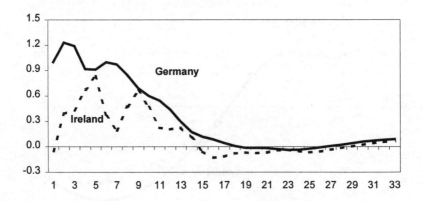

Figure 8.2a. Impulse response to a monetary policy tightening in France: GDP

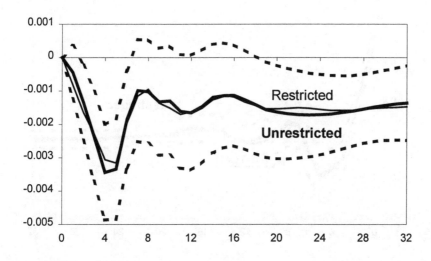

Figure 8.2b. Impulse response to a monetary policy tightening in France: inflation

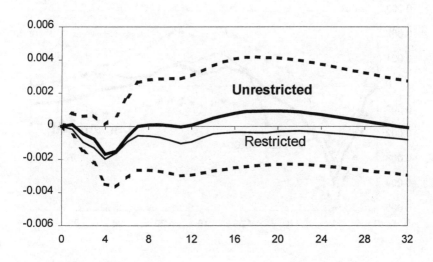

Figure 8.2c. Impulse response to a monetary policy tightening in France: interest rates

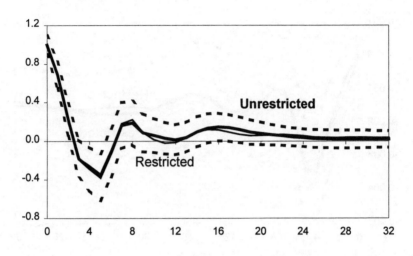

Figure 8.3a. Impulse response to a monetary policy tightening in Italy: GDP

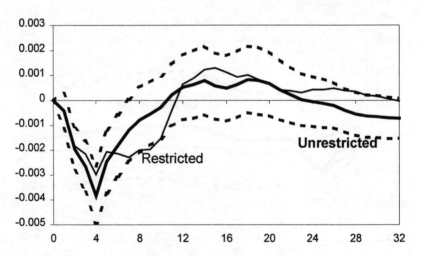

Figure 8.3b.   Impulse response to a monetary policy tightening in Italy:
inflation

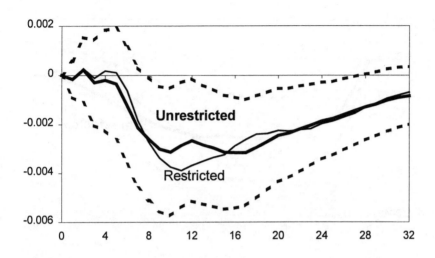

Figure 8.3c.   Impulse response to a monetary policy tightening in Italy:
interest rates

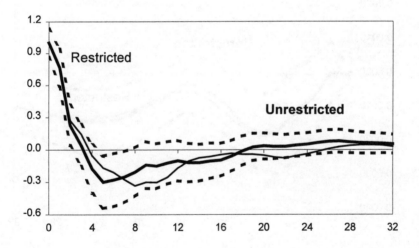

Figure 8.4a.   Impulse response to a monetary policy tightening in Spain:
*   GDP*

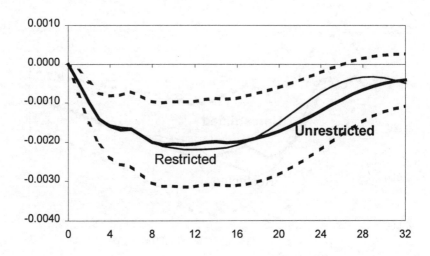

Figure 8.4b.   Impulse response to a monetary policy tightening in Spain:
*   inflation*

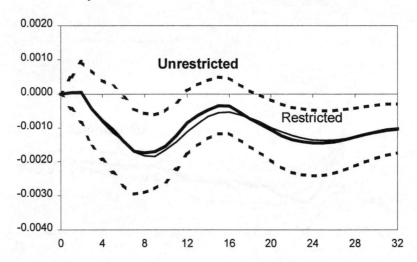

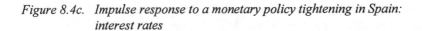

Figure 8.4c.   Impulse response to a monetary policy tightening in Spain: interest rates

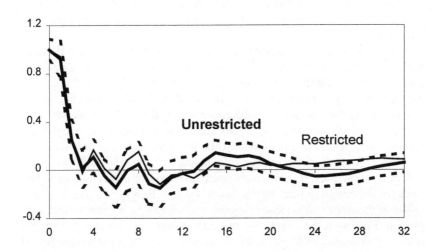

4. CONCLUSIONS

Monetary policy in the EMU is now founded on the aggregate evolution of the macro economy in the area as a whole. Because of this, it will only be used as a stabilization policy against aggregate shocks, losing its previous role as a tool of policy management at the national level. Fiscal policy within each country remains as the unique policy tool to counteract asymmetric shocks within the area. However, the efficiency of fiscal policy will be determined by the aggregate stance of monetary policy, the policy mix, and by the propagation mechanism of monetary policy in each economy. In this sense, it is necessary to evaluate the impact of monetary policy in the key macroeconomic variables within each country. In particular, this is even more relevant in the absence of a domestic exchange rate policy, which could be used to mitigate the effects of the asymmetric shock.

In this chapter, we first examined how domestic monetary policy has responded to changes in the monetary policy of the German Bundesbank. We find that all central banks respond to a Bundesbank monetary contraction with a tightening of their own. However, those countries with closer economic ties with Germany seem to respond faster and in a closer mapping of the monetary policy of the Bundesbank. The larger economies, France, Italy and Spain, also respond to the Bundesbank contraction. But they do so to a lesser extent than the smaller economies. This may be due to the existence of country-specific shocks that affect these economies. Ireland, because of its close economic relationship with the USA and the UK, appears to play at its own tune.

Regardless of the extent of the response to a tightening by the Bundesbank, since January 1999 the magnitude of the changes in monetary policy is common for all countries. This, however, does not imply that all countries respond similarly to monetary policy. In fact, they do not. In the chapter, we examine how, even under the euro arrangement, the key variables in each country respond differently to a monetary policy innovation. Output responses are negative and persistent, while inflation responses are small and seldom significantly different from zero, in line with the price rigidities in the European economies. If these results were taken to heart, they would be bad news for the design of monetary policy in Europe. However, a closer examination of the empirical evidence suggests that the structural changes that took place in Europe in the late 1970s and early 1980s may explain part of this result. To evaluate this hypothesis it is necessary to restrict the sample period to begin in the mid 1980s and to introduce some measure of fiscal policy, such as the deficit, into the analysis.

Finally, the introduction of the euro only alters moderately the propagation mechanisms of monetary policy. However, since monetary policy is set at the aggregate EMU level, nothing guarantees that policy actions by the ECB are appropriate for any specific country in particular.

NOTES

1. The authors are at the Research Department of the Banco Bilbao Vizcaya Argentaria (BBVA). They have benefited from valuable suggestions by R. Doménech.
2. We assume that monetary policy is set by a group of individuals at a meeting and nobody knows for sure the decision this will group will collectively make.
3. Data are only available for Ireland on a yearly basis. We have used TRAMO and SEATS to interpolate quarterly series of the data.
4. In some cases however the consumer price index yields better results.
5. There is a debate in the literature over whether the variables should be included in levels or in first differences. We chose to include the variables in levels (logs) in line with the work of Sims (1992) and others.
6. We have also allowed for the German interest rate to be completely exogenous in the system. That is, it does not respond to any other variable either contemporaneously or at any leads or lags. The results are robust to this change in the specification.
7. The results are robust to changes in the ordering of output and prices. We chose to order output before prices in line with other work in the literature.

8. The error bands are calculated using the Monte Carlo integration method described in the RATS user manual example 10.1.
9. In France the response is not significantly different from zero for very long. But the average response remains below zero for several years.
10. The problem is that this restricts us to use monthly data since some central banks in Europe only gained their independence in the last decade.
11. Although identification of these shocks is not trivial when the policy decisions are made jointly.

BIBLIOGRAPHY

Alejano, A. and J.M. Peñalosa (1995), 'La Integración Financiera de la Economía Española: efectos sobre los mercados financieros y la política monetaria', *Documento de Trabajo del Banco de España*, No. 9525.

Ayuso, J. and J.L. Escrivá (1997), 'La Evolución de la Estrategia de Control Monetario en España', in *La Política Monetaria y la Inflación en España*, Servicio de Estudios del Banco de España, Madrid: Alianza Editorial.

Ballabriga, C. and S. Castillo (1999), 'BBVA-ARIES: un modelo de simulación y predicción para la economía de la UEM', *Documento de Trabajo*, No. 1/00, Servicio de Estudios del BBVA.

Balmaseda, M. and R.A. Braun (1998), 'Monetary Policy and the Term Structure of Interest Rates', mimeo.

Bernanke, B. and A. Blinder (1992), 'The Federal Funds Rate and the Channels of Monetary Transmission', *American Economic Review*, **82**, 901-921.

Bernanke, B.S. and I. Mihov (1997), 'What does the Bundesbank Target?', *European Economic Review*, **41**, 1025-1053.

Canzoneri, M., J. Vallés and J. Viñals (1996), 'Do Exchange Rates Move to Address International Macroeconomic Imbalances?', Working Paper No. 9626, Bank of Spain.

Christiano, L., M. Eichenbaum and C. Evans (1996), 'The Effects of Monetary Policy Shocks: Evidence from the Flow of Funds', *Review of Economics and Statistics*, **78**, 16-34.

Clarida, R., J. Gali and M. Gertler (1998), 'Monetary Policy Rules in Practice: some international evidence', *European Economic Review*, **42**, 1033-1067.

Clarida, R., J. Gali and M. Gertler (1999), 'The Science of Monetary Policy: a new-Keynesian perspective', *Journal of Economic Literature*, **37**, 1661-1707.

Clarida, R., J. Gali and M. Gertler (2000), 'Monetary Policy Rules and Macroeconomic Stability: evidence and some theory', *Quarterly Journal of Economics*, **115**, 147-180.

Cochrane, J.H. (1994), 'Shocks', National Bureau of Economic Research Working Paper No. 4698, April.

Coenen, G. and V. Wieland (2000), 'A Small Estimated Euro Area Model with Rational Expectations and Nominal Rigidities', Working Paper Series No. 30, European Central Bank, September 2000.

Cooley, T.J. and G.D. Hansen (1989), 'The Inflation Tax in a Real Business Cycle Model', *American Economic Review*, **79**, 733-748.

Cuadrado, M.P. and C. Melcón (1993), 'La Instrumentación de la Política Monetaria en los Países de la CE; Tipos de Interés Oficiales y de Intervención', *Boletín Económico*, Banco de España, April.

Doménech, R., M. Ledo and D. Taguas (2000), 'Some New Results on Interest Rate Rules in EMU and in the US', Working Paper 2/00, Research department, BBVA.

Escrivá, J.L. and J.L. Malo de Molina (1991), 'La Instrumentación de la Política Monetaria Española en el Marco de la Integración Europea', *Documento de Trabajo del Banco de España*, No. 9104.

Fagan, G., J. Henry and R. Mestre (2001), 'An Area-Wide Model (AWM) for The Euro Area', Working Paper Series, 42, European Central Bank, January 2001.

Gordon, D.B. and E.M. Leeper (1994), 'The Dynamic Impacts of Monetary Policy: an exercise in tentative identification', *Journal of Political Economy*, **102**, 1228-47.

Kim, S. (1996), 'Does Monetary Policy Matter in the G-6 countries? Using Common Identifying Assumptions about Monetary Policy Across Countries', mimeo.

Kim, S. (1997), 'Identifying European Monetary Policy Interactions: who stabilizes the intra-European exchange rate?', Bank of Spain, mimeo.

Leeper, E.M., C.A. Sims and T. Zha (1996), 'What does Monetary Policy Do?' *Brookings Papers on Economic Activity*, **1996**(2), 31-51.

Lucas, R.J. and N.L. Stokey (1987), 'Money and Interest in a Cash-in-Advance Economy', *Econometrica*, **55**, 491-513.

Malo de Molina, J.L. and J. Pérez (1990), 'La Política Monetaria Española en la Transición hacia la Unión Monetaria Europea', *Papeles de Economía Española*, **43**, 31-51.

Nieto, E. (1997), 'Efectos de las Perturbaciones de la Política Monetaria sobre la Estructura Temporal de Tipos en España', mimeo, CEMFI.

Romer, C. and D. Romer (1989), 'Does Monetary Policy Matter? A New Test in the Spirit of Friedman and Schwartz', *NBER Macroeconomics Annual*, 121-170.

Shioji, E. (1997), 'Spanish Monetary Policy: a structural VAR analysis', mimeo, Universidad Pompeu Fabra.

Sims, C.A. (1992), 'Interpreting the Macroeconomic Time Series Facts: the effects of monetary policy', *European Economic Review*, **36**, 975-1011.

Strongin, S. (1995), 'The Identification of Monetary Policy Disturbances. Explaining the Liquidity Puzzle', *Journal of Monetary Economics*, **35**, 463-497.

PART III

Convergence in the EU: Social and
Labour Market Issues

9. Some Theory on the Sustainability of Different Levels of Social Protection in a Monetary Union

Wim Meeusen and Glenn Rayp[1]

1. INTRODUCTION

In this chapter we analyse the long-run properties of a two-country Gross-man-Helpman type of 'expanding product variety' monopolistic competition model in which the equations expressing continuous clearing of the labour market are replaced by equations that impose continuous equilibrium on the social security budget (compare with Grossman and Helpman, 1991). We will assume that, although the process of product innovation is solely under the control of private firms, the accumulation of knowledge has partly a public character and thereby creates positive knowledge spillovers for other firms. The model will therefore exhibit sustainable (endogenous) growth, even if, for reasons of simplicity and transparency, physical and human capital accumulation is discarded.

At the same time, however, the economies, even in the long-run, will not necessarily operate at full employment levels since the labour markets do not automatically clear: the wage rates are the result of a bargaining process between unions and employers.

The government levies a uniform tax rate on labour and entrepreneurial income and finances in this way the payment of allowances to the unemployed. The basic research question is whether different levels of innovativity in the two countries, resulting for example from different levels of R&D-productivity, allow for lasting discrepancies in social protection under conditions of integrated goods markets.

We present the model in Section 2. We examine its long-run properties in Section 3, and the properties of its solution under different assumptions with respect to international knowledge spillovers in Section 4. In Section 5 we draw conclusions.

2. THE MODEL

We start from the familiar Dixit-Stiglitz specification of the utility of a representative consumer under conditions of monopolistic competition (Dixit and Stiglitz, 1977):

$$U = \left[\sum_{i=1}^{n+n^*} c_i^{(\sigma-1)/\sigma} \right]^{\sigma/(\sigma-1)} . \tag{9.1}$$

c_i represents the consumption of a good i by the representative consumer in both countries. n and n^* are the numbers of differentiated goods produced in both economies. The demand side of the economies is characterised by a uniform elasticity of substitution between goods, equal to $\sigma > 1$.

This utility is maximised under the following budget constraint:

$$\sum_{i=1}^{n} p_i c_i + \sum_{i=1}^{n^*} p_i^* c_{n+i} \leq e .$$

e is total expenditure by the representative consumer; p_i and p_i^* are the prices of the individual goods produced in country 1 and country 2 respectively.

A fundamental result from duality theory is that a price-index P of the following form is associated with u:

$$P = \left[\sum_{i=1}^{n} p_i^{1-\sigma} + \sum_{i=1}^{n^*} p_i^{*1-\sigma} \right]^{1/(1-\sigma)} . \tag{9.2}$$

From the first-order conditions follow the demand function of an individual consumer for a good of type i :

$$c_i = \left(\frac{p_i}{P}\right)^{-\sigma} \frac{e}{P} \qquad i = 1,...,n$$

$$c_{n+i} = \left(\frac{p_i^*}{P}\right)^{-\sigma} \frac{e}{P} \qquad i = 1,...,n^* \quad .$$

(9.3)

We obtain the total demand for good i by aggregating over the individual demands of all consumers:

$$x_i = C_i + C_i^* = (N + N^*)c_i = \left(\frac{p_i}{P}\right)^{-\sigma}\left(\frac{(N+N^*)e}{P}\right) = \left(\frac{p_i}{P}\right)^{-\sigma}\left(\frac{E+E^*}{P}\right)$$

$$i = 1,...,n$$

$$x_i^* = C_{n+i} + C_{n+i}^* = (N + N^*)c_{n+i} = \left(\frac{p_i^*}{P}\right)^{-\sigma}\left(\frac{(N+N^*)e}{P}\right)$$

$$= \left(\frac{p_i^*}{P}\right)^{-\sigma}\left(\frac{E+E^*}{P}\right) \qquad i = 1,...,n^* \quad .$$

(9.4)

N and N^* are the number of individuals, C_i, C_i^*, resp. C_{n+i} and C_{n+i}^* are the global consumption level of the domestic goods demanded by the consumers in their own and in the other country, and the goods produced in the foreign country demanded by domestic and foreign consumers, and E and E^* are total national spending in each economy on goods produced in both economies.

The demand for a good i, consequently, is negatively dependent on its relative price and positively linked to total demand. The choice of a 'numeraire' ensures complete determination of that expression. For that we follow Grossman and Helpman (1991) and assume that total nominal spending is equal to 1, which is another way of saying that the two countries form a monetary union in which the central bank follows a strict policy of zero-growth nominal money supply.

It holds in this case that

$$\sum_{i=1}^{n} p_i x_i + \sum_{i=1}^{n^*} p_i^* x_i^* = E + E^* = 1 \quad .$$

(9.5)

Following Sørensen (1994) and others, we keep the supply side of the economy as simple as possible. The $n + n^*$ goods are produced using in each country one and the same constant returns to scale production function with only one input, labour (l). Each good is produced by a single firm that enjoys its (relative) monopoly as a result of propriety rights obtained as innovator. As an expression of the production of goods we have therefore:

$$x_i = al_i \qquad (i = 1,...,n)$$
$$x_i^* = a^* l_i^* \qquad (i = 1,...,n^*) \quad . \tag{9.6}$$

a and a^* represent labour productivity and are assumed to be uniform over all production units in each country.

Profits per firm in each country can now be written as

$$\pi_i = p_i x_i - w_i l_i$$
$$\pi_i^* = p_i^* x_i^* - w_i^* l_i^* \quad .$$

w_i and w_i^* are the sectoral wage rates in each country.

If we assume that entrepreneurs take no account of the effect that a price change in the individual variety will have on the price index P, then the first-order condition for maximising profit are the following mark-up equations:

$$p_i = \left(\frac{\sigma}{\sigma - 1}\right)\frac{w_i}{a} \quad \text{resp.} \quad p_i^* = \left(\frac{\sigma}{\sigma - 1}\right)\frac{w_i^*}{a^*} \quad . \tag{9.7}$$

It is possible to simplify the model considerably if we now first consider wage formation.

With respect to the determination of the wage rate, we assume that all workers in the manufacturing sector of both countries are members of a trade union operating in their sector, exercising monopsony power over the labour supply, in the sense that it is the trade union that is solely responsible for wage bargaining. Note that this does not mean that there is no intersectoral labour mobility. However, it does mean that the trade union active in the sector only cares about the well-being of its own members.

The trade union organisations are not directly concerned with matters of government finance and therefore do not consider the equilibrium of the social security system as an external limitation. They behave in a utilitarian manner, which implies that they endeavour to maximise the global utility of their members:

$$l_i u_e + (M_i - l_i) u_u \quad , \text{resp.} \quad l_i^* u_e + (M_i^* - l_i^*) u_u \quad ,$$

where l_i are the employed union members, and M_i is the total member number. The subscripts e and u refer respectively to the utility of working and unemployed members (cf. Oswald, 1985). After reverting to indirect utility functions, we can describe the objective of the trade union organisations thus:

$$\underset{w_i(1-\tau)}{Max} \left\{ O_{Ui} = l_i \frac{w_i(1-\tau)}{P} + (M_i - l_i) \frac{b}{P} \right\} \quad , \text{resp.}$$

$$\underset{w_i^*(1-\tau^*)}{Max} \left\{ O_{Ui}^* = l_i^* \frac{w_i^*(1-\tau^*)}{P} + (M_i^* - l_i^*) \frac{b^*}{P} \right\} \quad . \tag{9.8}$$

b and b^*, the levels of the unemployment benefit (uniform across sectors in each country), are determined by the government and are therefore exogenous as far as the union is concerned. τ and τ^* are the uniform tax rates ($0 \le \tau, \tau^* < 1$).

The solution for the optimal gross sectoral wage rate, if the unions do not care about the effect of their claims on the overall price level, has again a mark-up form:

$$w_i = \frac{\sigma}{(\sigma - 1)} \frac{b}{(1 - \tau)} = w \quad \text{resp.} \quad w_i^* = \frac{\sigma}{(\sigma - 1)} \frac{b^*}{(1 - \tau^*)} = w^* . \tag{9.9}$$

The net money wages $w(1 - \tau)$ and $w^*(1 - \tau^*)$ are therefore uniform across sectors and are a fixed mark-up above the social security benefits b and b^*. They are invariant with respect to the level of social security contributions. A rise in taxes, in other words, is fully recovered on the gross wage and employment adjusts itself accordingly (see, for example, Holmlund *et al.*, 1989, p. 27).

As a consequence of (9.9), we may now simplify the notation and drop the subscripts with respect to the variables p, π, l and x:

$$p_i = p \quad \text{and} \quad p_i^* = p^* ,$$

$$\pi_i = \pi \quad \text{and} \quad \pi_i^* = \pi^* ,$$

$$l_i = l \quad \text{and} \quad l_i^* = l^* \quad \text{and}$$

$$x_i = x \quad \text{and} \quad x_i^* = x^* \quad \text{for all} \quad i = 1,...,n, \text{ (resp. } n^*) \quad .$$

It now also holds that

$$npx + n^* p^* x^* = 1 \quad ,$$ (9.10)

$$P = \left(np^{1-\sigma} + n^* p^{*1-\sigma} \right)^{1/(1-\sigma)}$$ (9.11)

$$\pi = px - wl = \frac{px}{\sigma}, \quad \text{resp.} \quad \pi^* = \frac{p^* x^*}{\sigma} \quad .$$ (9.12)

If $v(t)$, resp. $v^*(t)$, denotes the value of the claim to the supposedly infinite stream of profits that accrues to the representative firm at time t, we get

$$v(t) = \int_t^\infty e^{-(R(\upsilon)-R(t))} \left(\frac{p(\upsilon)x(\upsilon)}{\sigma} \right) d\upsilon \quad \text{and}$$

$$v^*(t) = \int_t^\infty e^{-(R(\upsilon)-R(t))} \left(\frac{p^*(\upsilon) x^*(\upsilon)}{\sigma} \right) d\upsilon$$ (9.13)

$R(\upsilon)$ represents the cumulative discount factor.

Separate from their productive activity, entrepreneurs are also involved in R&D and innovation. They finance product development costs by issuing equity. If there are no knowledge spillovers, and if A, resp. A^* are the (constant) labour intensities of R&D activity, then the rate at which new products ('variants' in the terminology of Grossman and Helpman) are created is the following:

$$dn = \frac{l_R}{A} dt \quad \text{resp.} \quad dn^* = \frac{l_R^*}{A^*} dt \quad ,$$

where l_R and l_R^* are the economy-wide amounts of labour devoted to innovative activity.

If, on the contrary, part of the knowledge created in the innovative firm cannot be appropriated and spills over to the rest of the economy, then the above equation should be amended. If we assume that the knowledge stock K_R that becomes available for the 'other' firms reduces in a proportionate way the labour requirements necessary for designing new products, we get the following expression:

$$dn = \frac{l_R}{A/K_R} dt \quad \text{and} \quad dn^* = \frac{l_R^*}{A^*/K_R^*} dt \quad .$$

We incorporate the phenomenon of international knowledge spillovers in the model by assuming that K_R can be proxied by the number of variants in the own economy plus a fraction ψ of the number of variants in the other economy. This finally yields for the rate of innovation at each moment of time, under conditions of knowledge spillovers from R&D:

$$g \equiv \frac{\dot{n}}{n} = \frac{n + \psi n^* }{n} \frac{l_R}{A} \quad \text{and} \quad g^* \equiv \frac{\dot{n}^*}{n^*} = \frac{n^* + \psi n }{n^*} \frac{l_R^*}{A^*} \ . \qquad (9.14)$$

Free entry to innovative activity then means that an unlimited amount of additional workers will be hired for this purpose as long as the marginal returns of the newly hired researcher $((n+\psi n^*)v/A)\mathrm{d}t$ exceed the marginal cost $w\mathrm{d}t$. This is of course not compatible with a situation of general equilibrium as it means that labour demand would be unbounded. In the opposite case product development would come to a standstill. We must therefore conclude that the free entry condition takes the following form:

$$\frac{wA}{n + \psi n^*} \geq v, \ \text{resp.} \ \frac{w^* A^*}{n^* + \psi n} \geq v^* \qquad (9.15)$$

with equality holding whenever $\dot{n} > 0$, resp. $\dot{n}^* > 0$.

The tax rates τ and τ^*, the unemployment benefits b and b^* and the other social security allowances s and s^* are set by the government in terms of their own social preferences, and under the constraint that the social security budget balances at each moment of time:

$$(L - nl - g\frac{n}{n + \psi n^*}A)b + sL = \tau\,(nl + g\frac{n}{n + \psi n^*}A)\,w \ , \ \text{and}$$

$$(L^* - n^*l^* - g^*\frac{n^*}{n^* + \psi n}A^*)b^* + s^* L^* = \tau^*\,(n^*l^* + g^*\frac{n^*}{n^* + \psi n}A^*)\,w^* \ .$$

$$(9.16)$$

L and L^* are the active population. The 'other' social security allowances may refer to pensions in a pay-as-you-go system and to public health insurance. Its total amount is supposed to be proportional to the active population. It of course holds that $0 \leq s < b$. We will also assume, for simplicity, that s and s^* are given, e.g. by a law voted by the respective parliaments.

The balanced budget requirement then means that in actual fact the government disposes of only one free policy parameter. Because b and b^* are instruments expressed in money terms, the optimal value of which may therefore be assumed to vary over time, and because τ and τ^* are proportions, it seems to be more natural to concentrate on the latter as policy variable, and to treat the b's as being implicitly determined by (9.16), given τ and τ^*.

Finally, we need an equation explicitly expressing the fact that firms are valued at their fundamental value and that, as a result of it, there is no arbitrage on the capital market. This equation is obtained by differentiating equation (9.13). This yields

$$\dot{v} = rv - \pi \;, \text{ and } \dot{v}^* = rv^* - \pi^* \;. \tag{9.17}$$

r is of course the common rate of interest.

3. THE LONG-RUN PROPERTIES OF THE MODEL

In order to be able to proceed further in the analysis we now turn to the properties of the long-run balanced growth equilibrium of the model, hoping in this way to obtain relatively neat expressions.

We can considerably simplify the model by imposing the obvious long-run requirement that the current accounts are balanced, i.e. the national industrial product npx (resp. $n^*p^*x^*$) is equal to national expenditures on the goods markets E (resp. E^*). This implies that for the profits of the representative enterprise and its market value, we may now write:

$$\pi = \frac{px}{\sigma} = \frac{E}{n\sigma}, \text{ resp. } \pi^* = \frac{p^*x^*}{\sigma} = \frac{E^*}{n^*\sigma} \tag{9.18}$$

and, because of (9.13), assuming that the markets shares and the interest rate remain constant:

$$v = \frac{\pi}{r+g} = \frac{E}{n\sigma(r+g)} \text{ and } v^* = \frac{\pi^*}{r+g^*} = \frac{E^*}{n^*\sigma(r+g^*)} \;. \tag{9.19}$$

From (9.18) and (9.19) it follows immediately that

$$\frac{\dot{v}}{v} = \frac{\dot{\pi}}{\pi} = -\frac{\dot{n}}{n} = -g \text{ and } \frac{\dot{v}^*}{v^*} = \frac{\dot{\pi}^*}{\pi^*} = -\frac{\dot{n}^*}{n^*} = -g^* \;. \tag{9.20}$$

We shall also assume that, next to (endogenous) product innovation, there is also process innovation, which takes the form of a constant, but exogenous, rate of increase of labour productivity in the manufacturing sector of both countries ($\dot{a}/a$ = constant and $\dot{a^*}/a^*$ = constant).

We now can derive a number of simple relations between different rates of change, each time holding in both countries (in order not to burden the text unnecessarily we drop the equations for the other country).

Let us first consider the free-entry condition (9.15). In the long run it holds that

$$\frac{\dot{w}}{w} - gr(n + \psi n^*) = \frac{\dot{v}}{v} \quad , \tag{9.21}$$

from which it follows, since the growth rate of v is a constant and equal to minus g, that the growth rate of $(n + \psi n^*)$ should be a constant too. From this it follows in turn, given that the growth rates of the number of variants in the economy g and g^* must be supposed to be constants on the long-run growth path, that the proportion n/n^* of the number of variants in both economies must be a constant. It therefore holds that

$$gr(n + \psi n^*) = g = g^* \quad \text{and}$$
$$\frac{\dot{w}}{w} = 0 \quad . \tag{9.22}$$

From the price and wage mark-up equations (9.7) and (9.9) we can now see that

$$\frac{\dot{b}}{b} = 0 \quad ,$$
$$\frac{\dot{p}}{p} = \frac{\dot{w}}{w} - \frac{\dot{a}}{a} = -\frac{\dot{a}}{a} \quad . \tag{9.23}$$

Note that, because of the zero-growth monetary rule, the steady rise in labour productivity is reflected in a negative rate of change of the price-level and in the steady growth of real wages.

Together with the monetary zero-growth condition (9.10), this implies that the following relation must hold in the long run:

$$\frac{\dot{n}}{n} \equiv g = \frac{\dot{a}}{a} - \frac{\dot{x}}{x} \quad . \tag{9.24}$$

It is obvious that $\dot{a}/a$ cannot be anything else than the long-run rate of growth of the economy. From the production point of view, real income can indeed be defined as

$$GDP^R = \frac{GDP^N}{p} = nx + \frac{v\dot{n}}{p} = nx + \frac{v}{p}ng \quad .^2$$

Balanced growth means that the manufacturing sector and the R&D sector of the economy must grow at the same rate. From the above results it directly follows that the rate of growth of the economy (and of both its sectors) must therefore be equal to $\dot{a}/a$:

$$\text{rate of growth of } GDP^R \equiv \text{gr}(GDP^R) = \text{gr}(nx) = g + \frac{\dot{x}}{x}$$

$$= \text{gr}(\frac{v}{p}ng) = \frac{\dot{v}}{v} - \frac{\dot{p}}{p} + g = \frac{\dot{a}}{a} \quad .$$

From the necessary constancy in the long run of the market shares of both countries in a situation of balanced growth, and the equality of their rates of innovation it inevitably follows that the rates of process-innovating (Harrod-neutral) technological change must be identical in both countries, and therefore also their real rate of growth. From (9.4) it indeed follows that

$$x = \frac{p^{-\sigma}}{np^{1-\sigma} + n^* p^{*1-\sigma}} \quad \text{and therefore}$$

$$\frac{1}{x} - np = \frac{1-E}{x} = \frac{E^*}{x} = n^* p \left(\frac{p^*}{p}\right)^{1-\sigma} \quad . \tag{9.25}$$

If it holds that $\dfrac{\dot{E}}{E} = \dfrac{\dot{E}^*}{E^*} = 0$ then, after some transformations and making use of (9.23) and (9.24), (9.25) and its equivalent for the other country can be rewritten as follows:

$$g - g^* = (1-\sigma)(\frac{\dot{a}}{a} - \frac{\dot{a}^*}{a^*}) \quad \text{and} \quad \frac{\dot{x}}{x} - \frac{\dot{x}^*}{x^*} = \sigma(\frac{\dot{a}}{a} - \frac{\dot{a}^*}{a^*}) \tag{9.26}$$

The message of (9.26) is obvious: if the rate of Harrod-neutral technological progress in the own country is higher than abroad, then the constancy of the market shares would imply that its rate of innovation should be lower. Since different rates of innovation are incompatible with balanced growth, then – naturally enough – the rates of increase of labour productivity should be identical. Any other situation would lead to unbalanced growth and the elimination from the market of the country with the lowest rate of growth. As the rates of increase of a and a^* are exogenous in the model, the analysis of the long-run properties of the model under conditions of balanced growth is therefore only relevant for countries with a comparable level of development, so that the appeal to the standard neo-classical conclusions with respect to convergence in growth is warranted.

4. SOLUTION OF THE MODEL

It turns out that relatively few transparent analytical results can be obtained for the case where $0 < \psi < 1$. One has to revert in this case to simulations on a calibrated model to obtain solutions for g, b and b^* in terms of the policy variables τ and τ^* and the parameters σ, A and A^*.

In the following we will therefore concentrate on the special cases $\psi = 0$ and $\psi = 1$, but only after having established two significant expressions in the general case for the unemployment rate u and the real value of the unemployment benefit. From the equilibrium condition on the social security budget (9.16) it indeed immediately follows that the unemployment rate is given by the following:

$$u \equiv \frac{L - nl - g \dfrac{n}{n + \psi n^*} A}{L} = \frac{\sigma\tau - (\sigma - 1)(1 - \tau)\dfrac{c}{b}}{\sigma + \tau - 1} . \qquad (9.27)$$

It obviously holds that

$$\frac{\partial u}{\partial b} > 0 \text{ and } \frac{\partial u}{\partial \tau} > 0 .$$

These partial derivatives should be interpreted with care: the equilibrium condition on the social security budgets (equation (9.16)) implies b is not a free parameter but is a function of τ and indeed also of τ^*, which themselves can be regarded as being a function of the free parameters s and s^*. We have therefore

$$b = b\Big(\tau(s), \tau^*(s^*)\Big) \; . \tag{9.28}$$

We show elsewhere that in the absence of social security (b, s and τ equal to zero), in the one-country as well as in the two-country case, the model then reduces to the special case of the labour market clearing model of Grossman and Helpman (1991, chapters 3 and 9) (see Meeusen and Rayp, 2000).

From the mark-up equations (9.7) and (9.9) we can deduce the following expression for the unemployment benefit in domestic purchasing power terms:

$$\frac{b}{p} = a\left(\frac{\sigma - 1}{\sigma}\right)^2 (1 - \tau) \; . \tag{9.29}$$

4.1. The case $\psi = 0$

This case refers to the situation where knowledge spillovers are confined to the borders of the respective countries.

After putting $\psi = 0$ in equations (9.14) to (9.16), leaving open for the time being the possibility that g and g^* might be different, and defining $V = 1/(nv)$, i.e. the inverse of the aggregate equity value of all the firms in the corresponding country, we obtain, after having combined the free-entry condition, the wage mark-up equation and the 'monetary union' equation:

$$V = \frac{1}{wA} = \frac{\sigma - 1}{\sigma}\frac{1 - \tau}{bA} \Rightarrow VE = \frac{\sigma - 1}{\sigma}\frac{1 - \tau}{bA} apnl \; . \tag{9.30}$$

On the other hand we have that

$$nl = (1 - u)L - gA \; , \tag{9.31}$$

where u is given by (9.27).

Combining (9.30) and (9.31), again using the mark-up equations, yields

$$VE = \frac{\sigma}{\sigma - 1}\frac{1}{A}[(1 - u)L - gA]] \; .$$

Together with the no-arbitrage condition on the international capital markets (9.19), this results in a solution for g in terms of, essentially, *domestic* parameters and policy variables like L, A, s and τ:

$$g = \frac{\sigma - 1}{\sigma}\left[(1 + \frac{s}{b})\frac{1 - \tau}{\sigma + \tau - 1}\frac{L}{A} - r\right] , \tag{9.32}$$

although, surely enough, b is not solely domestically determined but also a function of parameters and decisions taken in the other country. It holds – under the earlier mentioned caveat with respect to the meaning of the partial derivatives (see (9.28)) – that

$$\frac{\partial g}{\partial \tau} < 0 , \quad \frac{\partial g}{\partial A} < 0 \text{ and } \frac{\partial g}{\partial b} < 0 . \tag{9.33}$$

Meeusen and Rayp (2000) show that this solution for the innovation rate for the two countries – like the corresponding cases examined by Grossman and Helpman (1991) – refers to a saddle-point equilibrium resulting from rational expectations of the respective national investors on the international capital market.

It is clear that in these conditions g and g^* will not necessarily be equal. The following equation, obtained in the same way as (9.26), will clarify the analysis:

$$\frac{\dot{E}}{E} - \frac{\dot{E}^*}{E^*} = g - g^* + (\sigma - 1)(\frac{\dot{a}}{a} - \frac{\dot{a}^*}{a^*}) . \tag{9.34}$$

The first possibility, namely that rates of Harrod-neutral technological progress differ between the two countries, and therefore the rates of growth of their economies, is of relatively little interest. The fastest growing economy will in the end take over the whole market. Evidently, its policy of social protection is sustainable.

If, as a second possibility, the growth rates of a and a^* become equal, by whatever spontaneous process of convergence in growth, without the rates of innovation becoming equal as well, then, because of (9.34), the most innovating economy will in the end drive out the other one. Its social policy would then of course also be sustainable. (9.32) and (9.33) make clear through which mechanisms such a superior rate of innovation might be achieved: a higher productivity of R&D (i.e. lower A), a lower tax rate, or lower unemployment benefits.

This leads us to the third possibility (discarding the fluke possibility that both terms in the right-hand side of (9.34) could exactly compensate): both the Harrod-neutral rate of technological progress and the innovation rate converge. The market shares then remain constant.
We now have:

$$(1+\frac{s}{b})\frac{1-\tau}{\sigma+\tau-1}\frac{L}{A}=(1+\frac{s^*}{b^*})\frac{1-\tau^*}{\sigma+\tau^*-1}\frac{L^*}{A^*} \ . \qquad (9.35)$$

One way to interpret (9.35) runs as follows: at equal s and s^* and an equal tax rate, the protection against unemployment can be higher in the own country if $L/A > L^*/A^*$ (that is, R&D-productivity is higher in the own country than abroad). Turning this argument around we may of course also say that the same b's can be sustained by lower tax rates in the own country than abroad if R&D-productivity is higher.

Simulation exercises, taking account of (9.28), show that the same type of conclusion can also be drawn with respect to sustainable differences in terms of the 'other' social security allowances.

4.2. The case $\psi = 1$

$\psi = 1$ means that international knowledge spillovers are complete and that there is therefore no redundancy in research efforts. There is one knowledge stock, proxied by $n + n^*$.

After having replaced A in expressions (9.30) to (9.32) with $A\, n/(n+n^*)$ we obtain the following result for the rate of innovation:

$$g = \frac{\sigma-1}{\sigma}\left[(1+\frac{s}{b})(1+\frac{n^*}{n})\frac{1-\tau}{\sigma+\tau-1}\frac{L}{A}-r\right] \ . \qquad (9.36)$$

With free trade of goods and services, and a uniform knowledge stock, convergence to a common long-run equilibrium on a balanced growth-path is assured. g and g^* should obviously be the same. The following implicit relation for n/n^* is now obtained:

$$\frac{n}{n^*} = \frac{1+\dfrac{s}{b}\dfrac{1-\tau}{\sigma+\tau-1}}{1+\dfrac{s^*}{b^*}\dfrac{1-\tau^*}{\sigma+\tau^*-1}}\frac{L/A}{L^*/A^*} \ ,$$

which is also what is obtained by Grossman and Helpman (1991, p. 245), under conditions where $A = A^*$ and in the absence of a social security system.

Much the same arguments as in the case of $\psi = 0$ concerning the sustainability of differences in social protection can be developed in this case, after correction for differences in the number of variants offered by both economies.

5. CONCLUSION

We analysed a model that can be considered as a generalisation of the Grossman-Helpman (1991) two–country 'expanding product variety' model of endogenous growth with knowledge spillovers. The proposed model no longer requires the labour market to clear and allows the governments of both countries to pursue a policy of social protection. We analysed the conditions under which differences in national levels of social protection are sustainable in the long run and, in particular, the way in which the financing burden of the social security system weighs upon the innovativity of the private sector, and therefore, implicitly, on the international competitiveness of the country.

The price that has to be paid for social protection, *ceteris paribus*, is, not unexpectedly, a lower rate of innovation. The model, however, shows that the government has other possibilities to compensate for this adverse effect or to mitigate its impact, the productivity level of R&D activity and a judicious choice of the tax rate being the most obvious ones. We showed that these possibilities are present irrespective of the degree in which international knowledge spillovers take place, albeit of course that policy margins are wider if knowledge creation is more confined to the national borders.

NOTES

1. Wim Meeusen is at the University of Antwerp (Faculty of Applied Economics) and Glenn Rayp is at the University of Ghent (Faculty of Economics and Business Administration). Correspondence address: wim.meeusen@ua.ac.be.
2. We use in this particular context the commonly used p variable as the GDP-deflator, rather than P, since the latter variable not only contains a component expressing average price changes, but also one expressing changes in 'quality'.

REFERENCES

Dixit, A. and J.E. Stiglitz (1977), 'Monopolistic Competition and Optimum Product Diversity', *American Economic Review*, **67**, 297-308.

Grossman, G. and E. Helpman (1991), *Innovation and Growth in the Global Economy*, Cambridge, Mass.: MIT Press.

Holmlund, B., K. Løfgren and L. Engstrøm (1989), *Trade Unions, Employment and Unemployment Duration*, Oxford: Clarendon Press.

Meeusen, W. and G. Rayp (2000), 'A Monopolistic Competition model of Social Security, Unemployment and Product Innovation', CESIT discussion paper 2000-09, University of Antwerp.

Oswald, A. (1985), 'The Economic Theory of Trade Unions: an introductory survey', *Scandinavian Journal of Economics*, **87**, 160-193.

Sørensen, J.R. (1994), 'Market Integration and Imperfect Competition in Labor and Product Markets', *Open Economies Review*, **5**, 115-130.

10. European Labour Markets under Convergence Pressure

Alain Borghijs and André Van Poeck[1]

1. INTRODUCTION

European labour markets are faced with two challenges. Firstly, about 15 million Europeans are officially unemployed and many more are not participating in the labour market. Reducing unemployment rates and enhancing employment growth are therefore high on the political agenda. Second, the introduction of the single European currency in combination with the Stability and Growth Pact has stripped European national policy-makers of the monetary and, to some degree also, fiscal instruments to stabilise their economies. These challenges set specific requirements for European labour markets. Section 2 of this chapter sketches the two challenges in more detail and translates them into requirements for European labour markets. Section 3 deals with the question of whether recent reform in the labour market has gone in the right direction to meet these requirements. Section 4 focuses on the future and deals with the role EMU may play in bringing about the necessary changes. Section 5 contains some concluding remarks.

2. EUROPEAN LABOUR MARKETS CHALLENGED

Despite the efforts of European policy-makers to stimulate labour market performance, unemployment rates have only marginally declined over the last decade. Labour market performance in the euro area is particularly bleak compared to other industrialised countries outside the euro area, as Table 10.1 illustrates[2].

Despite some contentment among policy-makers about the decline in equilibrium unemployment in the second half of the 1990s it is recognised that more work needs to be done to consolidate better labour market performance. The focus of the policy debate has thereby shifted from unemployment to employment. At a special meeting held by the European Council on 23-24 March 2000 in Lisbon the following text was agreed upon:

> The European Council considers that the overall aim [...] should be, on the basis of the available statistics, to raise the employment rate from an average of 61 percent today to as close as possible to 70 percent by 2010 and to increase the number of women in employment from an average of 51 percent today to more than 60 percent by 2010. Recognising their different starting points, Member States should consider setting national targets for an increased employment rate. (European Council, 2000)

Having set the targets to achieve better labour market performance, it is appropriate to look at ways to translate these targets into policy actions, which cannot be understood without clarifying the link between (bad) labour market performance and its institutional determinants.

It is now generally accepted that unfavourable labour market performances are often supported by inflexible labour market institutions giving incentives for real wage hikes or preventing a real wage decline in the wake of adverse supply shocks (Bean, 1994; Blanchard and Wolfers, 2000). Labour market characteristics that are assumed to support real wage hikes and downward real wage rigidity relate to the degree of centralisation, co-operation and co-ordination in the wage bargaining process, employment protection legislation (hiring and firing costs), the level and duration of unemployment benefits and the share of active labour market policy (education, mediation). We first discuss in some detail the relationship between the wage bargaining institutions (centralisation, co-operation and co-ordination) and labour market performance, after which the other labour market institutions will be analysed.

Wage negotiations can take place at the following levels of centralisation:
- firm- or plant-level (decentralised bargaining);
- industry-level (bargaining at the intermediate level);
- national or country-wide level (centralised bargaining).

With respect to the impact of the degree of centralisation of wage bargaining on labour market performance, there exist three views (Traxler and Kittel, 2000). The neo-liberal school favours the highest degree of 'marketisation' of wage bargaining. This view hinges on the alleged adverse effects of strong union bargaining power. The more decentralised the bargaining process, the less bargaining power trade unions can exert. This school considers high union coverage through legal extension mechanisms and high degrees of unionisation to be detrimental to labour market performance, as they increase the bargaining power of unions. The recommendation by the OECD to decentralise wage negotiations is inspired by this view.

The 'corporatist' school, in the terminology of Traxler and Kittel (2000), argues that countries with centralised bargaining have superior labour market performance. In contrast to the neo-liberal school, 'corporatists' do not assume that higher bargaining power automatically leads to higher wage demands. Centralised wage-setters are more aware of the negative externalities associated with high wages (see Calmfors (1993) for an overview of these externalities). In this view centralised bargaining is best suited for internalising these externalities. The hump-shape hypothesis (Calmfors and Driffill, 1988) combines both arguments, which results in superior labour market performance for both decentralised (high degree of competition) and centralised bargaining (high degree of internalisation) arrangements. Industry-level bargaining results in the least wage restraint and leads to inferior labour market performance.

The hump-shape hypothesis, a widespread view among labour economists nowadays, should be extended to hold for a monetary union (Danthine and Hunt, 1994; Calmfors, 1993). The concepts of union power and internalisation are maintained, but the incentives for trade unions in an open macroeconomic environment change. Two issues are relevant. Firstly, at the industry level, trade unions cannot exert monopoly power if they operate in an international product market. In an international industry that produces tradable goods, unilaterally raising the wage in one country would be harmful for the industry in that country. Secondly, at the national level, the incentive to internalise negative wage externalities may fade away if the country belongs to a monetary union. High wage demands in a single member state of the monetary union are unlikely to have a large impact on inflation of the union. In this sense, centralised bargaining in a monetary union is very similar to intermediate bargaining in an open economy.

The level of wage bargaining should further be supplemented by the degree of international co-operation regarding wage bargaining. Unmistakably, international trade union co-operation leads to an increase in union bargaining power as (international) competition among unions decreases. Especially in small open economies, trade union co-operation may increase union bargaining power considerably as the relevant macroeconomic environment becomes more closed. Yet, positive effects on the capability of internalising externalities can be expected from union co-operation at the national level between member states of a monetary union. The above-mentioned lack of internalisation can be overcome when centralised unions bargain co-operatively, taking into account the negative externalities of high wage demands for the entire union.

Table 10.1.   Equilibrium unemployment in the OECD countries[a]

EMU countries	1980	1985	1990	1995	1999	Non-EMU countries	1980	1985	1990	1995	1999
incr. NAIRU[b]											
Finland	4.3	3.9	5.6	10.6	9.0	Japan	1.9	2.7	2.2	2.9	4.0
Germany	3.3	4.4	5.3	6.7	6.9	Sweden	2.4	2.1	3.8	5.8	5.8
Italy	6.8	7.8	9.1	10.0	10.4						
stable NAIRU											
Austria	1.9	3.2	4.6	5.0	4.9	Australia	5.1	6.0	6.5	7.1	6.8
Belgium	5.5	6.8	8.4	8.0	8.2	New Zealand	1.6	5.1	7.0	7.5	6.1
France	5.8	6.5	9.3	10.3	9.5	Norway	2.2	2.6	4.6	4.9	3.7
Greece	4.6	6.5	8.4	8.8	9.5						
decr. NAIRU											
Ireland	12.8	13.2	14.1	10.8	7.1	Canada	8.9	10.1	9.0	8.8	7.7
the Nether-lands	4.7	7.5	7.5	6.1	4.7	Denmark	5.8	5.9	6.9	7.1	6.3
Portugal	6.1	5.4	4.8	4.2	3.9	Switzerland	2.3	2.9	3.0	3.3	2.4
Spain	7.8	14.4	17.4	16.5	15.1	UK	4.4	8.1	8.6	6.9	7.0
						United States	6.1	5.6	5.4	5.3	5.2
average NAIRU											
Average	5.8	7.2	8.6	8.8	8.1		4.1	5.1	5.7	6.0	5.5
St. dev.	2.8	3.6	4.0	3.4	3.2		2.4	2.6	2.3	1.9	1.7
Weighted average	5.5	7.1	8.8	9.2	8.9		4.8	5.3	5.2	5.1	5.3

Source: OECD (2000).
Notes: (a) : As a percent of the labour force. Equilibrium unemployment data are based on estimates of the NAIRU made for the OECD Economic Outlook (2000). An increase or decrease over the period 1990-99 is considered significant (in absolute terms) if it exceeds one standard deviation. The latter was calculated for each country over the 1980-99 period.
(b) : The NAIRU or non-accelerating inflation rate of unemployment can be defined as the rate of unemployment at which inflation is stable and which is not amenable to macroeconomic policy measures.

A different – third – theory builds on the concept of co-ordination in wage bargaining, which is defined as the degree of consensus between the bargaining partners (Soskice, 1990). It acknowledges the concepts of competition and internalisation that result in the Calmfors-Driffill hump-shape, but argues that these concepts are determined by the degree of co-ordination, rather than the degree of centralisation of wage bargaining. Instead of concentrating on the formal level at which wage negotiations take place, this theory focuses on the existence of mechanisms that co-ordinate the behaviour of trade unions and employer organisations. For highly centralised bargaining systems, the degree of co-ordination and centralisation are likely to be identical. More decentralised systems may, however, exhibit higher degrees of co-ordination than the formal level of centralisation may suggest. With respect to the impact of the degree of co-ordination of wage bargaining on labour market performance, it is found that higher levels of co-ordination result in better labour market performance (Soskice, 1990; Garibaldi and Mauro, 2001). This may be attributed to the higher internalisation capacity of co-ordinated arrangements. In this sense, the co-ordination theory is similar to the 'corporatist' school. Summarising the analysis of the wage bargaining institutions, it can be concluded that labour market performance depends on the degree of union bargaining power and the extent to which unions internalise negative wage externalities. These are determined by the degree of centralisation, co-operation and co-ordination of wage bargaining.

With respect to the other labour market institutions some authors (Scarpetta, 1996; Nickell and Layard, 1997; Elmeskov *et al.*, 1998; Garibaldi and Mauro, 2001) suggested that strict employment protection legislation may contribute to higher equilibrium unemployment and lower employment growth, especially among young persons and the low-skilled. This can be explained by the fact that high hiring and firing costs make firms reluctant to hire new and inexperienced workers. This decreases the outflow rate out of unemployment for these groups. As stricter employment protection also makes firms more reluctant to fire employees during a downturn of economic activity, it tends to decrease short-term unemployment. Consequently, the evidence that strict employment protection would increase total unemployment is not straightforward. Generous unemployment benefits are also found to have a negative impact on equilibrium employment and on wage flexibility (Plasmans *et al.*, 1999). Unconditional benefits reduce the downward pressure on wages and sustain (partially voluntary) unemployment, especially when the gap between unemployment benefits and the lowest wages is narrow. Another determinant of high unemployment in European labour markets may be found in the level of taxation. Daveri and Tabellini (2000) find that trade unions were able to shift part of the tax burden to employers, increasing labour costs and unemployment. Similarly, Garibaldi and Mauro (2001) find that low taxation is significantly associated with high employment growth.

Since these institutions simultaneously determine labour market performance, it may be expected that there exist several interaction effects between the different institutions. Nickell (1997) and Nickell and Layard (1997) find that the negative effects of a generous benefit system can be offset by an active labour market policy. If benefits are limited in time and conditional upon the willingness of the unemployed to follow retraining or other re-employment programmes, positive employment effects are noted as the employability of the average unemployed is increased. Taxation has a larger impact on labour market performance in combination with wage bargaining at the industry level. High bargaining power and poor internalisation of the unemployment effects result in higher wage demands by industry unions to compensate the effect of increases in taxation (Daveri and Tabellini, 2000; Elmeskov *et al.*, 1998). Considering these and other interaction effects, Belot and van Ours (2000) conclude that recent improvements in labour market performance in countries such as the Netherlands and Ireland have been due to a comprehensive set of reforms that takes account of these effects.

Given the persistent unemployment problem in most of the EMU countries and the apparent link between labour market performance and labour market institutions, it is clear that there is a need for reforming these institutions in a way that increases real wage flexibility and reduces the pressure for real wage hikes. It is expected that an appropriate set of reform measures will reduce equilibrium unemployment rates in the EMU countries. This is also the position taken by official institutions, like the IMF (views expressed in the World Economic Outlook and various European country reports), the EU (reflected in the annual Employment Guidelines) or the OECD (see the OECD *Jobs Study* (1994) and several follow-up reports (OECD, 1999)).

An argument that has attracted less attention in the debate but that may be equally important for a smooth functioning of the EMU is that the introduction of the single European currency itself puts pressure on European labour markets. EMU member states require a higher degree of nominal wage flexibility than countries with more autonomy over their policy instruments in case they are hit by an asymmetric shock (Feldstein, 1997; Pissarides, 1997; Calmfors, 2000) or in case common shocks have different effects due to structural differences between countries (Fase and De Bondt, 1999; Hughes Hallett *et al.*, 2000; Peersman, 2001). An example may clarify this point. Suppose a country is hit by an idiosyncratic negative demand shock. In order to rekindle demand for its products, the country may devalue its currency or lower the domestic interest rate. These options are, however, only available when countries do not take part in EMU. A country whose nominal exchange rate and interest rate are tied down by a monetary union would have to exert itself considerably more than a country with monetary autonomy. The main option for an EMU member to restore demand is to go through an adjustment process in the labour market (since the Stability and Growth Pact restricts the use of fiscal policy). Reduced demand (temporarily) raises unemployment above its equilibrium level and puts downward pressure on nominal wages. The duration of the adjustment process crucially depends on the amount of (downward) nominal inertia. The higher the degree of nominal wage rigidity, the longer actual unemployment exceeds its equilibrium value. If, moreover, the unemployed suffer from skill deterioration in the course of the adjustment process, the original level of equilibrium unemployment may not be attained again.

A similar situation arises when a common shock hits a set of countries that differ in their institutional structure. Even when the initial shock hits all countries equally hard, its impact in terms of (labour market) outcomes is likely to be different if countries are characterised by different degrees of nominal wage flexibility. This argument has gained relevance and attention with the introduction of the single currency. It is argued that a single monetary policy (which may be considered as a common shock) may lead to increasing divergences among EMU member states that are characterised by low, but different degrees of nominal wage flexibility. A monetary tightening, for example, would have a limited unemployment effect in member states in which nominal wage growth declines in accordance. However, countries characterised by a high degree of nominal wage rigidity would undergo an increase in real wages that may potentially result in higher unemployment. Reform of the institutions that allow for sufficient nominal wage flexibility in order to prevent unemployment divergences between EMU member states is therefore deemed necessary (Hughes Hallett *et al.*, 2000).

How urgent is the need for more nominal wage flexibility in EMU member states? In order to get an idea of the flexibility of nominal wages in EMU and non-EMU countries, we constructed an indicator that exploits the idea that the degree of nominal wage rigidity determines the size of the deviation between the actual unemployment rate and its equilibrium value when the economy is hit by a shock. When nominal wages are flexible, the shock is absorbed by wage changes such that unemployment deviations are small, whereas if nominal wages are rigid, shocks result in larger unemployment deviations. The indicator is reported in Figure 10.1 and is constructed as follows: for each country listed in Table 10.1, the absolute value of the difference is calculated between the actual unemployment rate and the equilibrium unemployment rate, as reported in the *Economic Outlook* (OECD, 2000). The figure shows the annual average difference for the group of EMU countries and non-EMU countries (defined as a large subset of non-EMU OECD countries). Higher average deviations are the result of larger shocks or a higher degree of nominal wage rigidity. Assuming that shocks are more or less of equal size in both groups, comparison of the indicators gives an idea of the amount of nominal rigidity in each of the two country groups. The solid and dashed lines in Figure 10.1 depict the indicator for the EMU and non-EMU groups over the period 1980-2000.

*Figure 10.1. Nominal wage rigidity in EMU and non-EMU countries,
1980-2000*

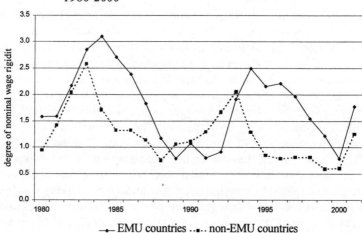

—◆— EMU countries ··■·· non-EMU countries

The figure indicates that nominal wage rigidity was generally higher in the EMU group. Excluding the EMU member states with the highest amount of rigidity does not alter this result. It can therefore be concluded that high nominal wage rigidity is a common feature of the EMU labour markets. Some interesting additional information can be obtained by decomposing the indicator in the average *downward* (actual unemployment is higher than equilibrium unemployment) and *upward* (actual unemployment is lower than equilibrium unemployment) deviation for each group in each year. In that way a distinction is made between downward and upward nominal wage rigidity respectively. Figure 10.2 displays the results of this decomposition for the EMU group and the non-EMU group.

The upper panel shows that downward nominal wage rigidity is higher in the EMU group than in the non-EMU group. This finding uncovers a second negative feature of European labour markets. Indeed, not only is equilibrium unemployment higher in EMU countries than outside the euro area, but negative economic shocks additionally lead to larger unemployment increases above the equilibrium unemployment rate. The lower panel of Figure 10.2 shows the opposite picture. Upward nominal wage rigidity is higher in the non-EMU group than in the EMU group. This suggests that the positive effects of buoyant economic activity are predominantly absorbed by nominal wage increases in the EMU countries, whereas in non-EMU countries upswings result in a decrease in unemployment below the level of the equilibrium value. Comparison of the two panels additionally reveals that downward nominal wage rigidity is higher than upward nominal wage rigidity.

Figure 10.2. Downward and upward nominal wage rigidity in (non-)EMU countries, 1980-2000

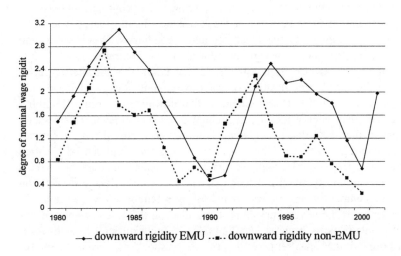

—♦— downward rigidity EMU ··■·· downward rigidity non-EMU

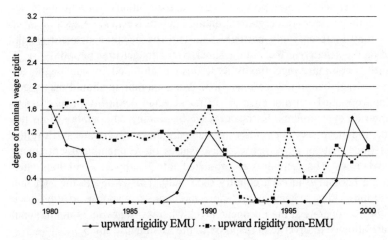

—♦— upward rigidity EMU ··■·· upward rigidity non-EMU

It can therefore be concluded that the need for more nominal wage flexibility in the EMU countries is particularly urgent in the downward direction. Pleading for more upward nominal wage flexibility is more ambiguous. On the one hand, increased upward flexibility prevents actual unemployment from falling far below its equilibrium value, but it dampens at the same time diverging unemployment evolutions between countries that react asymmetrically to positive shocks.

What determines the responsiveness of nominal wages? Four determinants have been advanced in the literature to explain the degree of nominal inertia. The first relates to the duration of wage contracts. Long contracts increase the probability that at some point – if a shock occurs – the negotiated wage may no longer correspond to the macroeconomic conditions. Wage indexation may compensate some of the rigidity induced by long contracts.

Secondly, it has also been established that nominal wage inertia varies with the degree of centralisation of wage bargaining (Fase and De Bondt, 1999; Calmfors, 2000). The argument is that downward nominal flexibility would be higher when wages are negotiated at the central level. This rests on the insight that centralised bargaining is more synchronised than decentralised bargaining and that it eliminates wage-staggering, and can be clarified by the following example. Suppose again that a member country of EMU is hit by a negative asymmetric demand shock. The need for wage moderation to restore competitiveness is acknowledged by a centralised wage-setter and agreed upon. If, however, bargaining takes place at the industry level at different points in time, wage moderation may be more difficult to achieve. If one of the industries has set its wage prior to the shock, concern over relative wages in other sectors may prevent large wage deviations from the wage-set in the 'leading sector' (an argument dating back to Keynes). Wages in other sectors may therefore only partially adjust to the negative demand shock, extending the negative effects of the shock over a longer time period.

Thirdly, nominal wage flexibility is also determined by the degree of European wage bargaining co-operation. Wage bargaining should take place at an appropriate level that ensures sufficient wage flexibility in reaction to asymmetric developments. European wage bargaining co-operation does not provide the necessary flexibility to dampen these divergences. Borghijs (2001) finds that an asymmetric shock causes more unemployment divergence when wage bargaining is co-ordinated at the European level than when wages are bargained in each country separately. This is due to the fact that trade unions adjust wages in the same direction in response to the shock when they co-operate at the European level, whereas wages set at the national level are allowed to diverge in response to the asymmetric shock.

A fourth strand of the literature stresses the importance of the inflation rate for the issue of nominal rigidity, especially in the downward direction (Akerlof *et al.*, 1996). The central idea is that both unions and employers are reluctant to cut nominal wages because it would hurt morale (Bewley, 1999). If inflation is high, downward nominal wage rigidity should be no obstacle to cut wage costs as wage moderation or real wage cuts can be achieved by slowing down the rate of nominal wage growth below the rate of inflation. If inflation is low, however, nominal wage cuts may be necessary to prevent unemployment increases.

Summarising the analysis in this section, it can be concluded that labour market reform in EMU is needed, firstly, to bring down equilibrium unemployment and, second, to ease the adjustment process in the wake of potential asymmetric developments between member states. With respect to the first reason, it is suggested that a higher degree of real wage flexibility could bring about positive employment effects. This could be achieved by decentralising wage bargaining, discouraging wage co-operation at the industry level and increasing wage bargaining co-ordination. A decrease in equilibrium unemployment rates could also follow from relaxing strict employment protection legislation and reducing the generosity of unemployment benefits in combination with more active labour market policies. With respect to the second reason it can be concluded that the introduction of the single currency further increases the need for (downward) nominal wage flexibility in EMU countries. Better labour market performance could be achieved by centralising wage bargaining, shortening wage contract duration, increasing inflation and discouraging European wage co-operation.

Table 10.2 summarises some suggestions for labour market reform. Note that the recommendations with respect to the degree of bargaining centralisation conflict.

Table 10.2.   Problems and cures on European labour markets

Problem	High equilibrium unemployment	Large (downward) unemployment deviations
Cure	Increase real wage flexibility	Increase (downward) nominal wage flexibility
Labour market reform	Decentralise wage bargaining Discourage wage bargaining co-operation at the industry level Increase bargaining co-ordination Reduce employment protection legislation Reduce unemployment benefits Increase active labour market policy	Centralise wage bargaining Discourage wage bargaining co-operation Reduce contract duration

3. PROGRESS IN LABOUR MARKET REFORM IN EMU AND NON-EMU COUNTRIES

The first section has highlighted the challenges European labour markets are confronted with. Equilibrium unemployment rates should be brought down (further) and appropriate adjustment mechanisms to limit divergence should be developed. This section investigates whether recent labour market evolutions have been successful in meeting these challenges. We do this by focusing on changes in the underlying labour market institutions. Particular attention will be paid to differences between the EMU and non-EMU countries.

The discussion focuses on the amount and nature of labour market reform that individual countries have implemented. Particular interest goes to the part EMU may have played in labour market reform. Has the prospect of joining EMU had a similar disciplining effect on labour market policy as it has had on monetary and fiscal policy? We evaluate the reform undertaken in individual countries by means of an indicator that measures the potential decrease in equilibrium unemployment that results from the reform measures undertaken. This section is concluded by a brief discussion of the issue of downward nominal wage rigidity.

An indicator of labour market reform, expressing the potential for unemployment reduction is constructed in Table 10.3, which is inspired by the work of Nickell and van Ours (2000) for the Netherlands and the UK. The table reports how a number of labour market institutions have evolved over the period 1990-95 and have potentially contributed to an unemployment decline. Nickell and van Ours include union bargaining power (through union density and coverage) and focus on the degree of wage bargaining coordination. Given its weaker link with equilibrium unemployment (see section 1), they do not consider employment protection legislation. The generosity of the unemployment benefit system is measured by the replacement rate. Expenditures for active labour market policy and the tax wedge are also considered. In order to compare changes in different institutions over different countries, every measure of institutional change is multiplied by its impact coefficient on unemployment. The latter are averages of estimated coefficients from several unemployment equations that link institutions to unemployment. The last column reports the total potential change in unemployment. This can be considered as a harmonised overall indicator of labour market reform. A negative sign for this labour market reform indicator points to an institutional change that could contribute to a decrease in equilibrium unemployment. The higher the number in absolute value the stronger the degree of labour market reform (provided the number is negative). In Table 10.3 countries are grouped as EMU member or non-EMU member. For every group averages are reported at the bottom of each column.

Table 10.3. *Equilibrium unemployment reduction and labour market reform, period 1990-95[a]*

	union density (b)	union coverage (b)	co-ordina tion (c)	replace- ment rate (b)	Tax wedge (b)	ALMP (c)	Labour market reform indicator
EMU countries							
the Netherlands	0	10	0	-5.4	-2.9	5.1	-0.58
Austria	-4	0	0	-5.4	6.5	-0.1	-0.18
Portugal	0	1	0	1.0	0	0.1	0.20
Germany	-4	2	0	-2.2	5.9	-0.6	0.34
France	-1	3	0	-0.2	3	1.5	0.36
Belgium	3	0	0	-2.8	2.4	-2.5	0.52
Spain	6	2	0	-1.8	2.5	-1.7	1.00
Italy	0	-1	2	16.8	2.7	-9.3	2.62
Finland	9	0	0	4.4	4.4	-18.7	3.89
Average	1	1.9	0.2	0.5	2.7	-2.9	0.91
non-EMU countries							
New Zealand	-15	-36	0	-3.3	-2.2	0.4	-5.36
Norway	2	-1	0	0	-3.8	6.3	-1.06
Australia	-6	0	-1.5	0.5	2	4.1	-0.32
Japan	-1	-2	0	0.3	-0.8	-3.2	0.02
US	0	0	0	0.8	-0.2	-1	0.17
UK	-5	0	-0.5	0	-1.2	-6	0.20
Canada	2	-2	0	-0.9	3.3	-0.9	0.38
Denmark	5	0	0	15.5	-1.6	14.3	0.39
Switzerland	0	-3	0	7.6	2.7	-31.4	4.37
Sweden	8	3	-0.5	-2.2	4.7	-71.8	9.40
Average	-1	-4.1	-0.3	1.8	0.3	-8.9	0.82
Impact coefficient	*0.9*	*0.93*	*-2.53*	*1.11*	*1.18*	*-1.11*	

Notes: (a) : for details on the definitions of the underlying concepts, see Van Poeck and Borghijs (2001);
(b) : in percentage points change in the period 1990-95;
(c) : index change in units.

It is striking that it is only in New Zealand that institutions have evolved in such a way that all changes contributed to lower unemployment. Most of the countries went through institutional changes that had opposing effects in terms of unemployment reduction. Only five out of nineteen countries re-formed their institutions in a way that is favourable to a reduction of equilib-rium unemployment. Comparison of the EMU group with the non-EMU group confirms the earlier finding that EMU has not functioned well as a catalyst for labour market reform. On average EMU countries score slightly worse (0.91) than the group of non-EMU countries (0.82), but the difference is not statistically significant. The averages for union coverage, co-ordination and the tax wedge, however, are significantly different between the two groups. Among EMU countries, the Netherlands and Austria have performed well, whereas among the non-EMU countries New Zealand, Norway and Australia have gone through an unemployment-reducing reform. Although the outcome for the EMU group is similar to that of the non-EMU group, different evolutions in the underlying institutions can be detected. In EMU, the worsening of the labour market reform indicator is primarily due to cuts in spending for active labour market policy and an increase in the tax wedge. Only wage bargaining co-ordination evolved in a positive way, although marginally. Moreover this positive effect is offset by an increase in union bargaining power. In the non-EMU group, reduced spending for active labour market policy stands out as the main cause for an increase in the indicator. Positive employment effects could follow from a decrease in union bargaining power. Both union density and coverage decreased over the observed period.

Let us now have a closer look at the determinants of labour market reform by means of the labour market reform indicator. Is labour market reform over the period 1990-95 driven by the level of equilibrium unemployment at the beginning of the 1990s? If so, we would expect to find a negative relationship between the labour market reform indicator and equilibrium unemployment. The correlation for the whole sample of countries is, however, only weakly negative (-0.172) and statistically insignificant (Figure 10.3).

Figure 10.3.   The equilibrium unemployment level and labour market reform indicator for EMU and non-EMU countries, 1990-95

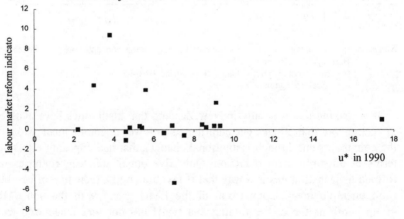

Figure 10.4a. The equilibrium unemployment level and labour market reform indicator for EMU countries, 1990-95

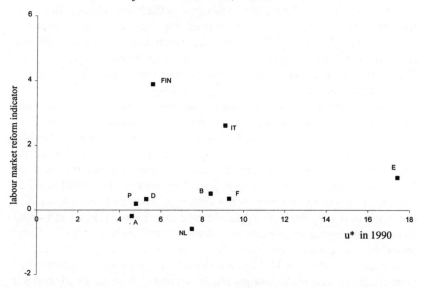

Figure 10.4b. The equilibrium unemployment level and labour market reform indicator for non-EMU countries, 1990-95

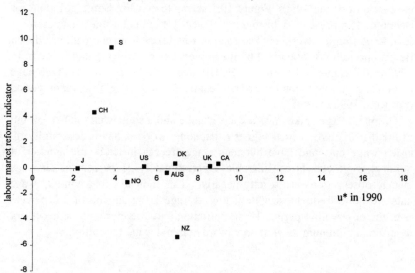

Splitting the sample into EMU countries and non-EMU countries confirms the results of the foregoing analysis. Not only is labour market change lower in EMU countries despite the worse situation in the labour market, there also appears to be no correlation between the amount of reform and the initial level of unemployment (0.066). The correlation is more apparent for the group of non-EMU countries (-0.425, with a significance level of 0.111). Countries with higher initial unemployment rates tend to have smaller labour market reform indicators. This is clearly shown in Figure 10.4b.

In the foregoing analysis the impact of the single currency on contract duration and downward nominal wage rigidity have remained untouched. They may, however, play a crucial role with respect to the issue of wage flexibility, next to the degree of centralisation of wage bargaining. To our knowledge, no empirical study has so far been conducted on the impact of (the transition to) EMU on the duration of wage contracts. The issue of downward nominal wage rigidity has recently attracted attention as inflation rates have steadily decreased over the 1990s. As explained in section 1, low inflation rates may increase the number of workers that resist nominal wage cuts and may increase equilibrium unemployment. The extent to which downward nominal wage rigidity has been eroded in countries with persistently low inflation has been addressed in a number of papers. In a repeat survey for Sweden, Agell and Lundborg (1995, 1999) find that resistance to nominal wage cuts persists, even in a low inflation environment. This conclusion is confirmed for the case of Switzerland by Fehr and Goette (2000). Smith (2000) on the other hand, finds no evidence of downward nominal wage rigidity in the UK for the first half of the 1990s. Figure 10.5 seems to confirm Smith's finding for Belgium. It represents a histogram of yearly nominal wage changes for a sample of Belgian workers. The sample was taken from the panel study on Belgian households organised by the universities of Antwerp and Liège from 1992 in the context of Eurostat's ECHP, and includes all workers who have remained in the same job for two consecutive periods. The observation period runs from 1993 to 1998.

Despite a large spike at zero wage change and a somewhat thinner left tail of the distribution – which suggests that some workers have successfully resisted wage cuts and have obtained wage freezes instead – the number of nominal wage cuts is considerable. Approximately 25 percent of all wage change observations are strictly negative. This indicates that nominal wage cuts are quite frequent, despite a low average inflation rate of 2.2 percent over the observation period. Higher inflation may therefore not be necessary to ensure a minimum level of downward nominal wage flexibility.

Figure 10.5. Wage change histogram of a sample of Belgian workers, 1993-98

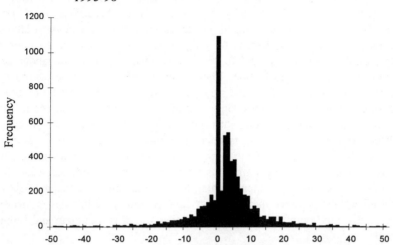

4. EMU AND LABOUR MARKET REFORM

The foregoing analysis has clarified the further need for labour market reform in the future, both to bring down equilibrium unemployment and to ease the adjustment process in the wake of asymmetric shocks. Despite the objective need for labour market reform, several countries have been reluctant to implement it, given the public resistance to cutbacks in the acquired level of social protection (Boeri *et al.*, 2001). This section addresses the question whether EMU may contribute to the necessary changes. We will first discuss the impact of EMU on the incentives of national governments to reform the labour market, after which we will focus on wage bargaining institutions and the behaviour of trade unions.

4.1. EMU and wage bargaining

It has already been indicated that union bargaining power, the extent of internalisation of wage externalities and the degrees of centralisation, co-operation and co-ordination of wage bargaining play an important part in labour market performance. We first discuss a number of issues relevant to the level of equilibrium unemployment, after which we focus on the issue of nominal wage flexibility.

Union bargaining power may come under pressure through increased product market competition in the euro-zone. More competition in the product market increases the elasticity of product demand. According to the Marshall-Hicks rule of labour demand – which states that the elasticity of labour demand is higher when demand for the product produced with that labour is more elastic – this would lead to an increase in the elasticity of labour demand and lower wages (Burda, 1999). Similar effects could be caused by increased transparency from the single currency, which facilitates the international comparison of wages. Unions in high-wage countries may be forced to cut wages to increase competitiveness and to achieve employment gains (Peters, 1995). The incentives to internalise negative wage externalities may increase because it has become impossible to devalue a national currency to correct excessive wage claims. This may lead to more moderate wage demands. An opposing argument leading to less internalisation under EMU is that all unions perceive themselves as smaller units of a broader monetary area. This may incite them to demand higher wages (Cukierman and Lippi, 1999).

Apart from these effects, EMU is also likely to have more structural consequences. More specifically, we argue that EMU increases the incentives for and lowers the costs of European trade union co-operation. This can be explained as follows: closer integration in the product market results in lower wages. This increases the pressure on unions to restore the original wage level, which can be achieved by an increase in bargaining power. Therefore, increasing economic integration increases the incentives for unions to negotiate at the European level, as this would increase their bargaining power. At the same time EMU lowers the barriers for European co-operation among labour unions through increased transparency, reduced uncertainty and a convergence of the institutional environment. Since nowadays wages are predominantly negotiated at the industry level in most European member states, it is not unlikely that European bargaining in the future will take place at the industry level. This evolution towards increased bargaining co-operation could therefore potentially lead to higher wage demands and higher unemployment. Summing up, the above arguments give no univocal indication as to whether EMU changes union behaviour such that equilibrium unemployment will decrease.

With respect to nominal wage flexibility, the following issues may be relevant. The first relates to the duration of wage contracts. If EMU increases the variability of economic activity, unions may prefer shorter contract periods (Calmfors, 2000). The second argument relates to the persistence of downward nominal wage rigidity in a low-inflation environment. If trade unions perceive the introduction of the single currency as a radical regime switch to a persistent low-inflation environment, traditional resistance against nominal wage cuts may erode in order to prevent job losses. These theoretical arguments would thus suggest that EMU would increase nominal wage flexibility. European wage co-operation, however, may counterbalance these positive effects.

4.2. EMU and labour market reform

In this section we address the question of whether EMU influences the incentives of national and European governing bodies to reform the labour market.

In general, countries have an incentive for labour market reform not only because it decreases equilibrium unemployment, but also because it brings down the inflation bias (Barro and Gordon, 1983). For individual countries inside the monetary union, the link between national labour market reform and inflation bias is, however, weak. Since reform in a single member state only brings equilibrium unemployment in the union down by a small amount, the benefits of a reduced inflation bias are only marginal. The incentives for labour market reform would therefore be smaller for countries in the EMU than for countries outside the EMU (Calmfors, 1998; Sibert and Sutherland, 2000). A second argument explaining why policy-makers could be more reluctant to carry out labour market reform in EMU as compared to policy-makers outside the EMU is the likely co-operation of the ECB in comparison to a national central bank in an encompassing policy framework. Rigid nominal wages prevent the real wage level from falling and the employment level from rising after the reform. A real wage decline could be achieved through combining labour market reform with a (temporary) monetary expansion. It is, however, unlikely that the ECB will co-operate in this policy mix. Finally, under EMU the pressure for fiscal consolidation, which was a prerequisite for entry, may subside. To the extent that labour market reform is fostered by the need to reduce budget deficits, there will be less pressure for reform (Bean, 1998; Calmfors 1998).

A common argument in favour of more labour market reform inside EMU is the so-called TINA argument ('There Is No Alternative'). Under EMU, monetary policy and more specifically competitive depreciations are no longer available to offset negative shocks. Therefore the only option that remains is to ensure that labour markets are sufficiently flexible to absorb the shocks, which can only be achieved through labour market reform. Another argument that points to more labour market reform inside EMU is that unemployment will be more volatile in EMU, as monetary policy is no longer available to stabilise asymmetric shocks. Insofar as governments are especially averse to bad unemployment outcomes, they will anticipate the problem and carry out precautionary labour market reform. Labour market reform may also be stepped up to attract inward flows of capital. To the extent that EMU increases the mobility of business through increased price transparency and economic integration, the location of business may become more sensitive to labour costs. This may increase competition between countries to reform the labour market in order to bring down labour costs (Bean, 1998; Calmfors, 1998; Calmfors 2001). Summing up the foregoing arguments, it remains unclear whether EMU will reduce or increase the incentives for national governments to reform the labour market.

At the European level, policy-makers have shown a keen interest in labour market reform. This has been inspired by the fact that some member states are characterised by high equilibrium unemployment and that labour market reform is considered necessary to ensure a viable EMU. To ensure that the necessary steps towards labour market reform would be taken by the member states, the Council of Ministers initiated in 1997 the 'Luxembourg Process' that formulates annual Employment Guidelines. These guidelines, focusing on employability, entrepreneurship, adaptability and equal opportunities, are aimed at reducing structural unemployment in Europe. They are supplemented by Broad Economic Guidelines, directed at increasing the flexibility of the labour market. The implementation of the Employment Guidelines is subject to annual control of the European Commission and the European Council.

Although these guidelines constitute a clear pressure on the European member states to impose labour market reform, the question remains as to whether member states are willing to implement the (often unpopular) guidelines. Above we developed arguments that cast doubt on the incentives for more labour market reform by national governments in the EMU countries. Since national and European governing bodies sometimes consist of the same people, incentives may be conflicting. Moreover, no retaliation mechanism in the case of non-implementation has been imposed.

5. CONCLUSION

European labour markets are under convergence pressure. The single European currency is introduced in a set of countries that are characterised by a high degree of real and (downward) nominal wage rigidity. This is reflected in high levels of equilibrium unemployment and large unemployment deviations away from equilibrium. We therefore plead for increased wage flexibility in European labour markets in order to bring down equilibrium unemployment as well as to limit divergent unemployment evolutions between EMU member states that react differently to economic shocks.

Labour market reform measures that could contribute to higher real wage flexibility are increasing bargaining co-ordination, decentralising wage bargaining, relaxing strict employment protection legislation, conditioning unemployment benefits and augmenting the share of active labour market policy. Nominal wage flexibility may benefit from centralising wage bargaining and shortening wage contracts. Although some measures have been implemented in the past decade, more should be done. It is particularly worrying in this respect that EMU countries have not been more diligent in reforming their labour markets than their counterparts outside the euro area, although labour market conditions in EMU would require more labour market reform. Whether the introduction of the single European currency itself provides the necessary incentive to step up reform remains hard to predict. Both arguments for and against more labour market reform in the EMU can be advanced. This alone should be sufficient to encourage policy-makers to take specific policy actions to make European labour markets capable of coping with the changing economic conditions.

NOTES

1. The authors are both at the Department of Economics of the University of Antwerp. Correspondence address: alain.borghijs@ua.ac.be.
2. We consider equilibrium unemployment rates to correct for differences in the business cycles among countries. Note, however, that the equilibrium unemployment rate is an estimated concept that cannot be observed. Equilibrium unemployment rates are therefore sensitive to the estimation technique.

REFERENCES

Agell, J. and P. Lundborg (1995), 'Theories of Pay and Unemployment: survey evidence from Swedish manufacturing firms', *Scandinavian Journal of Economics*, **97**, 295-308.

Agell, J. and P. Lundborg (1999), 'Survey Evidence on Wage Rigidity and Unemployment: Sweden in the 1990s', IFAU working paper no. 1999:2.

Akerlof, G., W. Dickens and G. Perry (1996), 'The Macroeconomics of Low Inflation', *Brookings Papers on Economic Activity*, **1999**(1), 1-59.

Barro, R.J. and D. Gordon (1983), 'A Positive Theory of Monetary Policy in a Natural Rate Model', *Journal of Political Economy*, **91**, 589-610.

Bean, C. (1994), 'European Unemployment: a survey', *Journal of Economic Literature*, **32**, 573-619.

Bean, C. (1998), 'The Interaction of Aggregate-demand Policies and Labour Market Reform', *Swedish Economic Policy Review*, **5**, 353-382.

Belot, M. and J. van Ours (2000), 'Does the Recent Success of some OECD Countries in Lowering their Unemployment Rates Lie in the Clever Design of their Labour Market Reforms?', CEPR Discussion Paper no. 2492.

Bewley, T. (1999), *Why Wages don't Fall During a Recession*, Cambridge, MA: Harvard University Press.

Blanchard, O. and J. Wolfers (2000), 'The Role of Shocks and Institutions in the Rise of European Unemployment: the aggregate evidence', *Economic Journal*, **110**, C1-C33.

Boeri, T., A. Börsch-Supan and G. Tabellini (2001), 'Would you like to Shrink the Welfare State? A Survey of European Citizens', *Economic Policy*, **32**, 7-50.

Borghijs, A. (2001), 'Does Product Market Integration lead to European Wage-Setting?', Faculty of Applied Economics Research Paper no. 2001-001, University of Antwerp.

Burda, M. (1999), 'European Labour Markets and the Euro: how much flexibility do we really need?', CEPR Discussion Paper no. 2217.

Calmfors, L. (1993), 'Centralisation of Wage Bargaining and Macroeconomic Performance: a survey', *OECD Economic Studies*, **21**, 161-191

Calmfors, L. (1998), 'Macroeconomic Policy, Wage-setting and Employment: what difference does the EMU make?', *Oxford Review of Economic Policy*, **14**, 125-151.

Calmfors, L. (2000), 'Wages and Wage-Bargaining Institutions in the EMU - a survey of the issues', IIES Seminar Paper no. 690, forthcoming in *Empirica*.

Calmfors, L. (2001), 'Unemployment, Labour Market Reform and Monetary Union', *Journal of Labor Economics*, **19**, 265-289.

Calmfors, L. and J. Driffill (1988), 'Bargaining Structure, Corporatism and Macroeconomic Performance', *Economic Policy*, **6**, 13-61.

Cukierman, A. and F. Lippi (1999), 'Labor Markets and Monetary Union: a strategic analysis', CentER Discussion Paper no. 99100.

Danthine, J.P. and J. Hunt (1994), 'Wage Bargaining Structure, Employment and Economic Integration', *Economic Journal*, **104**, 528-541.

Daveri, F. and G. Tabellini (2000), 'Unemployment, Growth and Taxation in Industrial Countries', *Economic Policy*, **30**, 47-88.

Elmeskov, J., J. Martin and S. Scarpetta (1998), 'Key Lessons for Labour Market Reforms', *Swedish Economic Policy Review*, **5**, 205-258.

European Council (2000), *Presidency Conclusions – Lisbon*, 23 and 24 March 2000, http://europa.eu.int/council/off/conclu/mar2000/mar2000_en.pdf .

Fase, M. and G. De Bondt (1999), 'Institutional Environment and Monetary Transmission in the Euro Area: a cross-country view', De Nederlandsche Bank Research Memorandum WO&E no. 599.

Fehr, E. and L. Goette (2000), 'The Robustness and Real Consequences of Downward Nominal Wage Rigidity', University of Zürich Institute for Empirical Research Working Paper no. 44.

Feldstein, M. (1997), 'The Political Economy of the European Economic and Monetary Union: political sources of an economic liability', *Journal of Economic Perspectives*, **11**, 23-42.

Garibaldi, P. and P. Mauro (2001), 'Anatomy of Employment Growth', mimeo, paper prepared for the 34th Economic Policy Panel Meeting, Brussels, October 19-20, 2001.

Hughes Hallett, A., Y. Ma and M. Demertzis (2000), 'The Single Currency and Labour Market Flexibility: a necessary partnership?', *Scottish Journal of Political Economy*, **47**, 141-155.

IMF, *World Economic Outlook*, various issues, Washington DC: IMF.

Nickell, S. (1997), 'Unemployment and Labor Market Rigidities: Europe versus North America', *Journal of Economic Perspectives*, **11**, 55-74.

Nickell, S. and R. Layard (1997), 'Labour Market Institutions and Economic Performance', University of Oxford Centre for Economic Performance Discussion Paper Series no. 23.

Nickell, S. and J. van Ours (2000), 'The Netherlands and the United Kingdom: a European unemployment miracle?', *Economic Policy*, **30**, 135-180.

OECD (1994), *The OECD Jobs Study: Evidence and Explanations*, Paris: OECD.

OECD (1999), *Implementing the OECD Jobs Strategy: Assessing Performance and Policy*, Paris: OECD.

OECD (2000), *Economic Outlook*, Paris: OECD.

OECD, *Employment Outlook*, various issues, Paris: OECD.

Peersman, G. (2001), 'The Transmission of Monetary Policy in the Euro Area: are the effects different across countries?', paper presented at an International Workshop on 'The European Macroeconomy: Integration, Employment and Policy Coordination' at the University of Antwerp, 9 and 10 November 2001.

Peters, T. (1995), 'European Monetary Union and Labour Markets: what to expect?', *International Labour Review*, **135**, 315-332.

Pissarides, C. (1997), 'The Need for Labor-Market Flexibility in a European Economic and Monetary Union', *Swedish Economic Policy Review*, **4**, 513-545.

Plasmans, J. *et al.* (1999), 'Generosity of the Unemployment Benefit System and Wage Flexibility in EMU: time-varying evidence in five countries', UFSIA, Department of Economics, Research Paper 99-043.

Scarpetta, S. (1996), 'Assessing the Role of Labour Market Policies and Institutional Settings on Unemployment: a cross-country study', *OECD Economic Studies*, **26**, 43-98.

Sibert, A. and A. Sutherland (2000), 'Monetary Union and Labor Market Reform', *Journal of International Economics*, **51**, 421-435.

Smith, J. (2000), 'Nominal Wage Rigidity in the United Kingdom', *Economic Journal*, **110**, C176-C195.

Soskice, D. (1990), 'Wage Determination: the changing role of institutions in advanced industrialized countries, *Oxford Review of Economic Policy*, **6**, 36-61.

Traxler, F. and B. Kittel (2000), 'The Bargaining System and Performance: a comparison of 18 OECD countries', *Comparative Political Studies*, **33**, 1154-1190.

Van Poeck, A. and A. Borghijs (2001), 'EMU and Labour Market Reform: needs, incentives and realisations', Faculty of Applied Economics Research Paper 2001-022, University of Antwerp.

11. Distorted Labour Markets and Revealed Comparative Advantage: a Note on the Single Market and the EU Periphery

Frank Barry and Aoife Hannan[1]

1. INTRODUCTION

Trade liberalisation, according to the Heckscher-Ohlin-Samuelson model of textbook trade theory, should cause labour-abundant regions to specialise into labour-intensive products and out of capital-intensive products.

The development of the Single European Market represented one such instance of trade liberalisation. It was concerned with the removal of remaining non-tariff barriers such as restrictive government procurement policies and differing national standards that inhibited inter-EU trade. We might therefore have expected the four poorest EU economies, Greece, Portugal, Ireland and Spain, to become more specialised in relatively labour-intensive sectors.

Of course, much discussion in recent years has focused on intra-industry trade, or two-way trade in varieties of the same product. This trade is likely to dominate when trading partners have fairly similar factor endowments; that is, when trade takes place between countries or regions with similar levels of income per capita (Krugman, 1981). However, in the lead-up to the Single Market the peripheral EU countries with which we are concerned had levels of GDP per head at or below 75 percent of the EU average. Trade economists therefore expected substantial interindustry as well as intra-industry adjustment (Krugman and Venables, 1990; Neven, 1990).

The EC Commission, in a special issue of *European Economy* (1990), developed a methodology, based on revealed comparative advantage, to predict the sectoral consequences for each EU country of the Single Market programme. In this chapter we explore, for the peripheral economies, the implicit factor intensity adjustments that the sectoral results emerging from the EC Commission study imply.

We find that, contrary to Heckscher-Ohlin-Samuelson theory, the Commission's results predict that Ireland and Spain will adjust towards more capital-intensive sectors. Portugal and Greece, on the other hand, in line with the Heckscher-Ohlin-Samuelson view, are predicted to adjust towards more labour-intensive sectors. These results of ours, on predicted dynamics, support the static findings of Neven (1990) and Barry and Hannan (1995), that Irish and Spanish exports at the time of the Single Market were not labour-intensive while those of Portugal and Greece were.

We hypothesise that the paradoxes arising in the cases of Ireland and Spain can be explained by the labour market distortions pervailing in these countries at that time. This is consistent with the theoretical arguments advanced by Brecher (1974).

2. REVEALED COMPARATIVE ADVANTAGE AND THE SINGLE MARKET

The Internal Market programme entailed the removal of remaining non-tariff barriers to trade within the EU. A special issue of the journal *European Economy* (1990) identified 40 out of the 120 NACE 3-digit manufacturing sectors as likely to be affected by the programme. These sectors were characterised by high price dispersion across states and were ones in which public procurement policies were deemed to be restrictive or in which differences in national standards were found to hinder trade.

In evaluating the implications for each individual EU country, the EC Commission developed a methodology based on indicators of how each EU state performed in each of these industrial sectors. The methodology was based on four static and three dynamic indicators, as follows:

The static indicators (averaged over 1985-87) include:

- the intra-community coverage ratio (the ratio of intra-EU exports to intra-EU imports);
- the extra-community coverage ratio (the ratio of extra-EU exports to extra-EU imports);
- an export specialisation index, which measures the ratio of the share of one sector's exports in total manufacturing exports for the country concerned versus the same share for the whole EU $(X_{ij}/X_{\cdot j})/(X_{iEU}/X_{\cdot EU})$;
- a production specialisation index similar to the previous indicator, except dealing with industrial production rather than exports.

A score of between +1 and -1 was awarded for each of these indicators, to yield a global score of between +4 and -4.[2] Sectors with high global scores (+3, +4) were considered to be in a favourable position to benefit from the effects of market integration while those with low scores (-4 or -3) were deemed to be in an unfavourable position.

These static indicators were supplemented by three dynamic indicators measuring historical movements in the first and third indicators above by comparing the difference between the 1980-82 and 1985-87 values of the indicators.[3]

The static and dynamic indicators are designed to measure a country's revealed comparative advantage. On the basis of the scores awarded in the European Economy special issue (and on subsequent work by the author of the Irish study, O'Malley, 1992) we classified these sectors as either 'S' (for those likely to be successful) or 'D' (those likely to decline). S-sectors were those in which countries had a revealed comparative *advantage*, while D-sectors were those in which countries had a revealed comparative *disadvantage*.

The allocation of an 'S' or a 'D' category to each sensitive sector was of course country-specific, based as it was on how each sector in each country had performed in terms of the indicators detailed above. For example, the clothing sector (NACE 453) performed poorly in Ireland over the course of the 1980s, in the sense that export performance was sluggish relative to import growth, leading to a 'D' classification in the Irish table. The performance of this sector had been very much stronger in the other peripheral countries, however, and so was classified as 'S' in the other three country tables.

The motor vehicles and accessories sector (NACE 351), on the other hand, had been performing well in both Ireland and Spain, and so was classified as 'S'. The equivalent sector in Portugal and Greece was classified as 'D' however, because of poor performance over the course of the 1980s.

Tables 11.1a to 11.1d present our summaries of the data contained in *European Economy* (1990). That study goes no further than identifying sectors in each country which it deems likely to succeed or fail in response to the introduction of the Internal Market.

Alongside each potentially successful (S) sector and each potentially declining (D) sector, we show the proportion of gross manufacturing output that the sector represented, (Y/YM), and its proportion of total manufacturing employment (L/LM).

Table 11.1a. Greece: classification of sectors to be affected by SEM

	NACE	Sector	Y/YM	L/LM
S	224	Production of non-ferrous metal	3.8	2.1
	341	Insulated wires and cables	1.0	0.6
	351	Motor vehicles	0.9	0.7
	417	Spaghetti and macaroni	0.4	0.4
	431	Wool industry	0.6	1.0
	432	Cotton industry	1.4	7.1
	436	Knitting mills	2.0	4.5
	453	Clothing	2.2	8.1
	471	Pulp and paper manufacturing	1.2	1.5
	481	Rubber products	0.7	0.8
Total for 'S' Sectors			*14.2*	*26.8*
D	222	Steel tubes	0.7	0.7
	247	Glass and glassware	0.3	0.5
	248	Ceramic goods	0.9	1.8
	251	Basic industrial chemicals	4.2	2.3
	255/6	Paints, varnishes and inks; other chemical products	0.5	0.4
	257	Pharmaceuticals	1.5	2.0
	314	Structural metal products	0.7	0.9
	315	Boilermaking	0.1	0.2
	316	Tools, finished metal goods	3.0	4.1
	325	Plant for mines and steel	0.0	0.1
	328	Other machinery and equipment	0.5	1.0
	342	Electrical machinery	0.6	1.2
	343	Electrical appliances, batteries and accumulators	0.2	0.3
	344	Telecommunication equipment	0.3	0.6
	346	Domestic electrical appliances	1.1	1.4
	347	Electric lamps	0.1	0.1
	352	Car bodies, trailers and caravans	0.2	0.2
	362	Rolling stock	0.3	1.1
	411	Manufacturing of veg. and oils	1.5	0.6
	412	Meat	0.9	0.8
	413	Manufacturing of dairy products	1.9	1.4
	419	Bread and flour confectionery	0.5	1.1
	424	Distilleries and alcohol	0.5	0.4

Table 11.1a (continued)

427	Brewing and malting	1.1	1.0
428	Soft drinks	1.0	1.1
438	Carpets and floor coverings	0.6	0.9
441	Leather tanning and finishing	0.5	0.4
442	Leather industry	0.0	0.1
451	Footwear	0.7	1.9
455	Household textiles	0.2	0.2
467	Wooden furniture	0.3	0.8
472	Processed paper	1.2	1.2
483	Plastic products	1.8	2.5
494	Manufacturing of sports goods & toys	0.2	0.3
Total for 'D' Sectors		*28.1*	*33.6*

Table 11.1b. Ireland: classification of sectors to be affected by SEM

	NACE	Sector	Y/YM	L/LM
S	247	Glass and glassware	0.9	1.9
	251	Basic industrial chemicals	2.3	1.2
	257	Pharmaceuticals (M)	6.0	2.8
	322/5	Machine tools (M); plant for mines and steel (M)	0.4	0.6
	323	Textile machinery (M)	0.0	0.1
	324	Food and chemical machinery (M)	0.1	0.2
	326	Transmission equipment (M)	0.1	0.1
	327	Other machinery (M)	0.0	0.0
	330	Office and data-processing mach.(M)	13.2	3.8
	341	Insulated wires and cables (M)	0.8	2.1
	344	Telecommunication equipment (M)	2.7	2.6
	345	Radios, TVs etc. (M)	2.1	1.1
	346	Domestic electrical appliances (M)	1.0	1.3
	351	Motor vehicles	0.2	0.4
	364	Aerospace equipment	0.5	1.1
	372	Medical and surgical equipment (M)	1.7	2.3
	413	Dairy products	12.0	3.8
	421	Cocoa and chocolate	2.5	1.2
	427	Brewing and malting	5.1	1.6
	428	Soft drinks (M)	1.6	1.3
	432	Cotton industry (M)	0.8	0.4

Table 11.1b (continued)

481	Rubber products (M)	0.7	1.0
491	Jewellery	0.2	0.9
494	Toys and sports goods	0.3	0.3
Total for 'S' Sectors		*55.1*	*32.1*
248	Ceramic goods	0.2	0.4
256	Other chemical products (M)	0.8	0.7
321	Agricultural machinery (M)	0.4	0.6
342	Electrical machinery (M)	0.6	1.1
347	Electric lamps (M)	0.1	0.1
361	Ship building	0.1	0.3
417	Spaghetti and macaroni	0.0	0.0
431	Wool industry	0.4	1.9
438	Carpets and floor coverings (M)	0.3	0.4
451	Footwear	0.2	0.6
453	Clothing	1.4	6.5
455	Household textiles	0.2	0.5
493	Photographic labs	0.1	0.1
Total for 'D' Sectors		*4.8*	*13.2*

Table 11.1c. Portugal: classification of sectors to be affected by SEM

	NACE	Sector	Y/YM	L/LM
S	247	Glass and glassware	1.0	1.3
	248	Ceramic goods	1.1	2.3
	316	Tools, finished metal goods	2.7	4.9
	324	Food and chemical machinery	0.1	0.2
	341	Insulated wires and cables	0.9	0.6
	352	Car bodies, trailers and caravans	0.4	0.8
	361	Shipbuilding	1.0	2.7
	415	Seafood	1.1	1.4
	425	Wine and champagne	0.1	0.2
	427	Brewing and malting	0.9	0.5
	428	Soft drinks	0.6	0.5
	431/2	Wool/cotton textiles	8.7	15.2
	436	Knitwear industry	3.3	4.7
	438	Carpets and floor coverings	0.5	0.7
	439	Miscellaneous textile industries	0.7	1.5

Table 11.1c (continued)

	451	Footwear	2.3	3.9
	453	Clothing	4.0	7.6
	455	Household textiles	0.3	0.5
Total for 'S' Sectors			*29.7*	*49.5*
D	251	Basic industrial chemicals	5.3	1.2
	256	Other chemical products	2.6	1.0
	257	Pharmaceuticals	1.5	1.3
	260	Man-made fibres	0.7	0.3
	315	Boilermaking	0.4	0.7
	321/2/5	Agricultural machinery, machine tools, plant for mines and steel	0.2	0.4
	323	Textile machinery	0.2	0.3
	328	Other machinery and equipment	1.0	1.3
	330	Office and data processing machinery	0.2	0.2
	342	Electrical machinery	0.6	0.9
	343	Electrical appliances, batteries and accumulators	0.3	0.2
	344/5	Radio & TV, telecommunication equipment	2.3	2.1
	346	Domestic electrical appliances	0.4	0.3
	347	Electric lamps	0.3	0.5
	351	Motor vehicles	2.4	0.8
	353	Motor vehicle parts & accessories	1.1	0.7
	362	Rolling stock	0.3	0.2
	363	Cycles, motorcycles and parts	0.3	0.4
	371/2	Precision instruments; medico-surgical equipment	0.1	0.1
	416	Grain milling	2.4	0.6
	417	Spaghetti and macaroni	0.3	0.1
	419	Bread and flour confectionery	1.6	3.9
	421	Cocoa and chocolate	0.4	0.5
	481	Rubber products	0.8	0.9
Total for 'D' Sectors			*25.7*	*18.9*

Table 11.1d. Spain: classification of sectors to be affected by SEM

	NACE	Sector	Y/YM	L/LM
S	248	Ceramic goods	0.9	1.5
	341	Insulated wires and cables	0.5	0.4
	346	Domestic electrical appliances	1.0	0.9
	351	Motor vehicles	10.0	4.9
	425	Wine and champagne	1.6	1.1
	431	Wool/cotton textiles	0.2	0.3
	432	Cotton industry	0.9	1.1
	451	Footwear	0.9	1.9
	453	Clothing	1.9	4.0
	455	Household textiles	0.4	0.7
	481	Rubber products	1.3	1.6
	491	Jewellery	0.2	0.3
	494	Toys and sports goods	0.3	0.4
Total for 'S' Sectors			*20.0*	*19.0*
D	247	Glass and glassware	0.9	1.0
	251	Basic industrial chemicals	3.8	1.2
	256	Other chemical products	1.7	1.3
	257	Pharmaceuticals	1.9	1.6
	315/321	Boilermaking, agricultural machinery	0.4	0.7
	322	Machine tools	0.6	0.7
	323	Textile machinery	0.3	0.3
	324	Food and chemical machinery	0.3	0.6
	325	Plant for mines and steel	0.9	1.0
	326	Transmission equipment	0.2	0.3
	327	Other machines and equipment	0.2	0.4
	330	Office and data-processing machinery	0.5	0.1
	342	Electrical machinery	1.4	2.0
	344	Radio and TV, telecommunication	1.1	1.3
	345	Radio and TV	0.7	0.8
	347	Electric lamps	0.3	0.5
	361	Shipbuilding	0.7	1.9
	362	Rolling stock	0.3	0.7
	364	Aerospace equipment	0.3	0.4
	372	Medico-surgical equipment	0.1	0.1
	417	Spaghetti and macaroni	0.1	0.1
	421	Cocoa and chocolate	0.7	0.8

Table 11.1d (continued)

427	Brewing and malting	0.9	0.7
428	Soft drinks	1.1	0.9
438	Carpets and floor coverings	0.2	0.2
493	Photo and cine labs	0.1	0.1
Total for 'D' Sectors		*19.5*	*19.5*

Sources: Eurostat, *Structure and Activity of Industry*, Annual Enquiry – Main Results, supplemented by OECD STAN database and Irish Census of Industrial Production, various years.

Note: Totals for 'S' and 'D' sectors may be different from the sums of the displayed sector percentages because of rounding errors.

In the Irish case we see that the strong sectors comprised 55 percent of output and only 32 percent of employment; they were therefore capital- rather than labour-intensive. The weak sectors on the other hand comprised 5 percent of manufacturing output but 13 percent of employment, and were therefore labour-intensive.[4]

This methodology therefore predicted that the impact of further trade liberalisation would be to increase the capital intensity of Irish industry.

One important objection to this methodology is that multinational companies, which are known to engage in substantial transfer pricing, dominate many of these sectors in Ireland.[5] Thus the apparent output of these sectors is likely to be inflated.

To correct for this we remove from our data the sectors that are dominated by multinational companies. These sectors were ones in which current employment in foreign companies in Ireland was substantially greater (typically by a factor of three or more) than employment in indigenous industry.[6] These sectors are denoted by the letter 'M' in brackets in the table.

Removing these multinational-dominated sectors, however, does not change our results. The strong indigenous sectors were still relatively capital-intensive (comprising 24 percent of output and 12.4 percent of employment) and the weak indigenous sectors were still relatively labour-intensive (with 2.6 percent of output and 10.3 percent of employment).[7]

Therefore the predicted structural transformation of the economy was not a function just of continuing crowding-out of indigenous industry by the multinational sector. The revealed comparative advantage analysis predicted a continuing shift out of labour-intensive sectors even within indigenous industry as trade liberalisation proceeded.

Spain, according to the revealed comparative advantage methodology, was also predicted to become more capital-intensive. The strong sectors comprised a little over 20 percent of output compared to under 19 percent of employment (making them capital-intensive), while these proportions were equal for the weak sectors.

For Greece and Portugal on the other hand the strong sectors appear la-bour-intensive relative to the weaker ones. This is immediately apparent for Portugal where the strong sectors comprised 49 percent of employment and only 30 percent of output, while the weak sectors comprised 19 percent of employment and just under 26 percent of output.

The Greek case was somewhat less clear-cut since both the weak and the strong sectors were labour-intensive relative to the remainder of industry (i.e. those sectors not deemed likely to have been affected by the internal market). Nevertheless the labour intensity of the strong sectors (with a labour-output ratio of $1.9 = 26.8/14.2$) was greater than that of the weak sectors (where the labour-output ratio is 1.2). Therefore the labour intensity of manufacturing was predicted to rise as trade liberalisation proceeded.

Both Greece and Portugal, therefore, unlike Ireland and Spain, were deemed likely to specialise further into labour-intensive sectors, as Heck-scher-Ohlin-Samuelson theory predicts.

What accounts for the paradox that arises in the cases of Ireland and Spain? Our preferred explanation is based on labour-market distortions. If real wages were excessively high in the latter two countries then labour-intensive industries would be disappearing at an excessively rapid pace. These sectors would then have scored lower in the indicators of revealed comparative advantage than would have been the case if labour markets were more flexible.

This point has been developed in a theoretical framework by Brecher (1974) who points out that 'it may be incorrect to infer flexible-wage com-parative advantage from the observed minimum-wage pattern of trade'.[8]

Prima facie evidence on the degree of labour market distortions in Ireland and Spain versus the relative flexibility of labour markets in Greece and Portugal is provided by unemployment rates. Irish and Spanish unemploy-ment averaged 15.6 percent and 18.9 percent respectively between 1985 and 1993, compared to an EU average of 9.6, while the equivalent figures for Portugal and Greece were 5.9 and 7.9 percent.[9]

If these distortions were to remain, then the revealed-comparative-advantage predictions implicitly predicated upon their continuance would be likely to be borne out, and both Ireland and Spain would produce a more capital-intensive mix of goods than might be expected on the basis of their raw factor endowments.[10] Indeed, our results on this are consistent with the static evidence reported by Barry and Hannan (1995) and Neven (1990).

3. STATIC EVIDENCE ON FACTOR INTENSITIES AND REVEALED COMPARATIVE ADVANTAGE

The Barry-Hannan evidence is presented in Table 11.2, which compares the composition of exports of the four peripheral EU economies.

Table 11.2.   *Composition of exports (1992)*

	Ireland	Spain	Greece	Portugal
Food, live animals, beverages, tobacco	24%	14%	28%	7%
Crude materials (hides, wool, etc.)	3%	2%	5%	7%
Chemicals	19%	8%	4%	4%
Basic manufactures	8%	19%	23%	23%
Machinery, transport equipment	27%	43%	4%	22%
Miscellaneous manufactures	16%	9%	23%	34%

Source: UN International Trade Statistics Yearbook (1992).

Table 11.2 reveals that Irish exports were concentrated not just in the Food and Agricultural sectors (as are most of the other peripheral economies), but also in the most modern of the manufacturing sectors (Chemicals and Machinery and Transport Equipment). Note the very small proportion of exports emanating from the 'Basic manufacturing' category (which included rubber and paper products, textiles, yarns, fabrics, glass, and iron and steel tools) and 'Miscellaneous manufactures' (which included furniture, clothing, footwear, printed and plastic materials, and toys) in comparison with Portugal and Greece. These were arguably the most labour-intensive sectors. Ireland shared this somewhat 'warped' industrial structure with Spain, the other high-unemployment EU economy.

Neven (1990) produces a different measure of revealed comparative advantage, reproduced in Table 11.3. This shows the deviation from the national average, in each of five categories of industries, of net exports to the EU as a percentage of domestic production. This is a measure, then, *adjusted for overall deficits or surpluses*, of the extent to which countries were *net exporters* in any particular industrial category.

*Table 11.3.   Revealed comparative advantage: net exports/domestic output
(adjusted for overall trade balance) (%)*

	Natural resources	Av. K/ Av. L	High labour	High capital	High human capital
Belgium	7.5	8.4	-91.8	18.3	-10.3
Denmark	28.5	-11.6	-26.5	-9.1	n.a.
France	1.7	-2.6	-9.8	0.2	1.4
Germany	-4.0	-0.4	-26.2	-20.0	5.8
Greece	-1.7	7.0	80.0	-1.3	-98.7
Ireland	16.5	-9.1	-61.3	-9.5	11.2
Italy	-14.9	6.1	36.1	3.1	-5.2
Netherlands	12.0	n.a.	-74.4	-17.2	-10.1
Portugal	12.2	4.4	79.4	10.2	-35.8
Spain	0.6	2.4	8.7	2.4	-6.6
UK	-0.8	1.0	-2.2	2.8	-4.8

The same broad picture emerges from this table. Greece and Portugal (and to a lesser extent Italy) were specialised in labour-intensive industries (clothing, footwear and ceramics), sectors from which the high unemployment countries, Spain and Ireland, were notably absent. It might be argued, in the Irish case at least, that *absolute advantage* (in the form of very low rates of corporation tax) has attracted high-tech foreign multinationals to Ireland, leading to this apparently unbalanced industrial structure. The fact that our dynamic analysis predicts that indigenous industry would also become more specialised in capital-intensive sectors suggests that labour-market distortions also play some role in resolving the puzzle.

4. CONCLUDING COMMENTS

In this chapter we made use of the revealed comparative advantage study carried out by the EU Commission to analyse the sectoral and spatial effects of the Single European Market. On the basis of this study we classified, for the four peripheral EU economies, the sectors in which each was predicted to do well (the 'S' sectors) and those in which each was predicted to do badly (the 'D' sectors). We then compared the factor intensities of the two groups of sectors.

We saw that Greece and Portugal, in line with the Heckscher-Ohlin-Samuelson model, were predicted to specialise more in labour-intensive sectors. Ireland and Spain, in contrast to the Heckscher-Ohlin-Samuelson view, however, were predicted to specialise more in capital-intensive sectors. This was in fact a continuation of the direction in which these economies have been specialising, evidence on which is presented for the Irish case by Brulhart and McAleese (1995) and Gray (1993).

We pointed out that this is consistent with Heckscher-Ohlin-Samuelson theory, as demonstrated by Brecher (1974), when the model is amended to allow for labour-market distortions. Prima facie evidence of such distortions in the Irish and Spanish cases is provided by the high unemployment rates prevailing in these countries at that time, in contrast to the very low rates prevailing in Portugal and Greece.

Our argument is also consistent with earlier findings of Neven's (1990) who pointed to the discrepancy between Spain's relatively low labour costs and its failure to specialise in labour-intensive commodities. This could have been because Spanish labour costs, while low relative to the EU average, were nevertheless above equilibrium levels, which would have constrained the development of Spanish labour-intensive sectors.

NOTES

1. Frank Barry is at University College Dublin and Aoife Hannan is at the European University Institute in Firenze. This paper forms part of an EU-funded research project on Labour Market Effects of European FDI (HPSE-CT99-00017). Stimulating discussions with John Bradley and Wim Meeusen on the subject matter of the chapter are gratefully acknowledged. Address for correspondence: Frank.Barry@ucd.ie .

2. The scoring for static indicators is: -1 if the value of the indicator is smaller than 90%; 0 if the value of the indicator lies between 90 and 110%; and +1 if the value of the indicator is greater than 100%.

3. For the change in the intra-EU coverage ratio (a) and the change in the extra-EU coverage ratio (b), the scores awarded were: -1 if the change in X/M is smaller than -5%; 0 if the change in X/M lay between + and -5%; and +1 if the change in X/M is greater than +5%. The scores for the change in the export specialisation index (SI) (c) were: -1 if the change in the SI is smaller than 0; 0 if the change in SI is 0; and +1 if the change in SI is greater than 0 .

4. As we see in the case of Greece, there is no requirement that because one group is capital intensive the other must be labour-intensive, since the sectors affected by the Single Market comprise only a subset of the entire manufacturing sector.

5. That is, low rates of Irish corporate profits tax encourage companies to over-invoice when selling to affiliates abroad and to under-invoice for materials purchased from foreign affiliates, in order to maximise the amount of value added ascribed to production in the Irish economy.

6. This was a very rough guide as data distinguishing between indigenous and foreign-owned companies were available for the most part only for 2-digit NACE-coded sectors (from the Irish Census of Industrial Production). In such cases we assumed that the published numbers for the 2-digit sectors applied to the individual 3-digit subsectors.

7. Furthermore, when the dairy industry with its high gross output per head was excluded, it was clear that indigenous industry was more labour-intensive, in both potentially successful and potentially declining sectors, than its foreign-owned counterparts, as might have been expected.

8. He argues furthermore that under free trade a trade reversal (from capital-intensive to labour-intensive exports) in response to the removal of the wage constraint will always increase welfare.
9   Sources: OECD Economic Surveys (various years) for Greece, and OECD Quarterly Labour Force Statistics, vol. 1, 1995, for the remainder.
10. Barry *et al.* (2001) show that in the Irish case the favoured 'S' sectors did indeed expand over the SEM period (1987-96) while the threatened 'D' sectors contracted.

REFERENCES

Barry, F., J. Bradley and A. Hannan (2001), 'The Single Market, the Structural Funds and Ireland's Recent Economic Growth', *Journal of Common Market Studies*, **39**, 537-52.

Barry, F. and A. Hannan (1995), 'Multinationals and Indigenous Employment: an Irish disease?', *Economic and Social Review*, **27**, 21-32.

Brecher, R. (1974), 'Minimum Wage Rates and the Pure Theory of International Trade', *Quarterly Journal of Economics*, **88**, 98-116.

Brulhart, M. and D. McAleese (1995), 'Intra-Industry Trade and Industrial Adjustment: the Irish experience', *Economic and Social Review*, **26**, 107-129.

European Economy (1990), *The Impact of the Internal Market by Industrial Sector: The Challenge for the Member States*, Special Edition, Brussels: Commission of the European Communities.

Gray, A. (1993), *Employment Potential in Manufacturing*, Dublin: An Bord Tráchtála.

Krugman, P. (1981), 'Intra-industry Specialisation and the Gains from Trade', *Journal of Political Economy*, **89**, 959-973.

Krugman, P. and A. Venables (1990), 'Integration and the Competitiveness of Peripheral Industry', in J.B. Braga de Macedo and C. Bliss (eds), *Unity with Diversity within the European Economy: The Community's Southern Frontier*, Cambridge, UK: Cambridge University Press.

Neven, D. (1990), 'EEC Integration Towards 1992: some distributional aspects', *Economic Policy*, **10**, 14-62.

O'Malley, E. (1992), 'Industrial Structure and Economies of Scale in the Context of 1992', in *The Role of the Structural Funds: Analysis of Consequences for Ireland in the Context of 1992*, Dublin: Economic and Social Research Institute Policy Research Series Paper, **13**.

12. Social and Employment Policies in the EU: Convergence on a 'Third Way' Model?

Nick Adnett[1]

> To meet …new challenges, the Agenda must ensure the modernisation and deepening of the European social model and place the emphasis on the promotion of quality in all areas of social policy. Quality of training, quality in work, quality of industrial relations and quality in social policy as a whole are essential factors if the European Union is to achieve the goals it has set itself regarding competitiveness and full employment. (European Social Agenda, 2000, Section 4).

1. INTRODUCTION

Following the Luxembourg Jobs summit in November 1997, the EU implemented a common employment strategy with specific targets being transposed into policies by each member state in National Action Plans for Employment (NAPs). At Lisbon in March 2000 the European Council agreed the need to modernise social policy, the resulting European Social Agenda was ratified at their Nice meeting in December 2000. This renewed emphasis upon social and employment policies within the EU has coincided with a swing of political power to centre-left parties in the member states. In particular, the election victories of Blair and Schröder have been interpreted as a break with 'old' social democratic policy-making, which was perceived to have failed to deliver its core economic objectives (Glynn, 1998), and the emergence of a 'Third Way' response to neo-liberalism. A key element of the philosophy of 'modernising' social democrats is a rejection of the anti-market bias of the 'old' state intervention, and the acceptance of the need to re-design welfare systems and labour market regulations in the face of the needs of the 'New Economy'. The full nature and extent of these developments, and their consequences for the European social model, remain unclear. It is evident, however, that the economic and social objectives of labour market regulation within the EU are now more directly juxtaposed than previously, a tendency that Giddens (2000) suggests is inevitable in the new economic and social environment.

In this chapter we seek to explore behind the rhetoric of these developments and consider the consequences of these events for the design and co-ordination of economic and social policy-making in the EU. We neglect questions concerning the appropriateness of 'Third Way' and 'New Economy' labels (see respectively Giddens, 2000 and OECD 2000), in order to concentrate on both the extent and desirability of uniform reforms to labour market regulation in the EU. In the following section we introduce the case for modernisation, by outlining the evolution of Social Europe and establishing the main weaknesses of the European social model identified by its critics. We do not here assess these arguments. Blau and Kahn (1999) and Adnett (2001) survey the limited evidence available on the effects of Social Europe on relative economic and social performance. In the next section we briefly review the European Employment Strategy and examine how this approach is to be extended to all areas of social policy through the European Social Agenda. We then critically examine the present infatuation with targets, scoreboards and the benchmarking of policy initiatives. This discussion precedes a more detailed examination of the Luxembourg process and its impact upon national policy-making. Our case studies explore the continuing diverse approaches within the EU to working time regulations, temporary contracts and co-ordinated bargaining. Whilst we discover some common themes we also stress the diversity of behaviour, policy and outcomes in the member states.

The final section contains our conclusions, which we now summarise. It seems clear that the development of the European Employment Strategy has generated convergence in the targeting of employment policies in member states. Similar tendencies are likely across all areas of social policy as a result of the adoption of the European Social Agenda. The current political dominance of the centre-left in the national governments of the EU has encouraged the addition of a 'Third Way' spin to the packaging and presentation of policy initiatives. Investing in people and combating social exclusion are at the heart of most recent policy initiatives. However, detailed examination of specific policies indicates the extent of national differences. Whilst policy convergence is to be encouraged to the extent that it promotes symmetrical labour market adjustments to symmetrical shocks within the EU, differences in labour market fundamentals provide a rationale for tolerating, if not encouraging, national policy differences.

2. THE EVOLUTION OF THE EUROPEAN SOCIAL MODEL

At the Nice Summit the European Council described the European social model as being 'characterised by the indissoluble link between economic performance and social progress' (Presidency Conclusions, p.2). This description reflects that a continuing objective of European economic integration has been to promote both economic and social cohesion, an objective that is now formalised in Article 2 of the Treaty of the European Union. The economic history of the European social model has recently been reinterpreted by Eichengreen and Iversen (1999) reflecting a new orthodoxy. Strong European economic growth after the Second World War was based upon Fordist technology supported by solidaristic wage bargaining. Whilst centralised wage bargaining compressed the distribution of wages and was associated with the growth of welfare programmes and labour market regulation, these were sustainable given the prevailing production technologies. This can be termed 'Stage I' of Social Europe's evolution (see Table 12.1) With the emergence of flexible specialisation and the growth of holistic firms, labour market institutions and employment regulations no longer sustained the EU's competitiveness in the fast growing sectors of the global market (Gual, 1998). The perceived over-expansion of welfare and regulation was now identified as a cause of chronic unemployment amongst the unskilled, falling male participation rates (through early retirement and permanent disability), and slow employment growth in the high-tech and service sectors (OECD, 1994). In the UK this emergence of euro-sclerosis coincided with the political ascendancy of neo-liberalism. As a response the Thatcher government invoked a programme of de-regulation, privatisation and reform of employment and trade union legislation with the objective of creating more flexible labour markets. This can be classed as 'Stage II' in the Anglo-Saxon variant of the evolution of Social Europe (Table 12.1).

The establishment of EMU has intensified the concern that an EU Social Policy based upon levelling-up may be inconsistent with increased economic integration and continuing international competitiveness (Bean *et al.*, 1998). As Otmar Issing (2000), a member of the Executive Board of the European Central Bank, recently argued, orthodox economics indicates that what is required instead is greater labour costs variability between, and within, EU labour markets. Though perversely, integration itself tends to promote both greater wage interdependence and wage convergence (Andersen *et al.*, 2000). Finally, globalisation has been identified as a further reason why Social Europe is no longer sustainable. The growth of trade and capital mobility increases labour cost elasticity of demand for labour and rigidities in wage adjustments increase the employment consequences of regulating labour market behaviour. In extending this argument, Saint-Paul (1997) argues that Europe's rigid labour markets encourage a concentration on producing a small range of relatively secure goods and services at a late stage of their product life cycle. This specialisation is associated with low market growth, low innovation, low learning externalities and therefore a low potential for European economic growth. As international trade and capital mobility increase, an international product cycle becomes established with specialisation in new goods and services in those economies with decentralised wages and 'employment at will'.

Table 12.1.   The evolution of the European social policy

Stage I	
challenge	Fordism
prevailing philosophy	conservative-corporatist & social democratic
policy response	European social model

$$\Downarrow$$

Stage II (*)	
challenge	euro-sclerosis
prevailing philosophy	neo-liberalism
policy response	de-regulation & flexible labour markets

$$\Downarrow$$

Stage III	
challenge	new economy & globalisation
prevailing philosophy	third way(s)
policy response	regulation for competitiveness

Note: '*' : largely a British phenomenon

We noted earlier the consensus that 'old' social democracy's economic policies had failed to produce their desired objectives of full employment and a more egalitarian distribution of income and wealth. When this view is combined with recognition of the above economic trends and assorted insights from sociological and political research, then Gidden's 'Third Way' emerges. From this perspective traditional social democracy elevated rights above responsibilities, and modernising social democrats recognise that the modern globalised, knowledge economy requires a different steer:

Flexible markets are essential to respond effectively to technological change. Companies should not be inhibited by the existence of too many rules and regulations. (Giddens, 2000, page 7)

or

The essential function of markets must be complemented and improved by political action, not hampered by it. (Blair and Schröder, 1999)

Hence the championing of regulation for competitiveness: social regulations need to be assessed in terms of their impact on overall economic performance. This can be represented as 'Stage III' in our evolution of Social Europe (Table 12.1). Since, as we noted, in Europe neo-liberalism only inspired significant and sustained policy reform in Britain, in some ways the 'Third Way' is Anglo-centric. It rests upon an implicit assumption that social solidarity is insufficient to sustain Swedish or even Dutch-style corporatist policies. These two countries have shown that it is possible to combine social solidarity and a dynamic economy, though doubts remain as to the sustainability of these models over time.

3. THE LUXEMBOURG PROCESS AND THE EUROPEAN SOCIAL AGENDA

The Luxembourg Process has co-ordinated the packaging and targeting of member states' employment policies around a four-pillar (with currently 19 guidelines) structure of improving employability, entrepreneurship, adaptability and equal opportunities (outlined in Table 12.2). Funk (1999) provides a summary of the origins of this European Employment Strategy and its recent history. Member states have to annually transform these guidelines into medium-term National Action Plans (NAPs) which currently incorporate the following horizontal objectives:

- raising overall employment rates; extending lifelong learning, and strengthening social partner involvement. NAPs are submitted for scrutiny to the Council and Commission. At the supra-national level the Commission produces an annual report reviewing labour market trends, adjusting guidelines if appropriate and assessing individual NAPs. Throughout the EU, the current emphasis is on a range of 'Third Way' measures derived often from Scandinavian experience:

- activating of passive policies; targeting of the long-term unemployed and socially excluded; increasing incentives to re-enter and remain in paid work; reducing tax burdens on employers; increasing working time flexibility; active ageing policies, and promoting lifelong learning.

Table 12.2.   Guidelines for member states' employment policies 2001

Pillar 1: Improving Employability

- tackling youth and long-term unemployment
- adopting an employment-friendly approach to benefits, taxes and training
- developing policies for active ageing
- developing skills for the new labour market in the context of lifelong learning
  - improving quality of education and training
  - developing e-learning for all citizens
  - assisting the acquisition or upgrading of skills of the unemployed
- enhancing active policies to improve job matching
- promoting a labour market open to all

Pillar 2: Developing Entrepreneurship

- making it easier to start up and run businesses
  - reducing overhead, administration and start-up costs
  - encouraging the take up of entrepreneurial activities
- exploiting new opportunities for job creation
- developing actions at the local and regional level
- making the taxation system more employment- and training-friendly

Pillar 3: Encouraging Adaptability of Businesses and Their Employees

- modernising work organisation
  - achieving the required balance between flexibility and security
  - assisting the development of an appropriate regulatory framework
- supporting adaptability in enterprises

Pillar 4: Strengthening Equal Opportunities Policies for Women and Men

- adopting a gender mainstreaming approach
- tackling gender gaps in employment, unemployment and pay
- reconciling work and family life

Following the Lisbon Summit, the Commission was required to develop a strategy for modernising the European social model. Not only was the EU 'to become the most competitive and dynamic knowledge-based economy', Lisbon also set a goal of full employment in a society more adapted to the personal choices of women and men. The resulting European Social Agenda was approved at the Nice European Council; Table 12.3 summarises its main priorities within the six strategic priorities. The intention is that on the basis of reports from the Commission and Council and together with a regularly updated scoreboard, the European Council will, with the assistance of the social partners, monitor its progress annually at its spring meetings, starting in Stockholm in March 2001.

Table 12.3. The European Social Agenda: a summary

1. More and Better Jobs

- increase active employment by improving policies for reconciling work and family life and by encouraging particular target groups to gain and retain employment
- strengthen the coordinated strategy for employment
- focus more on attaining quality in work
- develop preventive and reintegration strategies to combat long-term unemployment
- develop local and regional employment strategies
- improve effective access to lifelong education and training
- promote employment in, and adjustments to, the information society
- facilitate mobility for European citizens.

2. Create a New Balance Between Flexibility and Security

- involve workers more in managing change
- develop the Community strategy on health and safety at work
- disseminate good practice with respect to modernising and improving work relations and review existing Directives protecting workers facing mass redundancies and employer changes and bankruptcy.

3. Fight Poverty, Exclusion and Discrimination to Promote Social Integration

- implement national two-year plan for combating poverty and social inclusion
- exploit new information and communication technologies to reduce social exclusion
- ensure follow-up to national action plans on minimum guaranteed resources provided by social protection systems
- disseminate experiences of urban policy in combating social and spatial segregation
- evaluate ESF in terms of impact on social inclusion and implementation of existing anti-discriminatory legislation.

Table 12.3 (continued)

4. Modernising Social Protection

- assist the development of national strategies to guarantee secure and viable pensions
- encourage reforms to social protection that make work pay, promote secure income and reconcile work and family life
- strengthen co-operation and assist monitoring and evaluation in social policy.

5. Promoting Gender Equality

- integrate the concept of gender equality into all areas of the Social Policy Agenda
- increase women's access to decision-making
- promote gender equality in areas other than employment and professional life
- increase awareness, pool resources and share experience on gender issues
- extend initiatives to promote gender equality at work, particularly with regard to pay
- better reconcile work and family life, particularly by encouraging quality child care.

6. Strengthening Social Policy Aspects of Enlargement and in External Relations

---

- prepare for enlargement by exchanging views and information to assist compliance with employment, poverty, social protection and social exclusion policies
- develop a concerted approach to international social policy issues within multilateral institutions
- strengthen the social dimension of co-operation policy.

The Agenda seeks both to strengthen social policy as a productive factor, whilst making it more effective in protecting individuals and reducing inequalities and the degree of social exclusion. More accessible labour markets and a rising employment rate (target of 70 percent by 2010) are claimed to be the key to promoting both social inclusion and the sustainability of retirement pension systems. This requires, as the Agenda explains, a need to study 'the implications of the interaction between economic growth, employment and social cohesion when defining the policies of the Union'.

The European Employment Strategy and European Social Agenda call for much more extensive policy evaluation. The Lisbon Summit agreed greater emphasis on establishing quantitative and qualitative indicators, benchmarking against best world practice and target setting to be combined with periodic monitoring, evaluation and peer review organised as 'mutual learning processes'. The emphasis at Lisbon was on a 'new' open method of co-ordination as the means of spreading best practices and achieving greater convergence towards the EU's main goals. We assess the appropriateness of this emphasis in the following section.

4. MONITORING AND EVALUATING SOCIAL POLICY: BENCHMARKING AND CONVERGENCE

One key consequence of the Luxembourg process has been to gain acceptance for the need for greater monitoring and evaluation of social and employment policies. The open method of co-ordination encourages exchanges of information and identification of best practice, but more significantly has created a new culture based around indicators, target setting and benchmarking. The European Social Agenda makes clear that this culture is to spread across all areas of social policy. Overall, the aim appears to be to imitate the macroeconomic convergence process, creating a similar resolve to converge towards a joint set of verifiable and regularly updated targets (Schmid *et al.*, 1999).

One common underlying assumption of much neo-liberalist and 'Third Way' analysis is that government failures cause significant inefficiencies in the public provision of goods and services. Extending or imitating market forces has become a shared policy response, aimed at generating a new performance culture in the (smaller) public sector. Whilst market-testing and privatisation has been the preferred response of the neo-liberals, 'Third Way' advocates have been more willing to initially encourage 'competition by comparison' by publicising performance indicators for different providers. Benchmarking is a tool for raising efficiency where the performance of one organisation is measured against a standard, either absolute or relative to the performance of other organisations (Cowper and Samuels, 1997). The presumption is that any deviation of performance from the benchmark should be investigated and lead both to targeted changes in behaviour and continuing monitoring. Benchmarking of results thus tends to lead to the benchmarking of processes. As Schmid *et al.*. (1999) explain, the ultimate aim of benchmarking is to establish a controlled learning process supported by monitoring and scientific analysis.

The appropriateness of such methods rests upon issues concerned with comparability and transferability (Tronti, 1998). The inputs and outputs of individual employment policies cannot always be easily isolated. For example, individual active labour market policies may have little impact on social inclusion if assessed separately from interdependent reforms to taxation and benefit systems. Local, regional and national differences in social and workplace cultures and norms affect outcomes, obscuring the contribution of individual policies to comparative policy performance. The continuing differences, not just in workplace norms of behaviour, but also in gender balances, systems of taxation and social protection and degrees of social solidarity in the EU also contribute to national and regional differences in choosing and weighting appropriate goals. For example, a low overall employment rate is a problem in the UK where household income is highly sensitive to labour market participation. In the Netherlands redistributive policies, both employment and income, partially protect households from the consequences of low participation (Tronti, 1998). Such differences complicate the choice of suitable common performance indicators and prevent the identification of best practice.

Linked with the extension of target setting has been the 'Third Way' championing of evidence-based policy-making. Increasingly policies are initially piloted with the results used to refine their full implementation. Practice often appears to diverge from the original intentions, with policy-makers responding to the results from formative studies rather than awaiting the results from more precise measurement. It seems clear that the time-horizon of policy-makers is shorter than those evaluating the new policies. Identifying best practice and encouraging policy transfer within such an environment becomes even more complicated.

Overall, we agree with Tronti (1998) who concludes a discussion of how to evaluate labour market policies in member states as follows:

> ... in order to obtain meaningful and desirable results, convergence must not be based only on the blind imitation of the best performers. Labour market benchmarking implies a complex scientific, social and political process, whose success requires the accomplishment of many interrelated tasks. Among these are: understanding the reasons behind performance gaps, learning from better performers, evaluating the operative implications of institutional changes and adopting them through policy-making (while keeping social consensus), maintaining (or creating) a strong link between research and policy-making, through increased monitoring and evaluation analysis. (Tronti, 1998, page 511).

5. LABOUR MARKET REFORMS AND EMPLOYMENT POLICIES – POST-LUXEMBURG

In this section we initially try to ascertain some of the general consequences of the Luxembourg process, before examining three more detailed case studies of policy: working-time, temporary contracts and wage-fixing processes. First, however, we consider whether integration and associated institutional competition are inevitably leading to convergence of policy.

Contrary to the predictions of simple factor price equalisation models and the fears of high social protection member states, continued European economic integration appears to have produced no 'race to the bottom' (Freeman, 1998a; Andersen *et al.* , 2000; Teague, 2000). Product market integration has, as yet, not created major pressures on wages, regulations or the welfare state. In general, international evidence suggests that if the EU wishes to maintain labour market institutions that have a net negative spillover effect on labour productivity then, depending upon the particular measure, the costs are absorbed in three ways. The adjustment is through falling nominal wages, rising consumer prices and/or the depreciating exchange rates. The first two mechanisms are available to individual member states who wish to pursue their own policy agenda. The ability to sustain these costs over time depends crucially upon how the particular regulatory measure affects the dynamics of productivity growth.

Whilst the distinct national employment policies of Britain, Germany and Sweden were the centre of interest at the beginning of the 1990s, fashions have changed. Currently, those of Denmark, the Netherlands (Visser, 1998; Barrell and Genre, 1999; Hartog, 1999; Nickell and van Ours, 2000) and more recently Ireland, Italy and Spain have moved centre stage. This change partly reflects disenchantment with the consequences of neo-liberalist freeing of labour markets and doubts about the sustainability of the German and Swedish style corporatist models. To an extent, the 'Third Way' championing of the need to target human capital investments and the correction of government failures in the provision of social insurance now appears at the centre of policy-making in the EU. The 'Third Way' spin evident in the current guidelines for member states' employment policies (summarised above in Table 12.2) and those for the Social Policy Agenda (Table 12.3 above) clearly illustrates this point. However, the recent encouragement given to member states to lower VAT rates on certain labour intensive services, seems a throwback to 'old' social democratic policy-making.

In part the 'soft convergence' process seeks to progress the European social dimension without further legislation, but it permits a great diversity of strategies and policies at the national level (Abraham, 1999). The Joint Employment Reports for 1999 and 2000 confirm (see also EIRO, 1999) this diversity. At one extreme we have the UK. It has a more competitive approach to labour market regulation, strong welfare to work employment policies, low implicit tax on labour, absence of training plans in collective agreements and weak social partner involvement in policy-making. At the other extreme we have France, which has generally retained high labour taxes and championed strengthening regulation, such as in its flagship policy of tighter working time restrictions.

Notwithstanding this diversity, the Luxembourg process appears to have co-ordinated the packaging and targeting of employment policies around the four-pillar structure of improving employability, entrepreneurship, adaptability and equal opportunities. What is less evident from the Joint Employment

Reports is any real convergence of policies; indeed policies under Pillar I (equal opportunities) and particularly Pillar III (encouraging adaptability of business and their employees) appear to have been diverging. In general such divergence should not be disparaged. As Plantenga and Hansen (1999) show for the case of equal opportunities, the diversity of national institutional, social and cultural arrangements rules out policy convergence. Similarly consider Pillar I (improving employability) where there has been a general strengthening of incentives to work and active labour market policies targeted at the long-term unemployed. Martin's (2000) survey of active labour market policies across the OECD illustrates that there are no 'magic bullets' in solving the unemployment problem. The impact of employment policies on labour market behaviour is dependent upon the particular national institutional environment and the associated macroeconomic and microeconomic policy measures. We now illustrate this proposition further by considering three policy areas: working-time restrictions, temporary contracts and co-ordinated bargaining.

6. WORKING-TIME RESTRICTIONS

Belgium, France, Germany, Italy and the Netherlands have all introduced reductions in working hours in recent years as a key element in their employment policies (see Roche *et al.*, 1996 and Hunt, 1998). The EU's Employment Guidelines for 2000 urged social partners

> to agree and implement a process in order to modernise the organisation of work, including flexible working arrangements, with the aim of making undertakings productive and competitive and achieving the required balance between flexibility and security. Subjects to be covered may, for example, include ... the reduction of working hours...

Collectively agreed frameworks on working time are indeed becoming a more common feature of local (Austria, Italy and Finland) or sectoral (Sweden) agreements, though some other member states view working time restrictions above those in the Working Time Directive as generally harmful. In competitive labour markets conventional economic analysis suggests that arguments for work-sharing suffer from the 'lump of labour fallacy'. That is, proponents of work-sharing assume that the total amount of work to be done is constant or that positive effects on productivity dominate. However, reducing working hours may raise unit labour costs by raising hourly wages, as employees seek to avoid income sharing and also face less competition from the unemployed. In addition, employers' fixed costs may rise due to additional hiring and training costs. In turn, any higher unit labour costs are likely to lead both to a substitution of capital for labour, and reduced international competitiveness, which together will lower domestic employment. Conventional demand theory thus suggests that work-sharing could have either a positive or negative effect on employment dependent upon which of these arguments dominate in a particular national labour market.

The survey of time-series and production function studies by Freeman (1998b) concludes that reductions in hours generated by market forces have generally created additional employment, whilst those generated by government policy have, at best, only a small positive effect. Bauer and Zimmermann (1999) provide an explanation for this conclusion; using German data they find that skilled workers and unskilled workers are largely complements in production. Since overtime is concentrated amongst the skilled, and unemployment amongst the unskilled, then a general reduction in overtime working lowers production and unskilled employment. Consistent with this finding is Crépon and Kramarz's (2000) analysis of the 1982 mandatory reduction of working hours in France. They found large employment losses, especially amongst the lower-paid. In summary, labour supply factors, including the different skill composition of the employed and unemployed and a reluctance of those in employment to income-share, have severely limited the effectiveness of work-sharing policies. However, in those national labour markets where work-sharing can be combined with increased capital-sharing, through increased weekend and shift-working, then an appropriate policy mix may, as Freeman (1998b) and perhaps the most recent French experience suggest, be effective in raising employment levels. Timing may also be an important determinant of success. France introduced its recent working time restrictions at the point when economic recovery was generating the additional tax revenue to fund reduced social security contributions and encouraging agreement on flexible and innovative working time arrangements (EIRO, 1999). It appears that the timing, prevailing workplace behaviour, the degree of social solidarity and the particular policy mix are all important in determining the overall impact of work-sharing programmes.

7. TEMPORARY CONTRACTS

One of the earliest responses to improve the flexibility of labour markets in several member states was the championing of atypical contracts. While the implementation of policies regarding temporary contracts evolved differently in member states, their impact has also been very different. In Spain, large numbers of entrants were hired on temporary contracts as they displaced permanent contracts, whilst in Germany firms continued to hire apprentices for permanent jobs (Freeman, 1998a). These differences in part inspired the social partner negotiations that led to EU Directives on part-time and fixed-term contracts aimed at increasing the security of such workers. However, social partner negotiations have yet to be completed on the regulation of temporary agency work also identified in the Commission's 1995 consul-tation exercise. National policies have recently diverged as to whether to strengthen (Spain) or weaken (Italy and the Netherlands) controls on such temporary agency work (EIRO, 1999).

In addition, similar policies regarding temporary contracts in apparently similar European labour markets have had very different impacts. Differences in policy design and implementation appear to have a major impact upon the influence of the policy. Adam and Canziani (1998) compare the Italian and Spanish experience with fixed-term contracts. In Spain, temporary contracts provide jobs for around a third of the labour force, providing high numerical flexibility to employers. Indeed, more than 90 percent of new contracts in Spain are temporary (European Commission, 1999), though 1997 legislation, following agreement amongst the social partners, has sought to increase the number of permanent contracts. Currently, the probability of temporary workers becoming permanent workers is low and there is little incentive for employers to provide firm-specific training. The Spanish policy encouraged flexibility, albeit of a type which encouraged a 'low-skill' equilibrium, whereas Italian policy initially targeted a narrower segment of the labour force, though 50 percent of new entrants in large firms are now on temporary or part-time contracts (European Commission, 1999). Italian policy provided incentives for training and resulted in a much higher transition of temporary workers into permanent employment. Once again differences in the institutional and workplace environment, particularly the nature of the policy-mix, led to similar policy innovations generating very different labour market responses.

8. CO-ORDINATED BARGAINING

National wage-fixing processes have not been converging within the EU, though multi-tier collective bargaining institutions are common and quasi-centralised collective bargaining has been widely encouraged by member states seeking wage moderation (Teague, 2000). However, the extent of pay decentralisation remains uneven. Since 1980, the coverage of collective bargaining has generally been increasing, Britain apart, but trends in unionisation and the centralisation of wage-fixing have diverged. These developments suggest that some EU countries have found it easier to achieve macroeconomic targets by encouraging greater co-ordination of wage bargaining, whilst others have encouraged the fragmentation of the wage bargaining system (Nickell, 1998). For example, since 1983 unions in the Netherlands have become very co-operative, delivering wage moderation even under tight labour market conditions. This has contributed to the reduction in unemployment, whilst in Britain the same outcome has been promoted through a weakening of trade union bargaining power, partly induced by increased legal restrictions on union behaviour (Nickell and van Ours, 2000).

Finland, Greece and Ireland have attempted national incomes policy agreements in recent years (EIRO, 1999). Wage moderation can work well in small open economies with extensive international capital mobility, but requires institutions for co-ordinated bargaining which just do not exist in countries such as Britain and Spain. In such countries with fragmented bargaining the setting of 'wage norms' targeted at sustaining international competitiveness, such as those in Sweden and Belgium, seems unlikely to be desirable or effective. However, implicit co-ordination of collective bargaining across the EU is increasing, with a growing use of international comparisons being used to benchmark sectoral or local bargaining (EIRO, 1999). Overall, while national bargaining structure remain diverse in the EU, there is a new convergence in the functioning of these systems (Teague, 2000). EMU and the prioritising of competitiveness have standardised the macroeconomic framework for pay determination.

9. THIRD WAY OR THIRD WAYS IN MODERNISING SOCIAL EUROPE?

We have found that 'Third Way' philosophies and priorities have become influential in the targeting, presentation and packaging of EU social and employment policies. However, they have not promoted, to the same degree, a convergence in member states' actual policies. While the objectives of social policy-making have become more uniform, the processes by which member states seek to achieve those objectives remain diverse. This is to be expected: national variations in social and employment policies are desirable and sustainable even in the modern global economy. There is no 'law of one institution' and what is an appropriate modernising reform appears to depend upon both the current national economic environment and customary labour market behaviour. There is little evidence that institutional factors, workplace norms of behaviour and degrees of social solidarity are being harmonised across the OECD. Even within the EU this process appears to be very slow. The absence of appreciable convergence in labour market fundamentals within the EU implies that enforced policy convergence would be expensive in both economic and social terms. Moreover, both the benefits of increased flexibility and the costs of increased regulation may be lower than anticipated.

Freeman (2000) has argued, utilising the Coase theorem, that firms and workers adjust property rights in the light of existing regulations. What those regulations predominantly affect is the form of labour market adjustment and the distribution between firms and workers of the benefits from those adjustments, not overall labour market efficiency.

Our previous discussion suggests that there are factors that will prevent modernising reforms in accord with the shared 'Third Way' agenda from promoting a convergence of national social and employment policies. Reform has to discriminate between labour market rigidities that are dynamically harmful to economic and social cohesion, and those rigidities that may be benign or beneficial in the face of specific national product and labour market failures. Since policy changes are inevitably marginal, reform has to recognise the constraints imposed by existing policy and behaviour. Moreover, national reforms cannot be piecemeal: the existence of policy complementarities means that modernising reforms within national labour markets need to be co-ordinated and mutually consistent (Coe and Snower, 1997). It follows that given the diversity of national labour market behaviour and customs, the current infatuation with benchmarking at national and EU level may be dangerous: overly simplistic comparisons of individual policies across diverse markets are unlikely to be informative. Taking these propositions together they suggest that the setting of common broad targets for social and employment policy reform in the EU is to be preferred to the imposition of greater uniformity on national 'Third Way' reforms. This conclusion supports that drawn in the European Social Agenda which recognises that reform should be sensitive to: 'the need to take full account of the principle of subsidiarity and the differences between member states in social and labour traditions and situations'.

NOTES

1. The author is at Staffordshire University Business School.
   His e-mail address is N.J.Adnett@staffs.ac.uk.

REFERENCES

Abraham, F. (1999), 'A Policy Perspective on European Unemployment', *Scottish Journal of Political Economy*, **46**, 350-366.

Adam, P. and P. Canziani (1998), 'Partial De-regulation: fixed-term contracts in Italy and Spain', Centre for Economic Performance, Discussion Paper No. 386.

Adnett, N. (2001), 'Modernising the European Social Model: developing the guide-lines', *Journal of Common Market Studies*, forthcoming.

Andersen, T., N. Haldrup and J. Sørensen (2000), 'Labour Market Implications of EU Product Market Integration', *Economic Policy*, **30**, 105-133.

Barrell, R. and V. Genre (1999), 'Employment Strategies for Europe: lessons from Denmark and the Netherlands', *National Institute Economic Review*, **168**, 82-99.

Bauer, T. and K. Zimmermann (1999), 'Overtime Work and Overtime Compensation in Europe', *Scottish Journal of Political Economy*, **46**, 419-436.

Bean, C., S. Bentolila, G. Bertola and J. Dolado (1998), 'Social Europe: one for all?', London Centre for Economic Policy Research.

Blair, T. and G. Schröder (1999), *Europe: The Third Way - die Neue Mitte*, London: Labour Party and SPD.

Blau, F. and L. Kahn (1999), 'Institutions and Laws in the Labour Market', in O. Ashenfelter and D. Card (eds), *Handbook of Labour Economics*, vol. 3A, Amsterdam: Elsevier.

Coe, D. and D. Snower (1997), 'Policy Complementarities: the case for fundamental labour market reform', *IMF Staff Papers*, **44**, 1-35.

Cowper, J. and M. Samuels (1997), 'Performance Benchmarking in the Public Sector: the UK Experience', in OECD, *Benchmarking, Evaluation and Strategic Management in the Public Sector*, Paris: OECD.

Crépon, B. and F. Kramarz (2000), 'Employed 40 Hours or Not Employed 39: lessons from the 1982 mandatory reduction of the workweek', CEPR Discussion Paper No. 2358.

Eichengreen, B. and T. Iversen (1999), 'Institutions and Economic Performance: evidence from the labour market', *Oxford Review of Economic Policy*, **15**, 121-138.

EIRO (European Industrial Relations Observatory) (1999), *Annual Review*, http://www.eiro.eurofound.ie/1999/review.

European Commission (1999), *Joint Employment Report for 1999*, Brussels: European Commission.

Freeman, R. (1998a), 'War of the Models: which labour market institutions for the 21st century?', *Labour Economics*, **5**, 1-24.

Freeman, R. (1998b), 'Work-Sharing to Full Employment: serious option or populist fallacy?', in R. Freeman and P. Gottschalk (eds), *Generating Jobs: How to Increase Demand for Less-Skilled Workers*, New York: Russell Sage Foundation.

Freeman, R. (2000), 'Single-Peaked v. Diversified Capitalism: the relation between economic institutions and outcomes', *National Bureau of Economic Research Working Paper* No. 7556.

Funk, L. (1999), 'Towards a European Employment Pact: a third-way solution to persistent unemployment?', in L. Funk (ed.), *The Economics and Politics of the Third Way: Essays in Honour of Eric Owen Smith*, Hamburg: Lit Verlag.

Giddens, A. (2000), *The Third Way and its Critics*, Cambridge: Polity Press.

Glynn, A. (1998), 'Economic Policy and Social Democracy', *Oxford Review of Economic Policy*, **14**, 1-18.

Gual, J. (1998), 'The Employment Debate: employment performance and institutional change', in J. Gual (ed.), *Job Creation: The Role of Labor Market Institutions*, Cheltenham, UK and Lyme, USA: Edward Elgar, pp. 1-33.

Hartog, J. (1999), 'Wither Dutch Corporatism? Two Decades of Employment Policies and Welfare Reforms', *Scottish Journal of Political Economy*, **46**, 458-487.

Hunt, J. (1998), 'Hours Reduction as Work-Sharing', *Brookings Papers on Economic Activity*, **1998**(1), 339-381.

Issing, O. (2000), 'Europe: Common Money – Political Union?' *Economic Affairs*, March 2000, 33-39.

Martin, J. (2000), 'What Works among Active Labour Market Policies: evidence from OECD countries' experiences', *OECD Economic Studies*, **30**, 79-113.

Nickell, S. (1998), 'Employment Dynamics and Labour Market Institutions', in J. Gual (ed.), *Job Creation: The Role of Labor Market Institutions*, Cheltenham, UK and Lyme, USA: Edward Elgar.

Nickell, S. and J. van Ours (2000), 'The Netherlands and the United Kingdom: a European unemployment miracle?', *Economic Policy*, **30**, 135-180.

OECD (1994), *The OECD Job Study: Evidence and Explanations*, Vol. I and II, Paris: OECD.

OECD (2000), *Economic Outlook*, Paris: OECD.

Plantenga, J. and J. Hansen (1999), 'Assessing Equal Opportunities in the European Union', *International Labour Review*, **138**, 351-379.

Roche, W., B. Fynes and T. Morrissey (1996), 'Working Time and Employment: a review of international evidence', *International Labour Review*, **135**, 129-157.

Saint-Paul, G. (1997), 'Is Labour Rigidity Harming Europe's Competitiveness? The Effect of Job Protection on the Pattern of Trade and Welfare', *European Economic Review*, **41**, 499-506.

Schmid, G., H. Schütz and S. Speckesser (1999), 'Broadening the Scope of Benchmarking: radar charts and employment systems', *Labour*, **13**, 879-899.

Teague, P. (2000), 'Macroeconomic Constraints, Social Learning and Pay Bargaining in Europe', *British Journal of Industrial Relations*, **38**, 429-452.

Tronti, L. (1998), 'Benchmarking Labour Market Performance and Policies', *Labour*, **12**, 489-513.

Visser, J. (1998), 'Two Cheers for Corporatism, One for the Market: industrial relations, wage moderation and job growth in the Netherlands', *British Journal of Industrial Relations*, **36**, 269-292.

Index